Dumping in Dixie

Race, Class, and Environmental Quality

SECOND EDITION

Dumping in Dixie

Race, Class, and Environmental Quality

ROBERT D. BULLARD

WESTVIEW PRESS

Boulder ◆ San Francisco ◆ Oxford

Copyright © 1990, 1994 by Westview Press, Inc.

Published in 1994 in the United States of America by Westview Press, Inc., 5500 Central Avenue, Boulder, Colorado 80301-2877, and in the United Kingdom by Westview Press, 36 Lonsdale Road, Summertown, Oxford OX2 7EW

Library of Congress Cataloging-in-Publication Data
Bullard, Robert D. (Robert Doyle), 1946–
    Dumping in Dixie : race, class, and environmental quality / Robert D. Bullard.   — 2nd ed.
        p.   cm.
    Includes bibliographical references and index.
    ISBN 0-8133-1962-5 (hardcover). — ISBN 0-8133-1963-3 (paperback).
    1. Environmental policy—Southern States.   2. Waste disposal sites—Southern States—Location.   3. Afro-Americans—Southern States—Social conditions.   4. Southern States—Race relations. 5. Social justice.   6. Social surveys—Southern States.   I. Title.
HC107.A13B85   1994
363.72'8'0975—dc20   93-41558
                                                                              CIP

Printed and bound in the United States of America

    The paper used in this publication meets the requirements
(∞) of the American National Standard for Permanence of Paper
    for Printed Library Materials Z39.48-1984.

10   9   8   7   6   5   4   3   2

**To my mother,
Myrtle Bullard**

CONTENTS

◆

TABLES AND ILLUSTRATIONS

◆

Photos, following page 66

Leon White; Mrs. and Dr. Joseph Lowery, president of the Southern
Christian Leadership Conference; the Reverend Walter Fauntroy, a
congressional delegate; Ken Ferruccio; and Dr. James Green lead a
Warren County demonstration, 1982

Warren County protesters line the highway in an attempt to block
the dump trucks loaded with PCB-tainted dirt, 1982

Houston's Northwood Manor residents protesting the construction
of the Whispering Pines sanitary landfill, 1980

Houston's Holmes Road municipal garbage incinerator located in
the Sunnyside neighborhood, 1980

The Reverend Benjamin F. Chavis, Jr., at the National Press Club in
Washington, D.C., where he released the national study by the
Commission for Racial Justice concerning toxic wastes and race,
1987

Crews begin cleanup of lead-tainted soil in West Dallas, Texas,
neighborhood, 1992

A lone house stands in Reveilletown, Louisiana, after a buyout
from a nearby industry, 1992

PREFACE

◆

This book is a product of my interest as an environmental sociologist and my concern that the rights of African American and poor communities be protected. Many Americans—ranging from constitutional scholars to lay grassroots activists—recognize that environmental discrimination is unfair, unethical, and immoral. However, the practice is still legal. I carried out this research under the assumption that all Americans have a basic right to live, work, and play in a healthy environment. I made a deliberate effort to write a readable book that might reach a general audience while at the same time covering uncharted areas of interest to environmentalists, civil rights advocates, political leaders, and policy makers.

The issues addressed center on equity, fairness, and the struggle for social justice by African American communities. The struggles against environmental injustice are not unlike the civil rights battles waged to dismantle the legacy of Jim Crow in Selma, Montgomery, Birmingham, and some of the "Up South" communities in New York, Boston, Philadelphia, Chicago, and Los Angeles. The analysis chronicles the environmental justice movement in an effort to develop common strategies that are supportive of building sustainable communities of African Americans and other people of color.

In the South, African Americans just happen to make up the region's largest racial minority group. This analysis could have easily focused on Latino Americans in the Southwest or native Americans in the West. People of color in all regions of the country bear a disproportionate share of the nation's environmental problems.

As a sociologist at the predominantly African American Texas Southern University in Houston, I was asked in 1979 by attorney Linda McKeever Bullard (my wife) to conduct a study of the spatial location of all of the municipal solid-waste disposal facilities in Houston. The request was part of a class-action lawsuit (*Bean v. Southwestern Waste Management*) she filed against the city of Houston, the state of Texas, and the locally headquartered Browning Ferris Industries—the "Avis of garbage." The lawsuit stemmed from a plan to site a municipal landfill in a suburban, middle-income neighborhood of single-family home owners. *Bean v. Southwestern*

Waste Management was the first lawsuit in the United States that charged environmental discrimination in waste facility siting under the Civil Rights Act. The Northwood Manor neighborhood was an unlikely location for a garbage dump except that over 82 percent of its residents are African American.

In order to obtain the history of waste disposal facility siting in Houston—the only major U.S. city at the time that did not have zoning—government records (city, county, and state documents) had to be manually retrieved because the files were not yet computerized. On-site visits, windshield surveys, and informal interviews—done in a sort of "researcher as detective" role—were conducted as a reliability check. The Houston case predates some important landmark studies and events: the 1983 U.S. General Accounting Office study of off-site commercial hazardous-waste landfills in the South, the 1987 Commission for Racial Justice's *Toxic Wastes and Race*, the 1990 Gulf Coast Tenants Organization's and Southwest Organizing Project's letters to the "big ten" environmental groups accusing them of elitism and racism, the 1990 University of Michigan Conference on "Race and the Incidence of Environmental Hazards," and the 1992 *National Law Journal* study of Environmental Protection Agency (EPA) enforcement practices.

In the case of landfills in Houston, the task was made easier because of the city's terrain. Whenever a "mountain" was encountered—and quite a few were scattered across the urban landscape—I suspected an old dump site.

After collecting the data for *Bean v. Southwestern Waste Management* and interviewing citizens from other African American neighborhoods, we realized that the siting of local waste facilities was not random. Moreover, this was not a chicken or egg (which came first) problem. In all cases, the residential character of the neighborhoods had been established long before the industrial facilities invaded the areas. Many residents came to understand the research I was conducting and to recognize the noble profession of sociology as a field in which grandiose theories are developed, hypotheses formulated, and data collected that result in verification of the obvious: Most residents of segregated black Houston neighborhoods not only knew which days the garbage was collected but also knew the addresses of the existing and abandoned landfills and incinerators. Many of these same residents had spent much of their lives escaping from waste sites only to find waste landfill disputes following them to their new neighborhoods.

I was curious to know whether the Houston case was typical of other African American communities in the South—a region in which over half of all African Americans reside. The research focus was extended to include four additional African American communities. I decided to explore the thesis that African American communities in the South—the nation's Third World—because of their economic and political vulnerabilities, have been routinely targeted for the siting of noxious facilities; locally unwanted land uses, or LULUs; and environmental hazards. People in these communities, in turn, are likely to suffer greater environmental and health risks than is the general population.

In this book I seek to identify the major social and psychological impacts associated with the siting of noxious facilities (municipal landfills, hazardous-waste facilities, lead smelters, chemical plants) and their significance in mobilizing the African American community. The subjects were drawn from an array of mostly black areas, including neighborhoods in Houston and Dallas, Texas, and the communities of Alsen, Louisiana; Institute, West Virginia; and Emelle, Alabama.

Limited housing and residential options, combined with discriminatory facility practices, have contributed to the imposition of all types of toxins on African American communities through the siting of garbage dumps, hazardous-waste landfills, incinerators, smelter operations, paper mills, chemical plants, and a host of other polluting industries. These industries have generally followed the path of least resistance, which has been to locate in economically poor and politically powerless African American communities.

Poor African American communities are not the only victims of siting disparities, however. Middle-income African American communities are confronted with many of the same land-use disputes and environmental threats as their lower-income counterparts. Increased income has enabled few African Americans to escape the threat of unwanted land uses and potentially harmful environmental pollutants. In the real world, racial segregation is the dominant residential pattern, and racial discrimination is a leading cause of segregated housing.

Since affluent, middle-income, and poor African Americans live within close proximity of one another, the question of environmental justice can hardly be reduced to a poverty issue. The black middle-class community members in Houston's Northwood Manor neighborhood quickly discovered that their struggle was not unlike that of their working-class and poor counterparts who had learned to live with waste facilities. For those making environmental and industrial decisions, African American communities—regardless of their class status—were considered to be throwaway communities; therefore, land could be used for garbage dumps, transfer stations, incinerators, and other waste disposal facilities.

A growing number of African American grassroots activists have challenged public policies and industrial practices that threaten the residential integrity of their neighborhoods. Activists began to demand environmental justice and equal protection. The demands were reminiscent of those voiced during the civil rights era—they were for an end to discrimination in housing, education, employment, and the political arena. Many exhibited a growing militancy against industrial polluters and government regulatory agencies that provided these companies with permits and licenses to pollute.

After more than a decade of intense study, targeted research, public hearings, and grassroots leadership summits, environmental justice struggles have taken center stage. Environmental racism is out of the closet. Yet, all communities are *not* created equal. Some individuals, neighborhoods, communities, and regions have become the dumping grounds for all kinds of toxins. From West Dallas to West Harlem and from Southside Chicago to South-Central Los Angeles, people of color are demanding and in some cases winning solutions to their environmental dilemmas.

The decade of the 1990s is a different era from the late 1970s. Some progress has been made in mainstreaming environmental protection as a civil rights and social justice issue. When I started this work in 1979, few environmentalists, civil rights advocates, or policy makers understood or were willing to challenge the regressive and disparate impact of this country's environmental and industrial policies—policies that resulted in benefits being dispersed while burdens were localized. In the end, lower-income and people-of-color communities paid a heavy price in terms of their health and lowered property values.

Today, we see groups like the National Association for the Advancement of Colored People (NAACP), NAACP Legal Defense and Educational Fund, Lawyers' Committee for Civil Rights Under Law, Natural Resources Defense Council, Sierra Club Legal Defense Fund, American Civil Liberties Union, and Legal Aid Society teaming up on environmental and public health issues that differentially affect poor people and people of color. Environmental racism panels have become "hot" topics at conferences sponsored by law schools, bar associations, public health groups, scientific societies, environmental groups, and civil rights organizations.

Environmental justice has even trickled up to the federal government and the White House. Environmental justice activists and academicians were key actors who convinced the U.S. Environmental Protection Agency to create an Office of Environmental Equity. The Reverend Benjamin F. Chavis, executive director of the NAACP, and I were selected to work on President Bill Clinton's Transition Team in the Natural Resources Cluster (the EPA and the Departments of Energy, the Interior, and Agriculture). Yet, we are a long way from achieving a fair and just society in the environmental and other arenas.

The book is divided into seven chapters. I explore the barriers to environmental and social justice experienced by African Americans in Chapter 1 and also lay the foundation for understanding the factors that contribute to environmental conflicts, distributive impacts, and growing militancy among African American community residents. An overview of the sociological and ecological changes that have taken place in the southern region of the United States is presented in Chapter 2. Socio-historical information on the individual case studies is outlined in Chapter 3. This chapter includes detailed community profiles and background data on the environmental disputes investigated, the response of relevant actors, and a description of dispute resolution mechanisms.

The results of the household surveys are discussed in Chapter 4. These environmental surveys were used to supplement the more descriptive and qualitative analysis obtained from archival records and in-depth interviews with local opinion leaders. In Chapter 5 I examine the role of environmental racism in creating inequities between whites and people of color and the extent to which some at-risk populations, neighborhoods, and communities are underprotected by the government. In Chapter 6 I analyze the driving forces behind the fast-growing environmental justice movement and its emergent leadership. I also explore successful grassroots strategies and delineate a model environmental justice framework for decision making, equal protection, and pollution prevention.

In Chapter 7 I draw both from the interviews conducted with local opinion leaders and the empirically based household surveys to form generalizations on environmentalism in the African American community—both concern and activism. In this final chapter I delineate action strategies and recommendations for building consensus and mobilizing African Americans and other people-of-color groups on environmental justice issues. Finally, I offer prescriptions for diversifying mainstream environmental groups—strategies that can enhance the larger environmental movement in the United States and around the world.

Robert D. Bullard

ACKNOWLEDGMENTS

◆

A great many people helped in carrying out this study of environmentalism in the black community. First of all, the project could not have been undertaken without the financial support provided by grants from the National Science Foundation's Minority Research Initiation Program and Resources for the Future under its Small Grants Program. I appreciate the patience and understanding shown in the months it took to compile this material.

Much of the background work was completed while I was at Texas Southern University in Houston and at the University of Tennessee in Knoxville. I am grateful to L. Alex Swan, my department head at Texas Southern, and Tom Hood, my department head at the University of Tennessee, for providing me the support and release time needed to undertake the fieldwork that was spread over four states (Alabama, Louisiana, Texas, and West Virginia). I want to thank my two graduate students at the University of Tennessee, Glenn Johnson and Marilyn Mack, who assisted in the coding and cleaning of the survey data, and Reva Govil—my research assistant while I was a visiting scholar at the Energy and Resources Group at the University of California, Berkeley—who assisted in keying the data for computer processing.

I want to extend a special thanks to Professor Beverly H. Wright of Xavier University for her comments and suggestions on the initial manuscript draft. The final manuscript was prepared by my colleague Zizwe of the Black Student Programs with the assistance of an Intramural Grant from the University of California, Riverside, for which I am grateful. I also want to extend special thanks to a number of key community leaders who were invaluable in the fieldwork stage of this study: Louise Black of Houston; John Fullinwider of Dallas; Edwin Hoffman of Institute, West Virginia; Wendell Paris of Livingston, Alabama; and Mary McCastle of Alsen, Louisiana. I am also grateful for the contributions of my colleagues at the local colleges and universities for the use of their students as interviewers. They are Alma Page (Southern University), L. Alex Swan (Texas Southern University), Edwin Hoffman (West Virginia State College), and Jessie Jones (Bishop College).

Finally, I am indebted to the many community residents who took the time to talk to me and the interviewers about their personal experiences and the actions they have taken to secure a better quality of life for themselves and their families.

R.D.B.

CHAPTER ONE

◆

Environmentalism and Social Justice

The environmental movement in the United States emerged with agendas that focused on such areas as wilderness and wildlife preservation, resource conservation, pollution abatement, and population control. It was supported primarily by middle- and upper-middle-class whites. Although concern about the environment cut across racial and class lines, environmental activism has been most pronounced among individuals who have above-average education, greater access to economic resources, and a greater sense of personal efficacy.[1]

Mainstream environmental organizations were late in broadening their base of support to include blacks and other minorities, the poor, and working-class persons. The "energy crisis" in the 1970s provided a major impetus for the many environmentalists to embrace equity issues confronting the poor in this country and in the countries of the Third World.[2] Over the years, environmentalism has shifted from a "participatory" to a "power" strategy, where the "core of active environmental movement is focused on litigation, political lobbying, and technical evaluation rather than on mass mobilization for protest marches."[3]

An abundance of documentation shows blacks, lower-income groups, and working-class persons are subjected to a disproportionately large amount of pollution and other environmental stressors in their neighborhoods as well as in their workplaces.[4] However, these groups have only been marginally involved in the nation's environmental movement. Problems facing the black community have been topics of much discussion in recent years. (Here, we use sociologist James Blackwell's definition of the black community, "a highly diversified set of interrelated structures and

1

aggregates of people who are held together by forces of white oppression and racism."[5]) Race has not been eliminated as a factor in the allocation of community amenities.

Research on environmental quality in black communities has been minimal. Attention has been focused on such problems as crime, drugs, poverty, unemployment, and family crisis. Nevertheless, pollution is exacting a heavy toll (in health and environmental costs) on black communities across the nation. There are few studies that document, for example, the way blacks cope with environmental stressors such as municipal solid-waste facilities, hazardous-waste landfills, toxic-waste dumps, chemical emissions from industrial plants, and on-the-job hazards that pose extreme risks to their health. Coping in this case is seen as a response to stress and is defined as "efforts, both action-oriented and intrapsychic, to manage, i.e., master, tolerate, reduce, minimize, environmental and internal demands, conflicts among then, which tax or exceed a person's resources."[6] Coping strategies employed by individuals confronted with a stressor are of two general types: *problem-focused coping* (e.g., individual and/or group efforts to directly address the problem) and *emotion-focused coping* (e.g., efforts to control one's psychological response to the stressor). The decision to take direct action or to tolerate a stressor often depends on how individuals perceive their ability to do something about or have an impact on the stressful situation. Personal efficacy, therefore, is seen as a factor that affects environmental and political activism.[7]

Much research has been devoted to analyzing social movements in the United States. For example, hundreds of volumes have been written in the past several years on the environmental, labor, antiwar, and civil rights movements. Despite this wide coverage, there is a dearth of material on the convergence (and the divergence, for that matter) of environmentalism and social justice advocacy. This appears to be the case in and out of academia. Moreover, few social scientists have studied environmentalism among blacks and other ethnic minorities. This oversight is rooted in historical and ideological factors and in the composition of the core environmental movement and its largely white middle-class profile.

Many of the interactions that emerged among core environmentalists, the poor, and blacks can be traced to distributional equity questions. How are the benefits and burdens of environmental reform distributed? Who gets what, where, and why? Are environmental inequities a result of racism or class barriers or a combination of both? After more than two decades of modern environmentalism, the equity issues have not been resolved. There has been, however, some change in the way environmental problems are presented by mainstream environmental organizations. More important, environmental equity has now become a major item on the local (grassroots) as well as national civil rights agenda.[8]

Much of the leadership in the civil rights movement came from histori-cally black colleges and universities (HBCUs). Black college students were on the "cutting edge" in leading sit-in demonstrations at lunch counters, libraries, parks, and public transit systems that operated under Jim Crow laws. In *The Origins of the Civil Rights Movement*, Aldon D. Morris wrote:

> The tradition of protest is transmitted across generations by older relatives, black institutions, churches, and protest organizations. Blacks interested in social change inevitably gravitate to this "protest community," where they hope to find solutions to a complex problem.
> The modern civil rights movement fits solidly into this rich tradition of protest. Like the slave revolts, the Garvey Movement, and the March on Washington, it was highly organized. Its significant use of the black religious community to accomplish political goals also linked the modern movement to the earlier mass movements which also relied heavily on the church.[9]

Social justice and the elimination of institutionalized discrimination were the major goals of the civil rights movement. Many of the HBCUs are located in some of the most environmentally polluted communities in the nation. These institutions and their students, thus, have a vested interest in seeing that improvements are made in local environmental quality. Un-like their move to challenge other forms of inequity, black student-activ-ists have been conspicuously silent and relatively inactive on environmen-tal problems. Moreover, the resources and talents of the faculties at these institutions have also been underutilized in assisting affected communi-ties in their struggle against polluters, including government and private industries.

The problem of polluted black communities is not a new phenomenon. Historically, toxic dumping and the location of locally unwanted land uses (LULUs) have followed the "path of least resistance," meaning black and poor communities have been disproportionately burdened with these types of externalities. However, organized black resistance to toxic dump-ing, municipal waste facility siting, and discriminatory environmental and land-use decisions is a relatively recent phenomenon.[10] Black environ-mental concern has been present but too often has not been followed up with action.

Ecological concern has remained moderately high across nearly all seg-ments of the population. Social equity and concern about distributive im-pacts, however, have not fared so well over the years. Low-income and minority communities have had few advocates and lobbyists at the na-tional level and within the mainstream environmental movement. Things are changing as environmental problems become more "potent political issues [and] become increasingly viewed as threatening public health."[11]

The environmental movement of the 1960s and 1970s, dominated by the middle class, built an impressive political base for environmental reform and regulatory relief. Many environmental problems of the 1980s and 1990s, however, have social impacts that differ somewhat from earlier ones. Specifically, environmental problems have had serious regressive impacts. These impacts have been widely publicized in the media, as in the case of the hazardous-waste problems at Love Canal and Times Beach. The plight of polluted minority communities is not as well known as the New York and Missouri tragedies. Nevertheless, a disproportionate burden of pollution is carried by the urban poor and minorities.[12]

Few environmentalists realized the sociological implications of the not-in-my-backyard (NIMBY) phenomenon.[13] Given the political climate of the times, the hazardous wastes, garbage dumps, and polluting industries were likely to end up in somebody's backyard. But whose backyard? More often than not, these LULUs ended up in poor, powerless, black communities rather than in affluent suburbs. This pattern has proven to be the rule, even though the benefits derived from industrial waste production are directly related to affluence.[14] Public officials and private industry have in many cases responded to the NIMBY phenomenon using the place-in-blacks'-backyard (PIBBY) principle.[15]

Social activists have begun to move environmentalism to the left in an effort to address some of the distributional impact and equity issues.[16] Documentation of civil rights violations has strengthened the move to make environmental quality a basic right of all individuals. Rising energy costs and a continued erosion of the economy's ability to provide jobs (but not promises) are factors that favor blending the objectives of labor, minorities, and other "underdogs" with those of middle-class environmentalists.[17] Although ecological sustainability and socioeconomic equality have not been fully achieved, there is clear evidence that the 1980s ushered in a new era of cooperation between environmental and social justice groups. While there is by no means a consensus on complex environmental problems, the converging points of view represent the notion that "environmental problems and ... material problems have common roots."[18]

When analyzing the convergence of these groups, it is important to note the relative emphasis that environmental and social justice organizations give to "instrumental" versus "expressive" activities.[19] Environmental organizations have relied heavily on environmentally oriented expressive activities (outdoor recreation, field trips, social functions, etc.), while the social justice movements have made greater use of goal-oriented instrumental activities (protest demonstrations, mass rallies, sit-ins, boycotts, etc.) in their effort to produce social change.[20]

The push for environmental equity in the black community has much in common with the development of the modern civil rights movement that began in the South. That is, protest against discrimination has evolved from "organizing efforts of activists functioning through a well-developed indigenous base."[21] Indigenous black institutions, organizations, leaders, and networks are coming together against polluting industries and discriminatory environmental policies. This book addresses this new uniting of backs against institutional barriers of racism and classism.

Race Versus Class in Spatial Location

Social scientists agree that a multidimensional web of factors operate in sorting out stratification hierarchies. These factors include occupation, education, value of dwellings, source and amount of income, type of dwelling structures, government and private industry policies, and racial and ethnic makeup of residents.[22] Unfortunately, American society has not reached a color-blind state. What role does race play in sorting out land uses? Race continues to be a potent variable in explaining the spatial layout of urban areas, including housing patterns, street and highway configurations, commercial development, and industrial facility siting.

Houston, Texas, the nation's fourth largest city, is a classic example of an area where race has played an integral part in land-use outcomes and municipal service delivery.[23] As late as 1982, there were neighborhoods in Houston that still did not have paved streets, gas and sewer connections, running water, regular garbage service, and street markers. Black and Hispanic neighborhoods were far more likely to have service deficiencies than their white counterparts. One of the neighborhoods (Bordersville) was part of the land annexed for the bustling Houston Intercontinental Airport. Another area, Riceville, was a stable black community located in the city's sprawling southwest corridor, a mostly white sector that accounted for nearly one-half of Houston's housing construction in the 1970s.

The city's breakneck annexation policy stretched municipal services thin. Newly annexed unincorporated areas, composed of mostly whites, often gained at the expenses of older minority areas. How does one explain the service disparities in this modern Sunbelt city? After studying the Houston phenomenon for nearly a decade, I have failed to turn up a single case of a white neighborhood (low- or middle-income) in the city that was systematically denied basic municipal services. The significance of race may have declined, but racism has not disappeared when it comes to allocating scarce resources.

Do middle-income blacks have the same mobility options that are available to their white counterparts? The answer to this question is no. Blacks have made tremendous economic and political gains in the past three decades with the passage of equal opportunity initiatives at the federal level. Despite legislation, court orders, and federal mandates, institutional racism and discrimination continue to influence the quality of life in many of the nation's black communities.[24]

The differential residential amenities and land uses assigned to black and white residential areas cannot be explained by class alone. For example, poor whites and poor blacks do not have the same opportunities to "vote with their feet." Racial barriers to education, employment, and housing reduce mobility options available to the black underclass and the black middle class.[25]

Housing is a classic example of this persistent problem. Residential options available to blacks have been shaped largely by (1) federal housing policies, (2) institutional and individual discrimination in housing markets, (3) geographic changes that have taken place in the nation's urban centers, and (4) limited incomes. Federal policies, for example, played a key role in the development of spatially differentiated metropolitan areas where blacks and other visible minorities are segregated from whites, and the poor from the more affluent citizens.[26] Government housing policies fueled the white exodus to the suburbs and accelerated the abandonment of central cities. Federal tax dollars funded the construction of freeway and interstate highway systems. Many of these construction projects cut paths through minority neighborhoods, physically isolated residents from their institutions, and disrupted once-stable communities. The federal government is the "proximate and essential cause of urban apartheid" in the United States.[27] The result of the nation's apartheid-type policies has been limited mobility, reduced housing options and residential packages, and decreased environmental choices for black households.[28]

Environmental degradation takes an especially heavy toll on inner-city neighborhoods because the "poor or nearpoor are the ones most vulnerable to the assaults of air and water pollution, and the stress and tension of noise and squalor."[29] A high correlation has been discovered between characteristics associated with disadvantage (i.e., poverty, occupations below management and professional levels, low rent, and a high concentration of black residents [due to residential segregation and discriminatory housing practices]) and poor air quality.[30] Individuals that are in close proximity to health-threatening problems (i.e., industrial pollution, congestion, and busy freeways) are living in endangered environs. The price that these individuals pay is in the form of higher risks of emphysema, chronic bronchitis, and other chronic pulmonary diseases.[31]

Blacks and other economically disadvantaged groups are often concentrated in areas that expose them to high levels of toxic pollution: namely, urban industrial communities with elevated air and water pollution problems or rural areas with high levels of exposure to farm pesticides. Kruvant described these groups as victims:

> Disadvantaged people are largely victims of middle- and upper-class pollu-
> tion because they usually live closest to the sources of pollution—power
> plants, industrial installations, and in central cities where vehicle traffic is
> heaviest. Usually they have no choice. Discrimination created the situation,
> and those with wealth and influence have political power to keep polluting
> facilities away from their homes. Living in poverty areas is bad enough. High
> pollution makes it worse.[32]

Air pollution in inner-city neighborhoods can be up to five times greater than in suburban areas. Urban areas, in general, have "dirtier air and drinking water, more wastewater and solid-waste problems, and greater exposure to lead and other heavy metals than nonurban areas."[33] The difference between the environmental quality of inner-city and suburban areas was summarized by Blum:

> Suburbanites are exposed to less than half of the environmental health haz-
> ards inner-city residents face. ... The inner-city poor—white, yellow, brown,
> and black—suffer to an alarming degree from what are euphemistically
> known as "diseases of adaptation." These are not health adaptations, but dis-
> eases and chronic conditions from living with bad air, polluted water, and
> continued stress.[34]

All Americans, white or black, rich or poor, are entitled to equal protection under the law. Just as this is true for such areas as education, employment, and housing, it also applies to one's physical environment. Environmental discrimination is a fact of life. Here, environmental discrimination is defined as disparate treatment of a group or community based on race, class, or some other distinguishing characteristic. The struggle for social justice by black Americans has been and continues to be rooted in white racism. White racism is a factor in the impoverishment of black communities and has made it easier for black residential areas to become the dumping grounds for all types of health-threatening toxins and industrial pollution.

Government and private industry in general have followed the "path of least resistance" in addressing externalities as pollution discharges, waste disposal, and nonresidential activities that may pose a health threat to nearby communities.[35] Middle- and upper-class households can often shut out the fumes, noise, and odors with their air conditioning, dispose of their garbage to keep out the rats and roaches, and buy bottled water for drinking.[36] Many lower-income households (black or white) cannot afford such "luxury" items; they are subsequently forced to adapt to a lower-quality physical environment.

Minority and low-income residential areas (and their inhabitants) are often adversely affected by unregulated growth, ineffective regulation of industrial toxins, and public policy decisions authorizing locally unwanted land uses that favor those with political and economic clout.[37] Zoning is probably the most widely applied mechanism to regulate land use in the United States. Externalities such as pollution discharges to the air and water, noise, vibrations, and aesthetic problems are often segregated from residential areas for the "public good." Negative effects of nonresidential activities generally decrease with distance from the source. Land-use zoning, thus, is designed as a "protectionist device" to insure a "place for everything and everything in its place."[38] Zoning is ultimately intended to influence and shape land use in accordance with long-range local needs.

Zoning, deed restrictions, and other protectionist land-use mechanisms have failed to effectively protect minority communities, especially low-income minority communities. Logan and Molotch, in their book *Urban Fortunes: The Political Economy of Place,* contend that the various social classes, with or without land-use controls, are "unequally able to protect their environmental interests."[39] In their quest for quality neighborhoods, individuals often find themselves competing for desirable neighborhood amenities (i.e., good schools, police and fire protection, quality health care, and parks and recreational facilities) and resisting negative characteristics (i.e., landfills, polluting industries, freeways, public housing projects, drug-treatment facilities, halfway houses, etc.).

Zoning is not a panacea for land-use planning or for achieving long-range development goals. Implementation of zoning ordinances and land-use plans has a political, economic, and racial dimension. Competition often results between special interest groups (i.e., racial and ethnic minorities, organized civic clubs, neighborhood associations, developers, environmentalists, etc.) for advantageous land use. In many instances, exclusionary zoning, discriminatory housing practices by rental agents, brokers, and lending institutions, and disparate facility siting decisions have contributed to and maintained racially segregated residential areas of unequal quality.[40] These practices persist in spite of years of government intervention.

Why has this happened and what have blacks done to resist these practices? In order to understand the causes of the environmental dilemma that many black and low-income communities find themselves in, the theoretical foundation of environmentalism needs to be explored.

The Theoretical Basis
of Environmental Conflict

Environmentalism in the United States grew out of the progressive conservation movement that began in the 1890s. The modern environmental movement, however, has its roots in the civil rights and antiwar movements of the late 1960s.[41] The more radical student activists splintered off from the civil rights and antiwar movements to form the core of the environmental movement in the early 1970s. The student environmental activists affected by the 1970 Earth Day enthusiasm in colleges and universities across the nation had hopes of bringing environmental reforms to the urban poor. They saw their role as environmental advocates for the poor since the poor had not taken action on their own.[42] They were, however, met with resistance and suspicion. Poor and minority residents saw environmentalism as a disguise for oppression and as another "elitist" movement.[43]

Environmental elitism has been grouped into three categories: (1) *compositional elitism* implies that environmentalists come from privileged class strata, (2) *ideological elitism* implies that environmental reforms are a subterfuge for distributing the benefits to environmentalists and costs to nonenvironmentalists, and (3) *impact elitism* implies that environmental reforms have regressive distributional impacts.[44]

Impact elitism has been the major sore point between environmentalists and advocates for social justice who see some reform proposals creating, exacerbating, and sustaining social inequities. Conflict centered largely on the "jobs versus environment" argument. Imbedded in this argument are three competing advocacy groups: (1) *environmentalists* are concerned about leisure and recreation, wildlife and wilderness preservation, resource conservation, pollution abatement, and industry regulation, (2) *social justice advocates'* major concerns include basic civil rights, social equity, expanded opportunity, economic mobility, and institutional discrimination, and (3) *economic boosters* have as their chief concerns maximizing profits, industrial expansion, economic stability, laissez-faire operation, and deregulation.

Economic boosters and pro-growth advocates convinced minority leaders that environmental regulations were bad for business, even when locational decisions had adverse impacts on the less advantaged. Pro-growth advocates used a number of strategies to advance their goals, including public relations campaigns, lobbying public officials, evoking police powers of government, paying off or co-opting dissidents, and granting small concessions when plans could be modified.[45] Environmental reform proposals were presented as prescriptions for plant closures, layoffs, and economic dislocation. Kazis and Grossman referred to this practice as "job blackmail." They insisted that by "threatening their employees with a 'choice' between their jobs and their health, employers seek to make the public believe there are no alternatives to 'business as usual.'"[46]

Pro-growth advocates have claimed the workplace is an arena in which unavoidable trade-offs must be made between jobs and hazards: If workers want to keep their jobs, they must work under conditions that may be hazardous to them, their families, and their community. Black workers are especially vulnerable to job blackmail because of the threat of unemployment and their concentration in certain types of occupations. The black workforce remains overrepresented in low-paying, low-skill, high-risk blue collar and service occupations where there is a more than adequate supply of replacement labor. Black workers are twice as likely to be unemployed as their white counterparts. Fear of unemployment acts as a potent incentive for many blacks to stay in and accept jobs they know are health threatening.

There is inherent conflict between the interest of capital and of labor. Employers have the power to move jobs (and sometimes hazards) as they wish. For example, firms may choose to move their operations from the Northeast and Midwest to the South and Sunbelt, or they may move the jobs to Third World countries where labor is cheaper and there are fewer health and environmental regulations. Moreover, labor unions may feel it necessary to scale down their demands for improved work safety conditions in a depressed economy for fear of layoffs, plant closings, or relocation of industries (e.g., moving to right-to-work states that proliferate in the South). The conflicts, fears, and anxieties manifested by workers are usually built on the false assumption that environmental regulations are automatically linked to job loss.

The offer of a job (any job) to an unemployed worker appears to have served a more immediate need than the promise of a clean environment. There is evidence that new jobs have been created as a direct result of environmental reforms.[47] Who got these new jobs? The newly created jobs are often taken by people who already have jobs or by migrants who possess skills greater than the indigenous workforce. More often than not, "newcomers intervene between the jobs and the local residents, especially the disadvantaged."[48]

Minority residents can point to a steady stream of industrial jobs leaving their communities. Moreover, social justice advocates take note of the miserable track record that environmentalists and preservationists have on improving environmental quality in the nation's racially segregated inner cities and hazardous industrial workplaces, and on providing housing for low-income groups. Decent and affordable housing, for example, is a top environmental problem for inner-city blacks. On the other hand, environmentalists' continued emphasis on wilderness and wildlife preservation appeal to a population that can afford leisure time and travel to these distant locations. This does not mean that poor people and people of color are not interested in leisure or outdoor activities. Many wilderness areas and national parks remain inaccessible to the typical inner-city resident because of inadequate transportation. Physical isolation, thus, serves as a major impediment to black activism in the mainstream conservation and resource management activities.

Translating Concern into Action

A considerable body of literature show that the socioeconomic makeup of environmental activists and the environmentally concerned are markedly different. Activists tend to be drawn disproportionately from the upper middle class, while environmentally concerned individuals tend to come from all socioeconomic strata.[49] Since our focus is on activism rather than concern, social participation models seem most appropriate in explaining the varying levels of environmental activity within the black community. Two of the most prevalent perspectives on social participation rates are expressed in the "social psychological" and "resource mobilization" models.

The basic assumption of the social psychological perspective is that personal characteristics, such as deprivation, status inconsistencies, grievances, and alienation, are useful in explaining motivation for social movement involvement.[50] The resource mobilization perspective, on the other hand, places greater confidence in structural conditions that make individual participation more accessible, including economic resources, organization affiliation, leaders, communication networks, and mastery skills gained through wearing "multiple hats."[51] Given the issues that have drawn minorities into the environmental movement (e.g., social justice and equity issues) and the indigenous black institutions that have initiated and sustained the movement, an integrated model is used to explain the emergence of environmentalism in black communities.[52] That is, both psychological factors (e.g., environmental quality rating, deprivation and sense of inequitable treatment, personal efficacy, and acceptance of trade-offs) as well as structural factors (e.g., social class and organization affiliation) are important predictors of environmental activism that is emerging in black communities.

There is no single agenda or integrated political philosophy in the hundreds of environmental organizations found in the nation. The type of issues that environmental organizations choose can greatly influence the type of constituents they attract.[53] The issues that are most likely to attract the interests of black community residents are those that have been couched in a civil rights or equity framework (see Table 1.1). They include those that (1) focus on inequality and distributional impacts, (2) endorse the "politics of equity" and direct action, (3) appeal to urban mobilized groups, (4) advocate safeguards against environmental blackmail with a strong pro-development stance, and (5) are ideologically aligned with policies that favor social and political "underdogs."

Mainstream environmental organizations, including the "classic" and "mature" groups, have had a great deal of influence in shaping the nation's environmental policy. Classic environmentalism continues to have a heavy emphasis on preservation and outdoor recreation, while mature environmentalism is busy in the area of "tightening regulations, seeking adequate funding for agencies, occasionally focusing on compliance with existing statutes through court action, and opposing corporate efforts to repeal environmental legislation or weaken standards."[54] These organizations, however, have not had a great deal of success in attracting working-class persons, the large black population in the nation's inner cities, and the rural poor. Many of these individuals do not see the mainstream environmental movement as a vehicle that is championing the causes of the "little man," the "underdog," or the "oppressed."[55]

Recently emerged grassroots environmental groups, some of which are affiliated with mainstream environmental organizations, have begun to bridge the class and ideological gap between core environmentalists (e.g., the Sierra Club) and grassroots organizations (e.g., local activist groups in southeast Louisiana). In some cases, these groups mirror their larger counterparts at the national level in terms of problems and issues selected, membership, ideological alignment, and tactics. Grassroots groups often are organized around area-specific and single-issue problems. They are, however, more inclusive than mainstream environmental organizations in that they focus primarily on local problems. Grassroots environmental organizations, however, may or may not choose to focus on equity, distributional impacts, and economic-environmental trade-off issues. These groups do appeal to some black community residents, especially those who have been active in other confrontational protest activities.

Environmental groups in the black community quite often emerge out of established social action organizations. For example, black leadership has deep roots in the black church and other voluntary associations. These black institutions usually have a track record built on opposition to social injustice and racial discrimination. Many black community residents are affiliated with civic clubs, neighborhood associations, community improvement groups, and an array of antipoverty and antidiscrimination organizations. The infrastructure, thus, is already in place for the emergence

TABLE 1.1 Type of Environmental Groups and Issue Characteristics That Appeal to Black Community Residents

	Type of Environmental Group			
Issue Characteristic	Mainstream	Grassroots	Social Action	Emergent Coalition
Appeal to urban mobilized groups	-	+	+	+
Concern about inequality and distributional impacts	-/+	-/+	+	+
Endorse the "politics of equity" and direct action	-/+	+	+	-/+
Focus on economic-environment trade-offs	-	-/+	+	+
Champion of the political and economic "underdog"	-	-/+	+	+

-: Group is unlikely to have characteristic.
+: Group is likely to have characteristic.
-/+: Group in some cases may have characteristic.

Source: Adapted from Richard P. Gale, "The Environmental Movement and the Left: Antagonists or Allies?" *Sociological Inquiry 53* (Spring 1983): Table 1, p. 194.

of a sustained environmental equity movement in the black community. Black sociologist Aldon Morris contends that the black community "possesses (1) certain basic resources, (2) social activists with strong ties to mass-based indigenous institutions, and (3) tactics and strategies that can be effectively employed against a system of domination."[56]

Social action groups that take on environmental issues as part of their agenda are often on the political Left. They broaden their base of support and sphere of influence by incorporating environmental equity issues as agenda items that favor the disenfranchised. The push for environmental equity is an extension of the civil rights movement, a movement in which direct confrontation and the politics of protest have been real weapons. In short, social action environmental organizations retain much of their civil rights flavor.

Other environmental groups that have appealed to black community residents grew out of coalitions between environmentalists (mainstream and grassroots), social action advocates, and organized labor.[57] These somewhat fragile coalitions operate from the position that social justice and environmental quality are compatible goals. Although these groups are beginning to formulate agendas for action, mistrust still persists as a limiting factor. These groups are often biracial with membership cutting across class and geographic boundaries. There is a down side to these types of coalition groups. For example, compositional factors may engender less group solidarity and sense of "control" among black members, compared to the indigenous social action or grassroots environmental groups where blacks are in the majority and make the decisions. The question of "who is calling the shots" is ever present.

Environmentalists, thus, have had a difficult task convincing blacks and the poor that they are on their side. Mistrust is engendered among economically and politically oppressed groups in this country when they see environmental reforms being used to direct social and economic resources away from problems of the poor toward priorities of the affluent. For example, tighter government regulations and public opposition to disposal facility siting have opened up the Third World as the new dumping ground for this nation's toxic wastes. Few of these poor countries have laws or the infrastructure to handle the wastes from the United States and other Western industrialized nations.[58] Blacks and other ethnic minorities in this country also see their communities being inundated with all types of toxics. This has been especially the case for the southern United States (one of the most underdeveloped regions of the nation) where more than one-half of all blacks live.

Environmentalism and Civil Rights

The civil rights movement has its roots in the southern United States. Southern racism deprived blacks of "political rights, economic opportunity, social justice, and human dignity."[59] The new environmental equity movement also is centered in the South, a region where marked ecological disparities exist between black and white communities.[60] The 1980s have seen the emergence of a small cadre of blacks who see environmental discrimination as a civil rights issue. A fragile alliance has been forged between organized labor, blacks, and environmental groups as exhibited by the 1983 Urban Environment Conference workshops held in New Orleans.[61] Environmental and civil rights issues were presented as compatible agenda items by the conference organizers. Environmental protection and social justice are not necessarily incompatible goals.[62]

The Commission for Racial Justice's 1987 study *Toxic Wastes and Race in the United States* is a clear indication that environmental concerns have reached the civil rights agenda. Reverend Ben Chavis, the commission's executive director, stated:

> Race is a major factor related to the presence of hazardous wastes in residential communities throughout the United States. As a national church-based civil rights agency, we believe that time has come for all church and civil rights organizations to take this issue seriously. We realize that involvement in this type of research is a departure from our traditional protest methodology. However, if we are to advance our struggle in the future, it will depend largely on the availability of timely and reliable information.[63]

A growing number of grassroots organizations and their leaders have begun to incorporate more problem-focused coping strategies (e.g., protests, neighborhood demonstrations, picketing, political pressure, litigation, etc.) to reduce and eliminate environmental stressors. The national black political leadership has demonstrated a willingness to take a strong pro-environment stance. The League of Conservation Voters, for example, assigned the Congressional Black Caucus high marks for having one of the best pro-environment voting records.[64]

Many black communities, however, still do not have the organization, financial resources, or personnel to mount and sustain effective long-term challenges to such unpopular facilities as municipal and hazardous-waste landfills, toxic waste dumps, incinerators, and industrial plants that may pose a threat to their health and safety. Some battles are being waged on "shoestring" budgets. The problem is complicated by the fact that blacks in many cases must go outside their community to find experts on environmental issues. Lawyers, toxicologists, hydrologists, and environmental engineers in today's market are not cheap.

Institutional racism continues to affect policy decisions related to the enforcement of environmental regulations. Slowly, blacks, lower-income groups, and working-class persons are awakening to the dangers of living in a polluted environment. They are beginning to file and win lawsuits challenging governments and private industry that would turn their communities into the dumping grounds for all type of unwanted substances and activities. Whether it is a matter of deciding where a municipal landfill or hazardous-waste facility will be located, or getting a local chemical plant to develop better emergency notification, or trying to secure federal assistance to clean up an area that has already been contaminated by health-threatening chemicals, it is apparent that blacks and other minority groups must become more involved in environmental issues if they want to live healthier lives.

Black communities, mostly in the South, are beginning to initiate action (protests, demonstrations, picketing, political pressure, litigation, and other forms of direct action) against industries and governmental agencies that have targeted their neighborhoods for nonresidential uses including municipal garbage, hazardous wastes, and polluting industries. The environmental "time bombs" that are ticking away in these communities are not high on the agendas of mainstream environmentalists nor have they received much attention from mainstream civil rights advocates. Moreover, polluted black communities have received little national media coverage or remedial action from governmental agencies charged with cleanup of health-threatening pollution problems. The time is long overdue for placing the toxics and minority health concerns (including stress induced from living in contaminated communities) on the agenda of federal and state environmental protection and regulatory agencies. The Commission for Racial Justice's *Toxic Wastes and Race* has at least started government officials, academicians, and grassroots activists talking about environmental problems that disproportionately affect minority communities.

Nevertheless, the "Black Love Canals" exist and many go unnoticed. A case in point is the contamination of Triana, a small, all-black town in northern Alabama. Barbara Reynolds in *National Wildlife* described Triana as the "unhealthiest town in America."[65] Residents of this rural town of about 1,000 people were tested by the Center for Disease Control and were found to be contaminated with the pesticide DDT and the highly toxic industrial chemical PCB (polychlorinated biphenyl). Some of the residents were contaminated with the highest levels of DDT ever recorded. The source of the PCBs was not determined. However, the DDT was produced at nearby Redstone Arsenal Army missile base from 1947 to 1971 by Olin Chemical Company. DDT was banned in the United States in 1971. The manufacturing plant was torn down and over 4,000 tons of DDT residue remained buried in the area and eventually worked its way into Indian Creek, a popular fishing place of the Triana residents. Indian Creek is a tributary of the Tennessee River and is under the jurisdiction of the Tennessee Valley Authority (TVA).

While the elevated level of contamination of these black residents was documented as early as 1978, actions on the part of the U.S. Army or the federal government did not materialize. Clyde Foster, then mayor of Triana, spoke to this lack of concern and inaction on the part of government:

> I did not want a confrontation. I just wanted the scientific investigation to speak for itself. Why did the TVA suggest Triana be studied if DDT was not at all dangerous? How can it kill insects, fish, and birds and not be potentially

harmful to people? I knew the stuff was real stable, that it stays in a body for years. Who knows what effects massive doses could have over a long period of time? The TVA has known about the presence of DDT in the fish of Indian Creek for years, and I found later that the Army checked in 1977 and found a fish with one hundred times the safe DDT level. We received the TVA analysis of the fish from our freezers. Our fish had even higher DDT levels than those they had first tested. ... Many of us eat its [Indian Creek's] fish every day. Already there is a hardship among the very poor people who customarily derive sustenance from the river. Our whole community is upset. We needed some help.[66]

It was not until Mayor Foster filed a class-action lawsuit in 1980 against Olin Chemical Company that the problems of these citizens were taken seriously.[67] After many delays and attempts to co-opt the local citizens, the lawsuit was settled out of court in 1983 for $25 million. The settlement agreement had three main points. Olin Chemical Company agreed to (1) clean up residual chemicals, (2) set aside $5 million to pay for long-term medical surveillance and health care of Triana residents, and (3) pay "cash-in-pocket" settlements to each resident. The legal claim against the federal government was withdrawn in order to make the settlement with Olin. The tragedy at Triana is not an isolated incident. There are numerous other cases of poor, black, and powerless communities that are victimized and ignored when it comes to enforcing environmental quality standards equitably. These disparities form the basis for this study and the environmental equity movement.

A Note on the Research Approach

This study examines how community attitudes and socioeconomic characteristics influence activism and mobilization strategies of black residents who are confronted with the threat of environmental stressors. The research on which this study is based was carried out in 1987 and 1988. Initial contact, however, had been made with local opinion leaders in several of the study communities as far back as 1979, after the author had served as a consultant, adviser, workshop lecturer, and guest speaker at a number of community events. A good rapport had been built up over several years with key community actors. This familiarity with the communities greatly enhanced the data-gathering phase of the project. Several data sources were used in order to develop an understanding of the complexities of black environmental mobilization. Three data sources were used: (1) government documents and archival records, (2) in-depth interviews with local opinion leaders, and (3) household surveys.

Community Case Studies

Descriptive case studies were developed on each of the five communities selected for investigation. This analysis included demographic and economic profiles of the population as well as the socio-historical context in which the environmental disputes arose. Local black leaders and community organizations were identified through the reputational approach (i.e., asking a group of influentials "who were the most important leaders on the local environmental problem, excluding themselves") and newspapers articles, editorials, and feature stories. In-depth interviews (unstructured) were conducted with fifteen black opinion leaders. These interviews were used to supplement archival documents and the more structured interviews that were conducted in the household surveys.

Newspaper article clip files from local public libraries were especially helpful in tracking local problems, including their discovery, local reactions (citizens, government, and industry), and government and industry responses. The analysis also chronicled the efforts made by local citizen groups to reduce the threats, including political pressure, court action, disruptive and violent action, and indirect methods.

Household Surveys

The sample consisted of 120 black household heads randomly selected from each of the five study communities (600 households in all). A total of 523 household interviews were completed, an 87 percent response rate. Data were collected in the spring and summer of 1988. Interviewers were recruited from local colleges and universities and trained by the author. They were instructed on how to gain entry, establish rapport, and handle common problems that arise in interview surveys. The training of the student interviewers also involved practicing role-playing as both interviewer and respondent to sensitize them to the interview process. The student-interviewers were supervised by the author and a faculty representative from the local university, with the exception of Emelle, where the author supervised the interviewing because there was not a historically black college or university in the area. Student-interviewers were used from Texas Southern University (Houston), Bishop College (Dallas), Southern University (Baton Rouge), West Virginia State College (Institute), and Livingston University (Livingston, Alabama).

Interviewers were assigned a randomly generated list of addresses and area maps of the sampling subareas. The small number of nonblacks who entered the sampling frame were not interviewed. Because this is a study of black mobilization, only black household heads were interviewed. Each respondent was given a letter that explained the purpose of the survey and contained information on where the author and the local faculty supervisor could be contacted if there were questions. As a precautionary measure, local police commanders from the neighborhood districts were informed of the survey and the time period that interviewers would be in the field. This practice has proven to be a useful strategy in urban communities where crime and fear of victimization may deter people from cooperating (opening their doors) in face-to-face surveys. Two follow-up visits were made to the residence before contacting the next household on the list.

The interview schedule was developed and pre-tested in a Houston neighborhood that was similar to the one used in this study. All five case study communities received the same survey instrument. In addition to basic demographic data, information was gathered on residents' rating of environmental pollution, environmental deprivation, and economic trade-offs. We were also interested in assessing social participation and environmental activism rates of the respondents.

After a systematic review of the related literature and studies on environmentalism (locational conflict, distributive impacts, social justice and equity, and mobilization factors), six research questions were formulated. They were:

1. What factors are important in explaining black mobilization on environmental issues?
2. What types of dispute-handling techniques and mechanisms do black community residents use to resolve environmental conflicts?
3. Are the strategies used in the civil rights movement readily adaptable to an environmental equity movement?
4. Do indigenous black institutions and organizations possess the leadership, resources, and communication infrastructure to plan, initiate, and sustain an environmental equity protest movement?
5. What role do outside elites play in environmental protest movements in black communities?
6. How effective are economic incentives, compensation, and other monetary inducements in mitigating environmental disputes and locational conflict in black communities?

The six research questions form the basis of the analysis and provide the foundation on which the investigation rests. The descriptive case histories provide basic socio-demographic profiles of the communities and background material on the local environmental disputes and remedial actions that were taken by citizens, government, and private industry. The intent of this analysis is not to assign blame for a specific environmental problem. The aim is to provide insights into the economic and political dynamics of environmental decision making and impacts on minority communities.

The next chapter outlines the social, geopolitical, and ecological changes that have fueled the "growth machine" in the southern region of the United States. While the environmental problems and concerns discussed in our analysis are not unique to the South, the region provided an ideal laboratory for studying the growth-environment dilemma. More important, if black environmental mobilization is the focus, as was the case in this inquiry, one should go to the source. The southern United States appears to be the center of the black environmental equity movement.

CHAPTER TWO

◆

Race, Class, and the Politics of Place

The southern United States, with its unique history and its plantation-economy legacy, presents an excellent opportunity for exploring the environment-development dialectic, residence-production conflict, and residual impact of the de facto industrial policy (i.e., "any job is better than no job") on the region's ecology. The South during the 1950s and 1960s was the center of social upheavals and the civil rights movement. The 1970s and early 1980s catapulted the region into the national limelight again, but for different reasons. The South in this latter period was undergoing a number of dramatic demographic, economic, and ecological changes. It had become a major growth center.

Growth in the region during the 1970s was stimulated by a number of factors. They included (1) a climate pleasant enough to attract workers from other regions and the "underemployed" workforce already in the region, (2) weak labor unions and strong right-to-work laws, (3) cheap labor and cheap land, (4) attractive areas for new industries, i.e., electronics, federal defense, and aerospace contracting, (5) aggressive self-promotion and booster campaigns, and (6) lenient environmental regulations.[1] Beginning in the mid-1970s, the South was transformed from a "net exporter of people to a powerful human magnet."[2] The region had a number of factors it promoted as important for a "good business climate," including "low business taxes, a good infrastructure of municipal services, vigorous law enforcement, an eager and docile labor force, and a minimum of business regulations."[3]

The rise of the South intensified land-use conflicts revolving around "use value" (neighborhood interests) and "exchange value" (business interests). Government and business elites became primary players in affecting land-use decisions and growth potentialities. The "growth machine," thus, sometimes pitted neighborhood interests against the interests of industrial expansion. However, economic boosters could usually count on their promise of jobs as an efficient strategy of neutralizing local opposition to growth projects. Harvey Molotch emphasized the importance of jobs as a selling point in growth machine politics:

> Perhaps the key ideological prop for the growth machine, especially in terms of sustaining support from the working-class majority, is the claim that growth "makes jobs." This claim is aggressively promulgated by developers, builders, and chambers of commerce; it becomes part of the statesman talk of editorialists and political officials. Such people do not speak of growth as useful to profits—rather, they speak of it as necessary for making jobs.[4]

Competition intensified as communities attempted to expand their work force and lure new industries away from other locations. There was a "clear preference for clean industries that require highly skilled workers over dirty industries that use unskilled workers."[5] Many communities could not afford to be choosy. Those communities that failed to penetrate the clean industry market were left with a choice of dirty industry or no industry at all. These disparities typify the changing industrial pattern in the South.

Before moving to the next section, we need to delineate the boundaries of the South. We have chosen to use the U.S. Bureau of the Census South Region, sixteen states and the District of Columbia, as the study area (see Figure 2.1). The South has the largest population of any region in the country. More than 75.4 million inhabitants, nearly one-third of the nation's population, lived in the South in 1980.[6] All of the southern states experienced a net in-migration during the 1970s. The South, during the 1970s and 1980s, also grew at a faster rate than the nation as a whole—a factor that had important economic, political, and ecological implications.

The South also has the largest concentration of blacks in the country. In 1980, more than 14 million blacks lived in the region. Blacks were nearly one-fifth of the region's population. In the 1970s the region's black population increased by nearly 18 percent. In 1980, six of the southern states had black populations that exceeded 20 percent (35.2 percent of the population in Mississippi, 30.4 percent in South Carolina, 29.4 percent in Louisiana, 26.8 percent in Georgia, 25.6 percent in Alabama, and 22.4 percent in North Carolina).

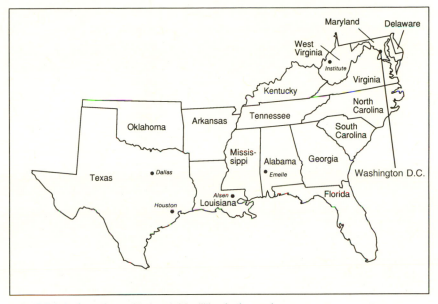

FIGURE 2.1   Locations of industrial facilities in the study area

Consequences of Uneven Development

The South has gone to great lengths to shed its image as a socially and eco-nomically "backward" region. However, slick public relations and image management campaigns have not been able to hide decades of neglect and underdevelopment. Many of the old problems remain, while new problems were created as a direct result of the new growth. Migrants to urban areas and incumbent residents who had marginal skills generally found themselves in the growing unemployment lines.[7] Individuals who do not have the requisite education often become part of the region's ex-panding underclass.

The South's new prosperity was mainly confined to metropolitan areas. Growth in the urban South heightened status differences between rich and poor and between blacks and whites. Poverty coexisted amid afflu-ence. Poverty, however, represented a source of cheap labor. The large pool of docile and nonunionized labor was part of the so-called "good business climate."[8]

William Falk and Thomas Lyson described the uneven economic devel-opment and plight of rural southerners in their book *High Tech, Low Tech, No Tech*. The authors wrote:

Not all citizens have benefited from the upturn in the southern economy. In fact, many may not have benefited at all. Blacks, women, and people living in rural areas have, in varying degrees, received little or none of the job opportunities and economic affluence that has washed over the region. The quality of life and opportunity for improvement for these "people left behind" have remained essentially unchanged over the last fifty years.[9]

Development disparities are heightened by business policies that direct jobs away from minority communities through the systematic avoidance of urban ghettos and rural blackbelt counties. The blackbelt represents geopolitical power (or the potential for empowerment). It also represents the epitome of American apartheid with its rigid segregation practices, second-class status for blacks, and staunch white resistance to black majority rule. Falk and Lyson studied 147 southern blackbelt counties (a band of counties with 40 percent or more black population extending from North Carolina to Louisiana) and discovered these areas lagging far behind other counties in the region, partly because of the concentration of unskilled, poorly educated workers. The authors summed up their findings by writing:

> If the SMSA counties are seen as the "pride of the South," the Black Belt can be viewed as the "Sunbelt's stepchild." The industrial growth and development that has washed over the region has left the 147 Black Belt counties with a residue of slow growth and stagnant and declining industries. ... High tech industries have virtually ignored the Black Belt. ... In short, by any yardstick of industrial development, the Black Belt remains mired in the backwater of the southern economy.[10]

The persistent problem of uneven development and economic disparities caused many writers to challenge the existence of a "New" South. Chet Fuller, a black journalist, traveled across the region in the late 1970s and discovered that "the much touted progress of some southern cities is more illusion than reality."[11] The region was portrayed as booming with industrial growth and expanding employment opportunities that were once closed to the black masses. The New South was promoted as a changed land where blacks could now share in the American Dream. Fuller argued that "power has not changed hands in the South, not from white hands to black hands."[12] What is "new" about an area where blacks are systematically denied access to jobs, housing, and other residential amenities?

Black communities still suffer from institutionalized discrimination. Discriminatory practices occur at various levels of government and affect the location of polling places, municipal landfills, and toxic-waste dumps. Discrimination, thus, involves a "process of defending one group's privilege gained at the expense of another."[13] Black communities and their inhabitants must defend themselves against hostile external forces that shape land-use decisions and environmental policies.

Why focus on the South? The South has always been home for a significant share of the black population. More than 90 percent of black Americans lived in the southern states at the turn of the century. A little more than one-half (53 percent) of all blacks were living in the region in 1980, the same percentage as in 1970.[14] In an effort to improve their lives, millions of rural blacks migrated from the South to other regions of the nation. From the mid-1940s to the late 1960s, nearly 4.5 million more blacks left the South than migrated to it. Beginning in the mid-1970s, however, the number of blacks moving into the South exceeded the number departing for other regions of the country. For the period 1975–1980, over 415,000 blacks moved into the South, while 220,000 left the region (or a net in-migration of 195,000 blacks), thereby reversing the longstanding black exodus. More than 411,000 blacks migrated to the South during the 1980–1985 period while 324,000 moved out of the region, a net in-migration of 87,000 blacks.[15]

As industry and jobs relocated to the region, job seekers followed. More than 17 million new jobs were added in the South between 1960 and 1985, compared to 11 million jobs added in the West, and a combined total of 13 million jobs added in the Midwest and Northeast.[16] The challenges that the South must face rest with how its resources—housing, jobs, public services, political representation, etc.—are shared with blacks who historically have not gotten their fair share of the region's amenities. The major reason for this discrepancy has been the location preferences of businesses. Industries that relocated to the South generally built new factories where they could find surplus white labor and "avoided places with a high ratio of poor and unskilled blacks."[17] The plight of millions of blacks has been exacerbated by the combination of economic recession (and depression-like conditions in many black communities), federal budget cuts, growing tension among individuals competing for limited jobs and other scarce resources, and the federal retreat on enforcement of civil rights and antidiscrimination laws.[18]

The social climate of the South was changed dramatically by the civil rights movement. Some gains were also made in the political arena. Most of these gains were made after the passage of the Voting Rights Act of 1965. There were 1,469 black elected officials in 1970, 4,912 in 1980, and 5,654 in 1984.[19] The number of black officeholders increased to 6,681 in 1987. There were twenty-three blacks in the U.S. Congress in 1989. This number represented only 5.3 percent of the 435 members of the U.S. House of Representatives. There were no blacks in the U.S. Senate.

Only four blacks from the Deep South were serving in Congress (Harold Ford of Memphis, Mickey Leland of Houston, John Lewis of Atlanta, and Michael Espy of Yazoo City, Mississippi) in 1989. Espy and Lewis were first elected in 1986. Espy became the first black elected to Congress from Mississippi since Reconstruction. Although some 53 percent of the nation's blacks live in the South, 62 percent of the black elected officials were found in the region.[20] In spite of the progress that has been made since the civil rights movement of the 1960s and 1970s, blacks remain underrepresented as political officeholders.[21] They are also underrepresented in policy-making boards and commissions, including industrial and environmental regulatory bodies. The interests of all-white industrial boards, zoning commissions, and governmental regulatory bodies may run counter to those of the black community. Until these policy-setting institutions are made more inclusive, we are likely to find an intensification of locational conflicts and charges of racial discrimination.

Endangered Environs

Millions of urban and rural blacks are physically trapped in inner cities while the job centers, especially for white-collar and service occupations, are moving to the suburbs. Housing discrimination, residential segregation, and limited public transportation severely limit the access of urban blacks to the job-rich suburbs. Many black workers must settle for nearby manufacturing jobs—the ones that have not moved out of the inner city. Because of their proximity to polluting industries, black communities have the most to gain from effective environmental enforcement mechanisms.[22]

Unlike their white counterparts, black communities do not have a long history of dealing with environmental problems. Blacks were involved in civil rights activities during the height of the environmental movement, roughly during the late 1960s and early 1970s. Many social justice activists saw the environmental movement as a smoke screen to divert attention and resources away from the important issue of the day—white racism. On the other hand, the key environmental issues of this period (e.g., wildlife and wilderness preservation, energy and resource conservation, and regulation of industrial polluters) were not high priority items on the civil rights agenda.

Social justice, political empowerment, equal education, fair employment practices, and open housing were major goals of social justice advocates. It was one thing to talk about "saving trees" and a whole different story when one talked about "saving low-income housing" for the poor. As a course of action, black communities usually sided with those who took an active role on the housing issue. Because eviction and displacement are fairly common in black communities (particularly for inner-city residents), decent and affordable housing became a more salient issue than the traditional environmental issues. Similarly, unemployment and poverty were more pressing social problems for African Americans than any of the issues voiced by middle-class environmentalists.

In their desperate attempt to improve the economic conditions of their constituents, many civil rights advocates, business leaders, and political officials directed their energies toward bringing jobs to their communities by relaxing enforcement of pollution standards and environmental regulations and sometimes looking the other way when violations were discovered. In many instances, the creation of jobs resulted in health risks to workers and residents of the surrounding communities.

Industrial policies remained paternalistic toward those who were less well-off. Polluting industries were brought into poor communities with little input from local community leaders.[23] When questions were raised by concerned citizens, the argument of jobs for local residents was used to quell dissent. Environmental risks were offered as unavoidable trade-offs for jobs and a broadened tax base in economically depressed communities. Jobs were real; environmental risks were unknown. This scenario proved to be the de facto industrial policy in "poverty pockets" and job-hungry communities around the world.

The South's unique history, traditions, and laws institutionalized employment, education, housing, and other forms of discrimination. A plethora of civil rights legislation was enacted to remedy inequities of Jim Crow laws and de facto segregation. Beginning in the 1970s the region was transformed into an economic "mecca."[24] Industrial growth was hailed as a panacea for the decades of neglect and second-class status accorded the region.

Even with the economic transformation, many of the region's old problems that were related to underdevelopment (e.g., poor education, large concentrations of unskilled labor, low wages, high unemployment, etc.) went unabated. New environmental problems were created with the influx of polluting industries. For example, in the 1970s four of the five states that led the nation in attracting polluting industries such as paper, chemical, and waste disposal firms were located in the South. These four states, Texas, South Carolina, North Carolina, and Florida, are not known for having strong environmental programs.[25]

Many industrial firms, especially waste disposal companies and industries that have a long history of pollution violations, came to view the black community as a "pushover lacking community organization, environmental consciousness, and with strong and blind pro-business politics."[26] These communities were ripe for exploitation. Residents of economically impoverished areas—intimidated by big corporations and deserted by local politicians—were slow to challenge private and governmental polluters of their neighborhoods. Moreover, the strong pro-jobs stance, a kind of "don't bite the hand that feeds you" sentiment, aided in institutionalizing risks at levels that are unacceptable in the larger society.[27]

According to nearly every quality-of-life indicator, black communities are worse off than their white counterparts. Environmental and land-use regulations are enforced on a less-than-routine basis in black communities. Because a large share of inhabitants in these communities are renters (many from low-income households) rather than home owners, it is difficult to organize and mobilize residents. This marginality also makes it hard for people to donate their time or money to fend off threats to the community. Logan and Molotch summarized this problem:

> Ghettos are organized less as attempts to defend the ongoing structure and institutional patterns of a specific neighborhood and more as assaults on the larger social order that denies basic resources to all deprived places and the people in them. It is organization around victimization. ... [T]he special vulnerability of black neighborhoods to outside penetration and the difficulties of organizing around turf issues are caused by racist patterns of exploitation, exclusion, and stigma.[28]

There is, of course, a "direct historical connection between the exploitation of the land and the exploitation of people, especially black people."[29] Southern historian David R. Goldfield sees southern ecology as being tied to the race issue. Goldfield predicted that "as race relations continue to improve, so will Southern ecology."[30] Southern ecology has been shaped largely by excessive economic boosterism, a blind pro-business climate, lax enforcement of environmental regulations, and industrial strategies that had little regard for environmental cost.

Rapid and unrestrained development has ruined or threatened the region's unique habitat. A classic example of this ecological destruction is the transformation of the life-giving Mississippi River into a "deadly mixture of sewage, industrial waste, and insecticides below fire-belching Baton Rouge."[31] Public Data Access, Inc., in a study commissioned by the environmental group Greenpeace, discovered some startling facts on the pollution problem in the East Baton Rouge parish, as counties are called in Louisiana:

> East Baton Rouge parish had more violators of emissions permits, commercial toxic waste facilities, employees in petrochemicals, and toxic waste generation than any other county along the [Mississippi] River, and, in addition,

ranked second or third for 6 toxic emissions measures, 3 toxic discharges measures, and for toxic waste landfills and incinerators.[32]

The entire Gulf Coast region, especially Mississippi, Alabama, Louisiana, and Texas, has been ravaged by "lax regulations and unbridled production."[33] Polluting industries exploit the pro-growth, pro-jobs sentiment exhibited among the poor, working-class, and minority communities.[34] Industries such as paper mills, waste disposal and treatment facilities, and chemical plants, searching for operation space, found these communities to be a logical choice for their expansion. Polluting smokestacks, to some individuals, were visible signs that plants were operating and employing people.

The smell of industrial operations was promoted as economic "progress." What civic-minded individual would advocate against economic progress? For example, a paper mill spewing its stench and poison in one of Alabama's poverty-ridden blackbelt counties led Governor George Wallace to declare: "Yeah, that's the smell of prosperity. Sho' does smell sweet, don't it."[35] Similar views have been reported of public officials in West Virginia's, Louisiana's, and Texas's "chemical corridor."[36]

Growing Black Militancy

Blacks did not launch a frontal assault on environmental problems affecting their communities until these issues were couched in a civil rights context beginning in the early 1980s. They began to treat their struggle for environmental equity as a struggle against institutionalized racism and an extension of the quest for social justice.[37] Just as black citizens fought for equal education, employment, and housing, they began to include the opportunity to live in a healthy environment as part of their basic rights. Moreover, they were convinced that disparate enforcement of environmental policies and regulations contributes to neighborhood decline much like housing discrimination, redlining practices, and residential segregation do.

Black resistance to environmental threats in the 1970s was confined to local issues and largely involved grassroots individuals. In the 1980s some changes occurred in the way black community groups and national advocacy groups dealt with the toxics issue. This new environmental activism among blacks did not materialize out of thin air nor was it an overnight phenomenon. It did, however, emerge out of the growing hostility to facility siting decisions that were seen as unfair, inequitable, and discriminatory toward poor people and people of color.

Toxic-waste disposal has generated demonstrations in many communities across the country.[38] The first national protest by blacks on the hazard-

ous-waste issue occurred in 1982. Demonstrations and protests were triggered after Warren County, North Carolina, which is mostly black, was
selected as the burial site for more than 32,000 cubic yards of soil contaminated with highly toxic PCBs (polychlorinated biphenyls), which had
been illegally dumped along the roadways in fourteen North Carolina
counties in 1978.

What was the source of the PCBs? The PCBs originated from the Ra-
leigh-based Ward Transfer Company. A Jamestown, New York, trucking
operation owned by Robert J. Burns obtained PCB-laced oil from the Ward
Transfer Company for resale. Faced with economic loss as a result of the
Environmental Protection Agency (EPA) ban on resale of the toxic oil in
1979, the waste haulers chose the cheap way out by illegally dumping it
along North Carolina's roadways. Burns and Ward were subsequently
sent to jail for the criminal dumping of the tainted oil.[39]

This dumping was the largest PCB spill ever documented in the United
States. More than 30,000 gallons of PCB-laced oil was left on 210 miles of
roadway in the state for four years before the federal EPA and the state of
North Carolina began clean-up activities. In 1982, after months of deliber-
ations and a questionable site selection exercise, North Carolina Governor
James B. Hunt decided to bury the contaminated soil in the community of
Afton located in Warren County. Local citizens later tagged the site
"Hunt's Dump."

The Afton community is more than 84 percent black. Warren County
has the highest percentage of blacks in the state and is one of the poorest
counties in North Carolina. The county had a population of 16,232 in 1980.
Blacks composed 63.7 percent of the county population and 24.2 percent
of the state population. Per capita income for Warren County residents
was $6,984 in 1982 compared with $9,283 for the state. The county ranked
ninety-second out of 100 counties in median family income in 1980. The
county unemployment rate was 13.3 percent in 1982 and 1983. More than
42 percent of the county's workforce commute out of the county for employment. Although the county lags far behind the rest of the state on a
number of economic indicators, over three-fourths of Warren County residents own their homes. More than 78 percent of the whites and 64 percent
of the blacks own their homes (nationally only 45 percent of blacks are
home owners).[40]

Why was Warren County selected as the PCB landfill site? The decision
made more political sense than environmental sense. In *Science for the People*, Ken Geiser and Gerry Waneck described the Warren County PCB siting decision:

> The site at Afton was not even scientifically the most suitable. The water table
> of Afton, North Carolina, (site of the landfill) is only 5-10 feet below the sur-

face, and the residents of the community derive all of their drinking water from local wells. Only the most optimistic could believe that the Afton land-fill will not eventually leach into the groundwater. Unless a more permanent solution is found, it will only be a matter of time before the PCBs end up in these people's wells.[41]

Black civil rights activists, political leaders, and area residents marched and protested against the construction of the Warren County PCB landfill. Dr. Charles E. Cobb, who was director of the United Church of Christ's Commission for Racial Justice in 1972, voiced his strong opposition to the Warren County PCB landfill and other siting decisions that make blacks and the poor bear a heavier burden than other communities. His directive to blacks was clear:

> We must move in a swift and determined manner to stop yet another breach of civil rights. We cannot allow this national trend to continue. If it means that every jail in this country must be filled, then I say let it be. The depositing of toxic wastes within the black community is no less than attempted geno-cide.[42]

Local county residents did organize. They formed the Warren County Citizens Concerned About PCBs. This time local citizens were not stand-ing alone. Grassroots groups were joined by national civil rights leaders, black elected officials, environmental activists, and labor leaders. For ex-ample, Reverend Leon White of the United Church of Christ's Commis-sion for Racial Justice, Reverends Joseph Lowery and Ben Chavis and Fred Taylor of the Southern Christian Leadership Conference, District of Co-lumbia Delegate Walter Fauntroy of the Congressional Black Caucus, and some 500 loyal supporters were able to focus the national limelight on the tiny black town of Afton.

The protests, however, did not stop the trucks from rolling in and dumping their loads. The state began hauling more than 6,000 truckloads of the PCB-contaminated soil to the landfills in mid-September of 1982. Just two weeks later, more than 414 protesters had been arrested. The pro-test demonstrations in Warren County marked the first time anyone in the United States had been jailed trying to halt a toxic waste landfill.[43]

The Warren County protesters even got encouragement from the chief of EPA's hazardous waste implementation branch, William Sanjour. He urged the demonstrators to "keep doing what you are going."[44] The EPA official questioned the disposal method selected over the alternatives (in-cineration and on-site neutralization). Sanjour's remarks at a rally at John Graham School in Warrenton reinforced what many of the protesters had suspected all along:

Landfilling is cheap. It is cheaper than the alternative. The people who like to use landfills such as chemical industries are very powerful. No amount of science, truth, knowledge or facts goes into making this decision. It is a purely political decision. What they listen to is pressure.[45]

Residents of Warren County were searching for guarantees that the state was not creating a future "superfund" site that would threaten nearby residents. Of course, no guarantees could be given since there is no such thing as a 100-percent safe hazardous-waste landfill—one that will not eventually leak. The question is not *if* the facility will leak but *when* the facility will leak PCBs into the environment.

Waste Facility Siting Disparities

Although the demonstrations in North Carolina were not successful in halting the landfill construction, the protests brought a sharper focus to the convergence of civil rights and environmental rights and mobilized a nationally broad-based group to protest these inequities. The 1982 demonstrations prompted District of Columbia Delegate Walter E. Fauntroy, who had been active in the protest demonstrations, to initiate the 1983 U.S. General Accounting Office (GAO) study of hazardous-waste landfill siting in the region.[46]

The GAO study observed a strong relationship between the siting of offsite hazardous-waste landfills and race and socioeconomic status of surrounding communities. It identified four offsite hazardous-waste landfills in the eight states that compose EPA's Region IV (i.e., Alabama, Florida, Georgia, Kentucky, Mississippi, North Carolina, South Carolina, and Tennessee). The data in Table 2.1 detail the socio-demographic characteristics of the communities where the four hazardous-waste landfill sites are located.

The four hazardous-waste landfill sites included Chemical Waste Management (Sumter County, Alabama), SCA Services (Sumter County, South Carolina), Industrial Chemical Company (Chester County, South Carolina), and Warren County PCB landfill (Warren County, North Carolina). Blacks composed the majority in three of the four communities where the offsite hazardous-waste landfills are located. Blacks make up about one-fifth of the population in EPA's Region IV. The GAO study also revealed that more than one-fourth of the population in all four communities had incomes below the poverty level, and most of this population was black.[47] The facility siting controversy cannot be reduced solely to a class phenomenon because there is no shortage of poor white communities in the region. One only has to point to southern Appalachia to see widespread white poverty in America. Nevertheless, poor whites along with their

TABLE 2.1 1980 Census Population, Income, and Poverty Data for Census Areas[a] Where EPA Region IV Hazardous-Waste Landfills Are Located (1983)

Landfill (State)	Population Number	% Black	Median family income ($) All Races	Blacks	Population below poverty level Number	%	% Black
Chemical Waste Management (Alabama)	626	90	11,198	10,752	265	42	100
SCA Services (South Carolina)	849	38	16,371	6,781	260	31	100
Industrial Chemical Co. (South Carolina)	728	52	18,996	12,941	188	26	92
Warren County PCB Landfill (North Carolina)	804	66	10,367	9,285	256	32	90

[a]Areas represent subdivisions of political jurisdictions designated by the census for data gathering.

Source: U.S. General Accounting Office, *Siting of Hazardous Waste Landfills and Their Correlation with Racial and Economic Status of Surrounding Communities* (Washington, D.C.; General Accounting Office, 1983), p.4.

more affluent counterparts have more options and leveraging mechanisms (formal and informal) at their disposal than blacks of equal status.

When the entire southern United States is studied, even more glaring siting disparities emerge. For example, there were twenty-seven hazardous-waste landfills operating in the forty-eight contiguous states with a total capacity of 127,897 acre-feet in 1987.[48] One-third of these hazardous-waste landfills were located in five southern states (i.e., Alabama, Louisiana, Oklahoma, South Carolina, and Texas). The total capacity of these nine landfills represented nearly 60 percent (76,226 acre-feet) of the nation's total hazardous-waste landfill capacity (see Table 2.2).

Four landfills in minority zip code areas represented 63 percent of the South's total hazardous-waste disposal capacity. Moreover, the landfills located in the mostly black zip code areas of Emelle (Alabama). Alsen (Louisiana), and Pinewood (South Carolina) in 1987 accounted for 58.6 percent of the region's hazardous-waste landfill capacity—although

TABLE 2.2 Operating Hazardous-Waste Landfills in the Southern United States and Ethnicity of Communities (1987)

Facility Name	Current Capacity in Acre-Feet[a]	Percent of Population in Zip code Area		
		Minority	Black	Hispanic
Chemical Waste Management (Emelle, AL)	30,000	79.5	78.9	0.0
CESCO International, Inc. (Livingston, LA)	22,400	23.8	21.6	1.8
Rollins Environmental Services (Scotlandville, LA)	14,440	94.7	93.0	1.5
Chemical Waste Management (Carlyss, LA)	5,656	6.8	4.6	1.7
Texas Ecologists, Inc. (Robstown, TX)	3,150	78.2	1.6	76.6
GSX Services of South Carolina (Pinewood, SC)	289	71.6	70.5	1.1
US Pollution Control, Inc. (Waynoka, OK)	118	37.3	23.2	12.3
Gulf Coast Waste Disposal Authority (Galveston, TX)	110	4.3	0.0	3.8
Rollins Environmental Services, Inc. (Deer Park, TX)	103	7.3	0.3	6.2

[a] Acre-feet is the volume of water needed to fill one acre to a depth of one foot. The total capacity of the nation's 27 hazardous-waste landfills was 127,989 in 1987.

Source: Commission for Racial Justice, *Hazardous Wastes and Race in the United States: A National Report on the Racial and Socio-Economic Characteristics of Communities with Hazardous Waste Sites* (New York: Commission for Racial Justice, 1987) Table B-10.

blacks make up only about 20 percent of the South's total population. These same three sites accounted for about 40 percent of the total estimated hazardous-waste landfill capacity in the entire United States.[49] Nationally, three of the five largest commercial hazardous-waste landfills are located in areas where blacks and Hispanics compose a majority of the population. These siting disparities expose minority citizens to greater risks than the general population.

It is not coincidental that the National Association for the Advancement of Colored People (NAACP) passed its first resolution on the hazardous-waste issue in 1983 after the national protest demonstration in Warren County, North Carolina. Subsequent protest actions were instrumental in getting the New York–based Commission for Racial Justice to sponsor its 1987 national study of toxic waste and race.[50] This national study, like the 1983 GAO report, found a strong association between race and the location of hazardous-waste facilities. Race was by far the most prominent factor in the location of commercial hazardous-waste landfills, more prominent than household income and home values. For example, the commission study found:

> Household incomes and home values were substantially lower when communities with hazardous-waste facilities were compared to communities in the surrounding county without such facilities. Mean household income was $2,745 less and mean value of owner-occupied homes was $17,301 less. The minority percentage of the population remained the most significant factor differentiating these groups of communities.[51]

Growing empirical evidence shows that toxic-waste dumps, municipal landfills, garbage incinerators, and similar noxious facilities are not randomly scattered across the American landscape. The siting process has resulted in minority neighborhoods (regardless of class) carrying a greater burden of localized costs than either affluent or poor white neighborhoods. Differential access to power and decision making found among black and white communities also institutionalizes siting disparities.

Toxic-waste facilities are often located in communities that have high percentages of poor, elderly, young, and minority residents.[52] An inordinate concentration of uncontrolled toxic-waste sites is found in black and Hispanic urban communities.[53] For example, when Atlanta's ninety-four uncontrolled toxic-waste sites are plotted by zip code areas, more than 82.8 percent of the city's black population compared with 60.2 percent of its white population were found living in waste-site areas. Despite its image as the "capital of the New South," Atlanta is the most segregated big city in the region. More than 86 percent of the city's blacks live in mostly black neighborhoods. As is the case for other cities, residential segregation and housing discrimination limit mobility options available to black Atlantans.

Siting disparities also hold true for other minorities and in areas outside the southern United States. Los Angeles, the nation's second largest city, has a total of sixty uncontrolled toxic-waste sites. More than 60 percent of the city's Hispanics live in waste-site areas compared with 35.3 percent of Los Angeles's white population. Although Hispanics are less segregated than the black population, more than half of them live in mostly Hispanic neighborhoods. The city's Hispanic community is concentrated in the eastern half of the city where the bulk of the uncontrolled toxic-waste sites are found.

On the other hand, large commercial hazardous-waste landfills and disposal facilities are more likely to be found in rural communities in the southern blackbelt.[54] Many of these facilities that are located in black communities are invisible toxic time bombs waiting for a disaster to occur.

Finally, the burden, or negative side, of industrial development has not been equally distributed across all segments of the population. Living conditions in many communities have not improved very much with new growth. Black communities became the dumping grounds for various types of unpopular facilities, including toxic wastes, dangerous chemicals, paper mills, and other polluting industries.

The path out of this environmental quagmire is clearly one that involves more communities in activities designed to reclaim the basic right of all Americans—the right to live and work in a healthy environment. A political strategy is also needed that can draw from a wide cross-section of individuals and groups who share a common interest in preservation of environmental standards. In his keynote address to the 1983 Urban Environment Conference on toxics and minorities, Congressman John Conyers of Detroit pinpointed this strategy. The black congressman saw broad-based groups (e.g., similar to those attending the New Orleans meeting) as having an "opportunity to raise the fairness issue in all dimensions, including the toxic threat to the poor, minority and working class Americans."[55]

CHAPTER THREE

◆

Dispute Resolution and Toxics: Case Studies

Most Americans encounter some type of unwanted land uses in or near where they live. Decisions surrounding the placement of needed (but unwanted) public facilities such as sewage treatment plants or municipal landfills, for example, have been hotly debated in community forums, planning boards, and city government. The usual consensus of these meetings is that few people want noxious facilities near their homes. Locational conflict involving unwanted land uses is inevitable. The question is, How will such conflicts be resolved? Unwanted land uses engender a sense of unfairness because they "gravitate to disadvantaged areas: poor, minority, sparsely populated, or politically underrepresented communities that cannot fight them off and become worse places to live after they arrive."[1]

Defining and Defending Against a Threat

White communities (middle- and lower-income areas) have been more successful than black communities in defending against unwanted industrial encroachment and outside penetration. Environmental organizations have won numerous siting concessions from government and private industry. However, the resolution of many environmental disputes has not affected all segments of the population in the same way. Some outcomes have had regressive impacts. The cumulative effect of not-in-my-backyard (NIMBY) victories by environmentalists appears to have driven the unwanted facilities toward the more vulnerable groups. Black neighborhoods are especially vulnerable to the penetration of unwanted land uses.

In the 1970s, environmentalists were able to institutionalize the communication networks, influence environmental policy, shape resolution techniques, and design dispute resolution mechanisms that reached deep into their communities. A decade later, blacks slowly began to move into this area—after much of the environmental damage had been inflicted.

The heightened level of environmental activism that emerged among blacks in the early 1980s served as a backdrop for this study. Because blacks do not have a long history of activism within mainstream environmental organizations, they were left to invent their own organizations or adapt their longstanding institutions to the environmental quality issue. Our analysis focuses on how black community residents defined the local disputes and the actions they used to eliminate the threat.[2]

Issue Crystallization and Focus

Issue crystallization refers to the main ideological focus taken by the citizen opposition and the opposition's perception of the relevant audiences' reaction. The citizen-defined issue areas included (1) conservation-environment, (2) public health, (3) equity and social justice, and (4) economic trade-offs.

Leadership Type

Regarding leadership type, we were interested in the "movers and shakers." Who spearheaded the local citizen opposition in the dispute and resolution process? Leadership types were grouped under (1) mainstream environmental organization, (2) grassroots environmental organization, (3) civil rights or social justice organization, and (4) emergent coalition organization. We were especially interested in the role (primary or secondary) played by outside groups in the mobilization and resolution phases.

Opposition Tactics

Citizen groups have pressed their opponents with a wide range of tactics and on many fronts. The most commonly used tactics include (1) governmental legal action, (2) governmental administrative action, (3) private legal action, (4) demonstrations, (5) petition and referenda, (6) lobbying, (7) press campaigns, and (8) violence. A special effort was taken to discover why local residents used certain tactics and not others.

Resolution Mechanisms

We emphasized the various methods and "appropriateness" of the dispute-handling mechanisms in resolving the problem. Resolution mechanisms come in a variety of sizes and shapes. However, we have used seven groupings: (1) legislation, (2) vote, (3) public hearing, (4) autocratic government decision, (5) adjudication, (6) arbitration and mediation, and (7) private bargaining and negotiation.

Outcomes

Citizens mobilized with the ultimate goal of defeating the opposition. In environmental disputes—as in other disputes—there are winners and losers. Sometimes it is not easy to declare clear-cut victories even after all the battles have been waged and the casualties counted. Nevertheless, outcomes of the environmental disputes were classified in three broad groups: (1) those having greater benefit for the opponents, i.e., resulting in closure, capacity reduction, or postponement; (2) those having benefits for the competing parties (these would be considered compromises), i.e., technical modification, relocation, compensation or fine; and (3) those having benefits that accrue largely to the industrial firm, i.e., approval.

Environmental dispute and resolution mechanisms were observed in five mostly black communities. Although different in some respects (size, density, housing occupancy, etc.), the areas share common barriers of institutional racism that limit mobility (physical and social) options. Urban, suburban, and rural black communities are not safe from the penetration of unwanted land uses. Land-use decisions involving the black community are usually made by individuals external to the community. Decision makers have few vested interests in establishing watchdog groups to monitor environmental quality in the urban ghettos or rural poverty areas in the blackbelt. Government inaction reinforces a system of exploitation, creates siting inequities, and exposes low- and middle-income black neighborhood residents to potential health risks.

It is no accident that the areas selected for this study are urban, suburban, and rural communities. The study areas also represent an economic mix, ranging from a low-income urban ghetto to a middle-class suburban neighborhood. The study areas are Houston's (Texas) Northwood Manor neighborhood (problem of municipal landfill siting), West Dallas (Texas) neighborhood (problem of lead contamination from a nearby smelter), Alsen (Louisiana) community (problem of toxic pollution from a hazardous-waste landfill and incinerator), Institute (West Virginia) community (problem of chemical emissions from a nearby industrial plant), and Emelle (Alabama) community (problem of living near the nation's largest hazardous-waste landfill). Summary characteristics of the study areas are presented in Table 3.1.

When looking at the various types of neighborhoods (e.g., urban versus rural), one runs the risk of comparing apples and oranges. It is quite apparent that somewhat different hurdles of organizing the community must be overcome in rural, sparsely populated areas from those in densely populated urban ghettos. When compared with rural community residents, urban residents, for example, may have (1) more resources at their disposal, i.e., finances, personnel, skills and communication networks, (2) easier access to voluntary organizations and action-oriented groups, (3) a larger pool of potential volunteers from which to draw supporters, and (4) their own elected or appointed representatives to lobby local government officials and policy makers. These hurdles, though difficult, are not impossible for rural community residents to overcome.

Many rural areas may not be able to match urban neighborhoods on a number of mobilization and organization resources. However, rural areas have not been without their pool of activist-leaders and dedicated followers. It was the action of the people in rural Warren County, North Carolina, in 1982 that focused national attention on toxics in the black community. Racism has forced African Americans to live apart from the larger society. It has also forced them to adapt strategies and institutions for their survival. This is true in urban and rural America—and the communities under investigation in this study.

The discussion now turns to descriptions of the case studies, the nature of the environmental disputes, and the strategies used by residents to resolve their problems.

Houston's Northwood Manor Neighborhood

In the 1970s, Houston was dubbed the "golden buckle" of the Sunbelt and the "petrochemical capital" of the world. The city experienced unparalleled economic expansion and population growth during the 1970s. By 1982, Houston emerged as the nation's fourth largest city with a population of 1.7 million persons spread over more than 585 square miles.[3] In 1980, the city's black community was made up of nearly a half million residents, or 28 percent of the city's total population. Black Houston, however, remained residentially segregated from the larger community. More than 81 percent of the city's blacks lived in mostly black areas with major concentrations in northeast and southeast sections of the city.

Houston is the only major city in the United States that does not have zoning. The city's landscape has been shaped by haphazard and irrational land-use planning, a pattern characterized by excessive infrastructure

TABLE 3.1 Profile of Study Areas and Nature of Environmental Problems

City/State	Community Size[a]	Facility Owner	Nature of Problem
Northwood Manor (Houston, TX)	8,449	Browning Ferris Industries	Municipal landfill
West Dallas (Dallas, TX)	13,162	RSR Corp.	Lead pollution
Institute (West Virginia)	1,450	Union Carbide	Chemical emission
Alsen (Louisiana)	1,104	Rollins Environmental Services	Hazardous waste
Emelle (Alabama)	626	Chemical Waste Management	Hazardous waste

[a]Community size refers to 1980 census areas--census tracts and enumeration districts--that are used by the census for data gathering.

chaos.[4] In the absence of zoning, developers have used renewable deed restrictions as a means of land-use control within subdivisions. Lower-income, minority, and older neighborhoods have had difficulty enforcing and renewing deed restrictions. Deed restrictions in these areas are often allowed to lapse because individuals may be preoccupied with making a living and may not have the time, energy, or faith in government to get the needed signatures of neighborhood residents to keep their deed restrictions in force. Moreover, the high occupancy turnover and large renter population in many inner-city neighborhoods further weaken the efficacy of deed restrictions as a protectionist device.

Ineffective land-use regulations have created a nightmare for many of Houston's neighborhoods—especially the ones that are ill equipped to fend off industrial encroachment. Black Houston, for example, has had to contend with a disproportionately large share of garbage dumps, landfills, salvage yards, automobile "chop" shops, and a host of other locally unwanted land uses. The siting of nonresidential facilities has heightened animosities between the black community and the local government. This is especially true in the case of solid-waste disposal siting.

Public officials learn fast that solid-waste management can become a volatile political issue. Generally, controversy centers around charges that disposal sites are not equitably spread in quadrants of the city; equitable siting would distribute the burden and lessen the opposition. Finding suitable sites for sanitary landfills has become a critical problem mainly because no one wants to have a waste facility as a neighbor. Who wants to live next to a place where household waste—some of which is highly toxic—is legally dumped and where hazardous wastes may be illegally dumped?

The burden of having a municipal landfill, incinerator, transfer station, or some other type of waste disposal facility near one's home has not been equally borne by Houston's neighborhoods. Black Houston has become the dumping grounds for the city's household garbage.[5] Over the past fifty years, the city has used two basic methods of disposing of its solid waste: incineration and landfill. The data in Table 3.2 show the location of the city-owned waste disposal facilities. Thirteen disposal facilities were operated by the city from the late 1920s to the mid-1970s. The city operated eight garbage incinerators (five large units and three mini-units), six of which were located in mostly black neighborhoods, one in a Hispanic neighborhood, and one in a mostly white area.

All five of the large garbage incinerators were located in minority neighborhoods—four black and one Hispanic. All five of the city-owned landfills were found in black neighborhoods. Although black neighborhoods composed just over one-fourth of the city's population, more than three-fourths of Houston's solid-waste facilities were found in these

TABLE 3.2 City of Houston Garbage Incinerators and Municipal Landfills

Neighborhood	Location	Incinerator	Landfill	Target Area[a]	Ethnicity of Neighborhood[b]
Fourth Ward	Southwest	1	1	Yes	Black
Cottage Grove	Northwest	1	-	Yes	Black
Kashmere Gardens	Northeast	2	-	Yes	Black
Sunnyside	Southeast	1	2	Yes	Black
Navigation	Southeast	1	-	Yes	Hispanic
Larchmont	Southwest	1	-	No	White
Carverdale	Northwest	1	-	Yes	Black
Trinity Gardens	Northeast	-	1	Yes	Black
Acres Homes	Northwest	-	1	Yes	Black

[a]Target areas are designated neighborhoods under Houston's Community Development Black Grant (CDBG) program.
[b]Ethnicity of neighborhood represents the racial/ethnic group that constitutes a numerical majority in the census tracts that make up the neighborhood.

neighborhoods. Moreover, lower-income areas, or "pockets of poverty," have a large share—twelve out of thirteen—of the city-owned garbage dumps and incinerators.

These environmental stressors compound the myriad of social ills (e.g., crowding, crime, poverty, drugs, unemployment, congestion, infrastructure deterioration, etc.) that exist in Houston's Community Development Block Grant (CDBG) target area neighborhoods.

The Texas Department of Health (TDH) is the state agency that grants permits for standard sanitary landfills. From 1970 to 1978, TDH issued four sanitary landfill permits for the disposal of Houston's solid waste. The data in Table 3.3 illustrate that siting of privately owned sanitary landfills in Houston followed the pattern established by the city. That is, disposal sites were located in mostly black areas of the city. Three of the four privately owned landfill sites are located in black neighborhoods.

Controversy surrounding landfill siting peaked in the late 1970s with the proposal to build the Whispering Pines landfill in Houston's Northwood Manor neighborhood. In 1980, the suburban neighborhood had a population of 8,449 residents, of whom 82.4 percent were black. The subdivision consists primarily of single-family home owners. It also sits in the midst of the predominately black North Forest Independent School District—one of the poorest suburban districts in the Houston area.

Northwood Manor residents thought they were getting a shopping center or new homes in their subdivision when construction on the landfill

TABLE 3.3 Privately Owned Houston Sanitary Landfills Permitted by the Texas Department of Health, 1970-1978

Site	Location	Year Permitted	Neighborhood	Ethnicity of Neighborhood
Holmes Road	Southeast	1970	Almeda Plaza	Black
McCarty	Northeast	1971	Chattwood[a]	White
Holmes Road	Southeast	1978	Almeda Plaza	Black
Whispering Pines	Northeast	1978	Northwood Manor	Black

[a]This predominately white neighborhood is located just north of the McCarty landfill. The Chattwood neighborhood lies within Houston's Settegast Target Area. The Settegast Target Area has undergone a dramatic racial transition from 40 percent black in 1970 to more than 70 percent black in 1980.

site commenced. When they learned the truth, they began to organize their efforts to stop the dump. It is ironic than many of the residents who were fighting the construction of the waste facility had moved to Northwood Manor in an effort to escape landfills in their former Houston neighborhoods.

Local residents formed the Northeast Community Action Group (NECAG)—a spinoff organization from the local neighborhood civic association—to halt the construction of the facility. They later filed a lawsuit in federal court to stop the siting of the landfill in their neighborhood. The residents and their black attorney, Linda McKeever Bullard, charged the Texas Department of Health and the private disposal company (Browning Ferris Industries) with racial discrimination in the selection of the Whispering Pines landfill site.[6] Residents were upset because the proposed site was not only near their homes but within 1,400 feet of their high school. Smiley High School was not equipped with air conditioning—not an insignificant point in the hot and humid Houston climate. Windows are usually left open while school is in session. Moreover, seven North Forest Schools—also without air conditioning—can be found in Northwood Manor and contiguous neighborhoods. (See Figure 3.1.)

The lawsuit that was filed in 1979 finally went to trial in 1984. The federal district judge in Houston ruled against the residents and the landfill was built. The class-action lawsuit, however, did produce some changes in the way environmental issues were dealt with in the city's black community. First, the Houston city council, acting under intense political pressure from local residents, passed a resolution in 1980 that prohibited city-owned trucks carrying solid waste from dumping at the controversial landfill. Second, the Houston city council passed an ordinance restricting

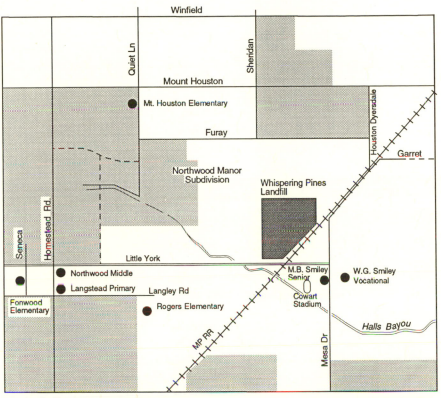

FIGURE 3.1 Location of Houston's Northwood Manor neighborhood and the Browning Ferris Industries Whispering Pines sanitary landfill

the construction of solid-waste sites near public facilities such as schools. This action was nothing less than a form of zoning. Third, the Texas Department of Health updated its requirements of landfill permit applicants to include detailed land-use, economic, and socio-demographic data on areas where they proposed to site standard sanitary landfills. Fourth, and probably most important, black residents sent a clear signal to the Texas Department of Health, city government, and private disposal companies that they would fight any future attempts to place waste disposal facilities in their neighborhoods. The landfill question appears to have galvanized and politicized a part of the Houston community, the black community, which for years had been inactive on environmental issues.

West Dallas (Texas)

Dallas is the seventh largest city in the nation with a population of 904,078 in 1980. The 265,594 blacks who live in Dallas represent 29.4 percent of the city's population. Dallas remains a racially segregated city with more than eight of every ten blacks living in majority black areas. West Dallas is just one of these segregated enclaves. The population of the West Dallas study area is 13,161 of whom more than 85 percent are black.[7] The neighborhood developed primarily as a rural black settlement on the fringe of the city. The area was one of the early dumping grounds for the city's solid waste. For years, West Dallas residents lived in squalor and had few basic services because they were outside the city boundaries.

One of the oldest institutions in the neighborhood is Thomas A. Edison School built in 1909. One of the oldest industries in the neighborhood is the 63-acre Murph Metals secondary lead smelter (later known as RSR Corporation). The company began operations in the neighborhood in 1934 near Thomas Edison School. West Dallas was annexed by the city in 1954. Two years later, a 3,500-unit public housing project covering more than 500 acres opened just north of the smelter. Many of the residents' homes were torn down as a "slum clearance" effort to make way for the massive public housing development. (See Figure 3.2.)

The Dallas Housing Authority is the chief landlord in the West Dallas neighborhood. Most of the privately owned housing near the public housing project is absentee-owned. Less than one-third of the housing in the area is owner-occupied. In the census tracts where the barracks-like public housing units are located, families are typically black, female-headed, and poor. More than two-thirds of the households have incomes below the poverty level.[8] The demand for privately owned housing in this low-income area that lies some four miles west of the sparkling "Big D" (as Dallas is affectionately tagged) skyline has been dampened by the concentration of public housing, systematic neglect by the city government, deteriorating infrastructure, and industrial pollution from the nearby RSR lead smelter.

The housing project, which was built in the mid-1950s, was located just fifty feet from the sprawling West Dallas RSR lead smelter's property line and in a direct path of the prevailing southerly winds. The secondary smelter recovered lead from used automobile batteries and other materials. During peak operation in the mid-1960s, the plant employed more than 400 persons. However, it pumped more than 269 tons of lead particles each year into the West Dallas air.[9] Lead particles were blown by prevailing winds through the doors and windows of nearby residents and onto the West Dallas streets, sidewalks, ballparks, and children's playgrounds. Few West Dallas residents can afford the luxury of air conditioners to contend with the long and hot Texas summers. People usually leave their windows open, sit underneath shade trees, or socialize outside on their porches to keep cool.

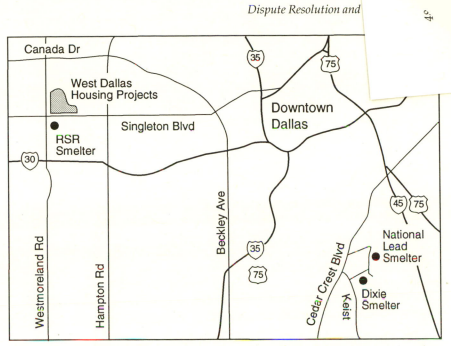

FIGURE 3.2   The West Dallas neighborhood and the nearby RSR Corporation lead smelter

The toxicity of lead has been known at least since the Roman era when the metal was widely used and lead poisoning cases were first documented. However, West Dallas residents were exposed to this environmental poison for five decades. Moreover, several generations of young children were subjected to unnecessary health risks associated with lead poisoning. In 1968 the city of Dallas enacted one of the strongest lead ordinances in the country. The ordinance prohibited the emission of lead compounds in excess of 5 $\mu g/m^3$ (micrograms per cubic meter) over any thirty-day period, and prohibited any particulate concentration greater than 100 $\mu g/m^3$. The ordinance, however, proved to be a worthless piece of legislation because city officials systematically refused to enforce its lead emission standards.

Dallas officials were informed as early as 1972 that lead was finding its way into the bloodstreams of the children who lived in two minority neighborhoods (West Dallas and East Oak Cliff) near lead smelters.[10] The Dallas Health Department study found that living near the smelters was associated with a 36 percent increase in blood lead level. Children near the smelters were exposed to elevated levels of lead in the soil, air, and households. The city was urged to restrict the emissions of lead to the atmosphere and to undertake a large screening program to determine the extent of the public health problem. The city failed to take immediate action on this matter.

After repeated violations of the lead ordinance, the city in 1974 sued the local smelters to force compliance. The suits were settled a year later after the firms agreed to pay fines of $35,000 and install pollution equipment. The city later amended its lead ordinance in 1976. The amended ordinance, however, was a much weaker version than its 1968 predecessor. The new ordinance—like the old version—was not enforced consistently, while lead companies in Dallas chronically and repeatedly violated the law. The Dallas Alliance Environmental Task Force, a citizen group appointed by the Dallas City Council in 1983 to address the health concerns of West Dallas, highlighted this point in its study:

> We believe that the City has missed many opportunities to serve and protect the community-at-large and two neighborhoods in particular in relation to the lead problem we now address. It is clear that the State and Federal governments have also failed in their opportunities to regulate an industry of this type with regard to the general welfare of citizens.[11]

The United States Environmental Protection Agency (EPA) in 1978 established the National Ambient Air Quality Standard, limiting airborne lead—an average of 1.5 micrograms per cubic meter of air averaged over a ninety-day period. Two years later the EPA—concerned about health risks associated with the Dallas lead smelters—commissioned another lead screening program. The 1981 study confirmed what was basically found a decade earlier: Children living near the lead smelters were likely to have greater lead concentrations in their blood than children who did not live near smelters. Soil-lead concentrations near the RSR smelter in West Dallas, for example, averaged nine times that in the control area, while the average near the Dixie Metals smelter in East Oak Cliff was thirteen times the norm.

Federal officials received the report in February 1981. The city and companies had the report three months later. West Dallas and East Oak Cliff residents, however, did not receive formal notification of the health risks associated with living so close to the lead smelters. It was not until June 1981 that the *Dallas Morning News* broke the headline-grabbing story of the "potentially dangerous" lead levels discovered by EPA researchers. The series of lead-related articles presented in the local newspapers triggered widespread concern, public outrage, several class-action lawsuits, and legal action by the city of Dallas and the state of Texas against the smelter operators.

Soil levels found around the West Dallas Boys Club—located just a short distance from the 300-foot smokestack of the RSR smelter—forced the directors to suspend outdoor activities. The first city-sponsored tests of soil at the Boys Club showed one sample that was sixty times the level considered potentially dangerous to children.

RSR voluntarily removed and replaced the soil at the Boys Club and at the nearby school. The West Dallas Boys Club, a program that enrolled more than 1,200 youths between ages 6 and 28, and the Maro Booth Day Care Center, a facility that served children from seventy-five low-income families, were later forced to close in 1983 because of the lead problem.[12]

After all of the publicity exposed the health threat, no immediate action was forthcoming by the EPA or the city to alleviate the lead contamination problem in West Dallas. Local opposition mounted against the company. At one meeting in the spring of 1983 more than 150 angry citizens packed a room in the George Loving Place public housing project to voice their opposition to a plan to move them out rather than close the lead smelter. Residents felt their plight was being ignored because they were poor, black, and politically powerless. Patricia Spears, a home owner, community leader, and operator of a West Dallas funeral home, summed up her community's dilemma: "If we lived in Highland Park or Northeast Dallas [affluent white areas], the lead plant would have been closed in 1981. Instead of them moving us, why don't they pull together and shut the lead plant down?"[13]

It was later revealed in the March 1983 hearings conducted by U.S. Representative Elliott H. Levitas (D-Ga.) that former EPA Deputy Administrator John Hernandez needlessly scrapped a voluntary plan by RSR to clean up the lead-contaminated "hot spots" in West Dallas. But Hernandez blocked the cleanup and called for yet another round of tests to be designed and conducted by the federal Centers for Disease Control (CDC) with the EPA and Dallas Health Department. The results of this study were available in February 1983. Although the new study showed a lower percentage of children affected than the earlier study had shown, it established the smelter as the dominant source of elevated lead in the children's blood.[14]

EPA officials from the Dallas regional office were especially critical of Hernandez's handling of the local lead issue and the general design of the 1983 Dallas lead study. The testimony of Dr. Norman Dyer, regional EPA chief of toxic substances, and Dr. William McAnalley, a former EPA toxicologist who resigned over the mismanagement of the Dallas lead problem, at the Levitas hearing sent shock waves through the federal EPA. They characterized the study findings as misleading and encompassing too large a study area. Moreover, the study did not look at blood lead levels of the children who lived downwind from the smelters, where the highly contaminated soil was found. This design was proposed by Dr. Dyer, but was turned down by the EPA in Washington as not "cost effective." In May 1983, the *Dallas Times-Herald* conducted this very analysis in West Dallas. The newspaper found that 34 percent of the children living in the areas where soil levels were above 1,000 parts per million (ppm) had elevated blood lead levels. More than 18 percent of the children who lived in areas where soil levels were above 300 ppm had elevated blood lead levels.[15] Hernandez's delay of cleanup actions in West Dallas was tantamount to "waiting for a body count."[16]

The Levitas hearings and the subsequent departure of EPA's top administrators thrust the handling of the Dallas lead problem into the national limelight. In March 1983, the Texas Air Control Board staff recommended that the state sue RSR for violating lead emission standards. One month later, the city of Dallas joined Texas Attorney General Jim Mattox in suing RSR in state district court in Dallas. The lawsuit did not seek to close the smelter but only sought the removal of tainted soil and reduced airborne emissions.

The lawsuit was settled out of court in June 1983 with RSR agreeing to a soil cleanup in West Dallas, a blood-testing program for children and pregnant women, and the installation of new antipollution equipment. The pollution control equipment, however, was never installed. In May 1984, the Dallas Board of Adjustments—an agency responsible for monitoring land-use violations—requested the city attorney to order the smelter permanently closed for violating the zoning code. Four months later, the Dallas Board of Adjustments ordered the West Dallas smelter permanently closed.[17] Although the smelter is now closed, much of the contaminated soil removed from "hot spots" remains on the site along with the contaminated equipment. West Dallas residents still have questions about the contaminated site itself and future land use in their neighborhood.

It is ironic that in its fifty years of operation the smelter had not obtained all of the necessary use permits for operating in the West Dallas residential neighborhood. The city not only had the legal means of forcing the company to comply with its lead emission ordinance but also had the legal power to close the smelter for violating its zoning ordinance. Slowly, it became apparent that the Dallas "secondary lead smelters are incompatible with residential neighborhoods."[18] It is unfortunate that many of the local residents had to pay a high health price for the city's ineptness in dealing with its black citizenry.

If nothing else, the plant closure was a tribute to the tenacity of the low-income black neighborhood to withstand the assaults of pollution, inept government officials, and institutionalized discrimination. D. W. Nauss, a *Dallas Times-Herald* reporter, captured the change in West Dallas residents:

> Once united only by poverty and powerlessness, the community has been brought together by the shared trauma of living with the lead smelter and the

need to save what little they have. The pollution problem also has awakened the community to other concerns, such as industrial development and housing redevelopment, and has made many residents for the first time cast a hard, distrusting eye toward city plans for the area.[19]

One of the long and bitter legal battles of the West Dallas residents who have lived in the shadow of the RSR lead smelter was finally resolved in an out-of-court settlement in the summer of 1985. The settlement, estimated at $20 million, was reached between RSR and Dallas Attorney Frederick M. Baron who sued on behalf of 370 children—almost all of whom were poor and black residents of West Dallas public housing—and 40 property owners. The agreement is one of the largest community lead-contamination settlements ever awarded. The settlement (with interest accruing over a thirty-year period) will funnel nearly $45 million to the children in periodic payments. Although no amount of money can ever repay the harm caused by lead poisoning of several generations of West Dallas children, the settlement does reveal that poor black communities are no longer willing to accept other people's pollution.

Another class-action lawsuit, Annie Young et al. v. RSR Corp. et al., by residents of West Dallas and East Oak Cliff neighborhoods has not been resolved. Residents of these two mostly black Dallas neighborhoods are charging the city and the lead smelter companies with discrimination in the placement of the plants and in enforcing local environmental standards. As in the case of Houston's Northwood Manor residents, the Dallas residents may discover that environmental discrimination is easier to document empirically than it is to prove in a court of law.

Institute (West Virginia)

Institute is located in Kanawha County, West Virginia. The county's population was 231,400 persons in 1980. The county's major population concentration is located in Charleston, the state capital.[20] Institute is located approximately six miles west of Charleston along Interstate 64 and West Virginia Route 25. It is an unincorporated community that lies between the cities of Dunbar on the east and Nitro on the south. Institute is confined on the south by the Kanawha River and mountains on the north.

Institute had a population of 1,450 inhabitants in 1980, down from 2,055 in 1970. Blacks compose over 90 percent of the community's population. The community has long been an area identified with black landowners. In 1891, the settlement was selected by the West Virginia State Legislature to be the site for the West Virginia Colored Institute—organized for blacks under the Second Morrill Act of 1890. Black citizens were influential in convincing the governor's site inspection committee to locate the school

k community found on the Kanawha River, near what is now
[1] The school's name was changed to West Virginia State College

Although the Institute community has remained mostly black since its founding, West Virginia State College has undergone a dramatic demographic transition. The historically black college now enrolls a predominately white student population. This transition began with the landmark 1954 Brown v. Board of Education U.S. Supreme Court decision that desegregated public schools. During the days of "Jim Crow" and segregation, both West Virginia State College and the nearby West Virginia Rehabilitation Center—a facility for handicapped individuals—were black institutions. West Virginia State College now enrolls more than 4,500 students, mostly white commuters from the Charleston area. Between 250 to 300 blind and disabled patients are enrolled in the Rehabilitation Center. A large share of the college's blacks students will live on campus or in the Institute community. (See Figure 3.3.)

The college and rehabilitation center are located adjacent to the Institute Union Carbide chemical plant. This plant is just one of the many chemical firms found along the 25-mile long Kanawha River Valley. The valley has more than twenty chemical plants that produce compounds used to make explosives, fertilizer, plastics, pesticides, automobile antifreeze, and other toxic and carcinogenic materials.[22] Some of the other well-known firms in the valley include American Cyanamid, Diamond Shamrock, Dupont, Monsanto, FMC, and Olin. Union Carbide, however, is the largest employer in the valley with some 7,000 workers in 1985. Statewide, more than 10,000 West Virginians were employed in the chemical industry.[23]

The Union Carbide chemical plants have been in the valley for six decades dating back to World War I. Dirty air and odors have long been a fact of life in the Kanawha Valley and in Institute. To some residents of the valley, Union Carbide has meant prosperity in an economically impoverished state. Without Union Carbide, some feel the area would be a "ghost valley."[24] The company represents the "sight and smell of money."[25] The average salary of a worker at the three local Union Carbide plants is more than $600 a week. To others, the polluting industries represent a potential health threat—a future Bhopal.

Local fears were heightened after the 1984 poison-gas leak at the Union Carbide plant in Bhopal, India, that killed more than 3,400 persons and maimed another 100,000. People became concerned that such an accident could happen in their community. This was especially the case for residents of Institute who live so close to and downwind from the Union Carbide plant. The plant also manufactured the same methyl isocyanate (MIC) responsible for the Bhopal disaster. The world's deadliest indus-

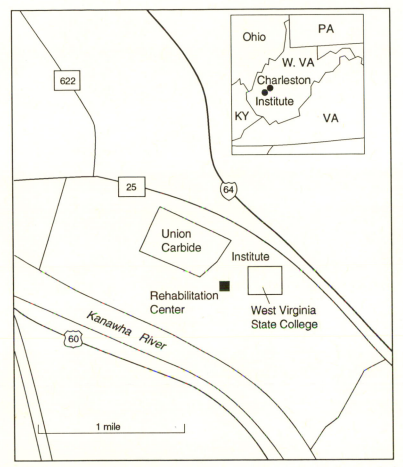

FIGURE 3.3   The community of Institute and the location of the Union Carbide chemical plant

trial accident was still fresh on the minds of the Institute residents when they first learned that the nearby plant made the same chemical a few hundred yards from their schools, homes, and churches. In the aftermath of the Indian tragedy, Union Carbide temporarily shut down the MIC unit at its Institute plant and spent more than $5 million on a safety and emergency warning system.[26] Federal officials subsequently inspected the plant and declared it safe for renewed operation.

The new safety and emergency system installed at the plant proved to be flawed. This fact was borne out on August 11, 1985, when a toxic mixture of aldicarb oxime—a mixture used to produce a pesticide called Temlik (used mostly on potatoes and bananas)—sent a poisonous plume of gas over Institute and sent 135 people to the hospital.[27] The leak continued for about fifteen minutes causing residents to experience breathing problems, burning eyes, chest tightness, headaches, nausea, and dizziness. It was only because of the change in the batching process—the chemical batching that ends with MIC was cut off at the aldicarb oxime step, one step from the final product—that Institute did not become another Bhopal. Plant officials did not sound a public alarm until twenty minutes after the leak began because of human error and incorrect readings on its new safety system's computers—instruments that measure such things as wind direction and velocity. The EPA subsequently ruled that Union Carbide's emergency notification took too long. EPA's investigation of the Institute plant revealed that this incident was not the only time the deadly MIC had leaked from the plant. The government investigation showed that 61 MIC leaks had occurred over the previous five years. These leaks ranged from one pound to more than ten pounds.[28]

These emissions are some of the more than 300 chemicals—at least 80 percent of them suspected to be injurious to health—that are continuously released into the air in the Charleston area. Most of these leaks are not accidents but are "allowable routine emissions." The Institute plant in 1981 alone, emitted "nearly 146 tons of butadiene, 11 tons of ethylene oxide, 50 tons of chloroform, 17 tons of propylene oxide, 10 tons of benzene, and, although it was not reported then, a harmless whiff of methyl isocyanate, or MIC—the lethal stuff of Bhopal."[29]

Local residents had become concerned about chemical emissions in the aftermath of Bhopal. Shortly after this tragedy, Edwin Hoffman, a history professor at West Virginia State College, organized a group called People Concerned About MIC. The group's credibility was enhanced when the aldicarb oxime leak occurred in Institute in the summer of 1985. On August 18, 1985, more than 300 angry residents marched against the Institute plant demanding an explanation from Union Carbide officials about the leak and the safety assurances they had been given earlier. Most of the people who participated in this protest were not "environmental types," but were ordinary citizens who were fed up with the "stink" in the Kanawha Valley. Anger against the Institute plant had been building for years. The 1985 leak made a bad situation worse. Claire Smith, whose family was hospitalized as a result of the leak, summed up the general feelings of the Institute residents: "We feel very fearful and very angry. This is family property passed down from my great-great-grandfather, but now I don't feel safe here anymore."[30] The residents wanted justice, i.e., protection from the threat posed by the nearby chemical plant. They demanded better emergency notification, more escape routes than the single two-lane road currently available to them, and relocation of the plant's most toxic chemicals out of their community.

The 1985 chemical leak heightened an already uneasy relationship that had existed for years between Union Carbide and the mostly black town. The community receives few economic benefits from the plant's location in its midst. Fewer than 10 percent of the Institute plant workforce are local residents. For years, officials at the Institute plant hired blacks in only the low-paying menial jobs, while whites were hired into the better-paying positions. Since the community was not incorporated, it received no direct tax benefits from the plant. Some Institute residents actually accuse Union Carbide of using its clout to keep the area unincorporated as a means to keep from paying taxes. Local residents often point to action by Kanawha County officials who authorized an incorporation election that left the plant outside the proposed Institute city limits—a position consistent with that held by Union Carbide but opposed by Institute residents. A group of local citizens appealed to the courts and the company offered to make payments to the city in lieu of taxes.[31] The Institute plant was subsequently sold to Rhone Poulenc, a French-owned chemical company. Change in ownership has not calmed the fears of local residents because the risks from toxic chemical leaks are still present.

Alsen (Louisiana)

Alsen is an unincorporated community located on the Mississippi River several miles north of Baton Rouge, Louisiana's state capital. The community had a population of 1,104 individuals in 1980 of whom 98.9 percent were black. Alsen developed as a rural community of black landowners to its present status as a stable, working-class suburban enclave. The median income for families in 1980 was $17,188. A total of 19.4 percent of Alsen's residents are below the poverty level, a percentage well below that of blacks nationally and in Louisiana. Typical homes in the area are woodframe or brick-veneer style. More than three-fourths (77.4 percent) of the year-round occupied homes in the community are occupied by owners and 22.6 percent by renters.[32] The community still maintains much of its small-town flavor. Many of the local residents have roots in the community dating back several generations.

Alsen lies at the beginning of the 85-mile industrial corridor where one-quarter of America's petrochemicals are produced. The chemical corridor begins in Baton Rouge and follows the Mississippi River down to the southeastern rim of New Orleans. The tiny town of Alsen sits in the shadow of Huey Long's skyscraper-capitol building and the towering petrochemical plants that dot the Mississippi River. This area also has been dubbed the "cancer corridor" because the air, ground, and water are full of carcinogens, mutagens, and embryotoxins. The area has been described as a "massive human experiment" and a "national sacrifice zone."[33]

The petrochemical industry has played an important role in Louisiana's economy, especially south Louisiana. More than 165,000 persons were employed in the state's petrochemical industry at its peak in 1982. This single industry accounted for one out of every three tax dollars collected by the state.[34] The Baton Rouge area has paid a high price—industrial pollution—for the concentration of so many chemical companies in its midst. These companies discharge more than 150,000 tons of pollutants into the city's air each year. The bulk of these air pollutants are in the form of sulfur dioxides, nitrogen oxides, carbon monoxides, and hydrocarbons. (See Figure 3.4.)

Louisiana is not a large state. It ranks thirty-one in land area of all states. Despite its relatively compact size, it managed to import more than 305.6 million pounds of hazardous waste in 1983.[35] Much of this waste was shipped into south Louisiana. In 1986, the state had 33.2 percent of the nation's total permitted hazardous-waste landfill capacity among active sites. Much of Louisiana's hazardous waste generated by the petrochemical industries is dumped in the Baton Rouge area. The only commercial hazardous-waste site in the Baton Rouge area is the Rollins Environmental Services facility, located adjacent to the Alsen community.

The Rollins site was the fourth largest in the nation, representing 11.3 percent of remaining permitted capacity in 1986.[36] The Rollins hazardous-waste landfill and incinerator have been a constant sore point for the nearby Alsen residents. The waste site has been the source of numerous odor and health complaints from nearby community residents and workers at the plant. The plant was cited for more than 100 state and federal violations between 1980 and 1985 but did not pay any penalties. Mary McCastle, a 72-year-old grandmother and Alsen community leader, summed up her community's running battle with Rollins:

> We had no warning Rollins was coming in here. When they did come in we didn't know what they were dumping. We did know that it was making us sick. People used to have nice gardens and fruit trees. They lived off their gardens and only had to buy meat. Some of us raised hogs and chickens. But not after Rollins came in. Our gardens and animals were dying out. Some days the odors from the plant would be nearly unbearable. We didn't know what was causing it. We later found out that Rollins was burning hazardous waste.[37]

Air quality in the Alsen community became a cause for alarm. Local residents began to question the company's right to spew pollutants on their community. Complaints were filed with the Louisiana Department

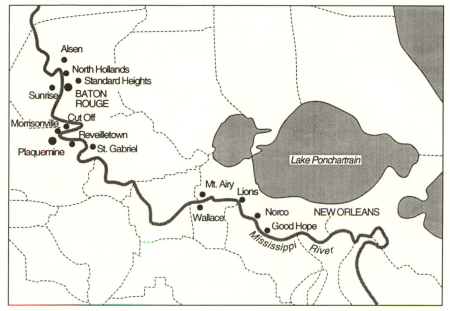

FIGURE 3.4 The community of Alsen and other communities contending with industry along the Lower Mississippi River Corridor

of Environmental Quality (LDEQ) with no immediate results. Although local citizens registered their displeasure with the waste facility's operation, they got little attention from state environmental officials. Annie Bowdry, the director of the Alsen Community Center—a nonprofit human services program—described the state's response (or lack of response) to Alsen's needs:

> Alsen is black and a nowhere place stuck out in the parish. It's not incorporated. It didn't count. It was not until after state environmental officials visited the community that citizen complaints were taken seriously. State officials could not believe that people endured everyday the terrible odors from the Rollins plant.[38]

In late 1980, residents began organizing to stop the contamination of their community. Local leaders recognized the fact that they were going up against a giant corporation. The annual revenue in Rollins from hazardous waste alone was more than $69 million. Citizens were also aware that the company provided jobs—although few Alsen residents worked at the company. Alsen residents were determined to take a stand based on what was best for the health and welfare of their community. In early 1981, local citizens filed a multimillion dollar class-action lawsuit against

Rollins. The lawsuit and subsequent state monitoring of the air quality problem in Alsen forced the company to reduce the pollutants from the waste site. Public opposition to the Rollins hazardous-waste facility intensified in the mid-1980s when citizen groups and environmentalists (Greenpeace, Sierra Club, and some local grassroots groups) turned out in force to oppose an application by the firm to burn PCBs at its incinerator. This protest was successful in blocking the PCBs burn.

Alsen residents were outraged that their lawsuit against Rollins dragged on for so long. Local citizens were angry that Louisiana DEQ officials took so long to believe the horror stories of Alsen's air pollution problem. They wondered why it was so difficult to resolve this problem. Admon McCastle, a native of Alsen, saw racism as the root of his community's dilemma:

> More than 15 years ago, a wealthy white property owner next to Rollins received a half million dollar settlement from the company for the death of his cattle after water spilled onto his pasture. Yet, Rollins has failed to recognize it is harming people, not cows, in the Alsen community. When I look at this, I have to say racism has played a big part in the company's actions and the state's inaction.[39]

After dragging on for more than six years, the lawsuit was finally settled out of court in November 1987. The settlement, however, splintered the community. Residents were polarized into "money versus health" factions. Each plaintiff in the lawsuit received "an average of $3,000 the day before Christmas."[40] There was a "take the money and run" atmosphere that prevailed in the battle-weary community. Opponents of the secret-settlement agreement point to the need for continual health monitoring in the community. This is not a small point since the plaintiffs were required to sign away their right to sue Rollins for any future health-related problems. Annie Bowdry lodged her opposition to the settlement:

> We wanted to establish a health clinic in Alsen that would be administered by the state [Louisiana] and paid for by Rollins. Since Rollins made the people sick, they should have to pay for the operation of the clinic. All at once, someone mentioned money and the health clinic proposal went out the window. My feelings about the whole thing is a dollar cannot buy my health. But if I knew I was contaminated in time, then maybe a cure for me could be found. If not for me, then maybe for my children.[41]

Overall, life in the Alsen community has improved since residents have become more informed on the hazardous-waste problem and convinced state officials to closely monitor air quality in their community. Although economic concessions were extracted from Rollins through an out-of-court settlement, the community was left without a health facility of its own. Moreover, the settlement agreement shielded the waste disposal company from any future health-related lawsuits by the Alsen plaintiffs. Alsen residents still must drive to Baton Rouge for health care services.

The community's pollution problem is far from over because numerous chemical plants are still clustered along the Mississippi River just a short distance from their homes. This problem will likely remain as long as the backbone of Louisiana's economy remains heavily dependent on its "chemical corridor." More important, increased public opposition and tougher environmental regulations have made it more difficult to site new hazardous-waste facilities. The Rollins hazardous-waste landfill and incinerator, thus, take on added state and regional importance.

Louisiana, dubbed the "sportsman's paradise," has become an environmental nightmare as a result of lax regulations, unbridled production of toxic chemicals, and heavy dependence on the petrochemical industry as the backbone of the state's economy.

Emelle–Sumter County (Alabama)

Sumter County is located in the heart of west Alabama's economically impoverished "blackbelt." The county's population in 1980 was 16,908, down from 27,000 in 1940 (a more than 40 percent decline). Blacks make up 69 percent of Sumter County. More than 33 percent of the county's population live below the poverty line. Blacks compose more than 90 percent of the county residents who live in poverty. The median family income for blacks in the county was only $11,015 in 1980.[42]

Sumter County has a legacy of farming and cotton production dating back to the plantation system of slavery and the sharecropper (tenant farmer) system that followed. Farming, a mainstay of the region, began to decline beginning in the 1970s. Many farmers were forced off their land, and others chose to sell their land for nonfarm uses. Land prices in the county, for example, decreased by 15–20 percent since 1981.[43] By the mid-1980s, cattle and timber had replaced the row crop form of agriculture in the county.

Sumter County and its neighboring blackbelt counties have been treated as a Third World region in our own backyard. Sumter County's per capita income ranks near the bottom (64th out of 67) of the state's counties. The area has been largely avoided by industry and failed by agriculture. The demise of agriculture has left a 20 percent countywide unemployment rate and a significantly higher black unemployment rate. It is not uncommon in many black communities in the county to have one-third of the workforce unemployed. These bleak economic conditions and cheap land made the county a likely candidate for polluting industries—especially waste disposal companies. (See Figure 3.5.)

In 1978, Chemical Waste Management (Chemwaste) opened the nation's largest hazardous-waste treatment, storage, and disposal facility in Sumter County. Chemwaste is a subsidiary of Waste Management, Inc.— a global conglomerate with gross receipts of $2 billion in 1986. Chemwaste is just one of the half-dozen firms that share the lucrative hazardous-waste disposal business with such firms as Browning Ferris Industries, Allied Signal, IT, IV International, and Rollins Environmental Services.

The Chemwaste facility was built near Emelle, a small, rural black community. The Emelle community study area consists of 626 residents. Blacks compose more than 90 percent of the community's population. About 42 percent of Emelle's population lived in poverty in 1980. Most residents live in single-family, woodframe houses. However, a sizable share of the people live in trailer homes scattered along the rural gravel and unpaved roads. This sleepy little town sits next to what has been dubbed the "Cadillac of dumps."[44] Booth Gunter and Mike Williams, two award-winning environmental reporters, described the Emelle facility:

> Chemical Waste Management, Inc., which runs the facility, boasts that it is the nation's Cadillac of toxic waste landfills—a claim confirmed by some geologists familiar with the site. Much of west Alabama is underlined by a layer of limestone called Selma chalk, which here averages 700 feet in thickness. The chalk is highly impermeable. The company claims it would take 10,000 years for waste escaping from the landfill's trenches to penetrate to the aquifer below the site. But for people living in the area, the aquifer, which provides drinking water for much of western Alabama, is the primary concern.[45]

The hazardous-waste operation was brought to the Emelle community without the input from local residents. The facility was "forced on the people."[46] No blacks held public office or sat on governing bodies, including the state legislature, county commission, or industrial development board (an agency that promotes industrial operation in the county) from predominately black Sumter County in 1978. It was not until 1984 that blacks took the majority of seats on the Sumter County Commission.[47] One year later, the first black was elected to the Alabama state legislature from the area.

Few residents knew that they were about to become the host community for the nation's largest hazardous-waste dump. Rumors circulated throughout the community about a "new industry" coming to town. The *Sumter County Record*, a local newspaper, touted the economic benefits of the industry with a banner headline that read "Unique New Industry Coming: New Use for Selma Chalk to Create Jobs."[48] Local residents mis-

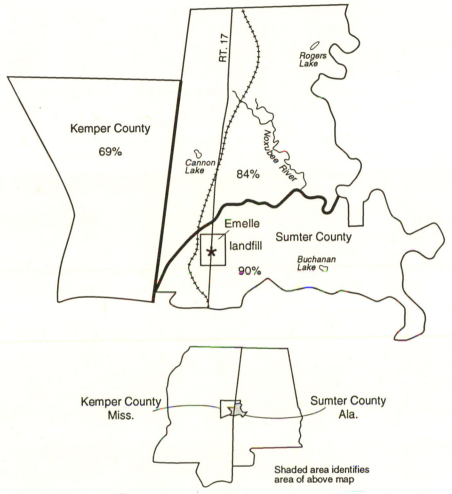

FIGURE 3.5 Sumter County, Alabama, and the Chemical Waste Management hazardous-waste landfill and racial composition of surrounding area

takenly thought the new job-generating industry moving into the area would be a brick factory.

It was more than two years after the site opened that residents learned that Alabama Governor George Wallace's son-in-law acquired the 2,400 acres of land, obtained the necessary permits with surprising ease, and immediately sold the package to Chemwaste. The deal is estimated at $15–$30 million over the lifetime of the agreement.[49] Chemwaste has subsequently purchased additional parcels of land, bringing its total to 3,200 acres in Sumter County.

The Emelle hazardous-waste site has not brought about an economic renaissance to this poor blackbelt county. Chemwaste, however, is the largest employer in Sumter County, providing more than 400 jobs with a payroll of nearly $8 million. The company pumps millions of dollars into Sumter and adjacent Greene counties with the goods and services it purchases. Chemwaste also pays Sumter County a user tax ($5 per ton) for hazardous waste disposed of at the site. The waste tax benefits a number of public services including schools (whose pupils are virtually all black), libraries, ambulance, and law enforcement. The waste disposal company also provides financial support and contribution for local charities such as the Boy Scouts and youth sports leagues.

The Chemwaste site in Emelle receives some of the most hazardous material in the nation including heavy metals, industrial solvents, and PCBs. It also receives hazardous wastes collected from the Superfund cleanup sites and from forty-eight states. It received more than 700,000 tons of waste in 1989. As in the case of all landfills, no one can really guarantee that buried wastes will not leak and return to cause future health problems.[50] The Chemwaste site is no exception. Wendell Paris, a black civil rights activist, contended that sending so much Superfund wastes to Emelle is "turning Sumter County into the pay toilet of America and local residents into hazardous waste junkies."[51] He summed up his community's concerns:

> People in this community have mixed emotions about the Chemwaste facility. Those that are more informed are clearly concerned about the health aspects of Sumter County residents, the water supply, and the overall pollution question. But the concerns from the general public of Emelle, we deal more with the economics, people being able to work and provide for their families. Our community needs jobs, but we also don't want to be poisoned. Jobs are scarce in this area. This trusting community was deceived. Of the 400–500 workers at the plant, roughly fifty Emelle and Geiger [another black community in the area] residents work at the plant. The large number of cars with out-of-state license plates at the plant tells the story of what this community is getting. We were promised jobs, but what we got was a giant hazardous-waste headache.[52]

Local concerns expressed by community leaders about the controversial landfill were not without merit. For example, Chemwaste has been fined for violations on a number of occasions. In June 1983, the Alabama Department of Environmental Management (ADEM) fined the company $150,000 for failing to complete a lining system. In December 1984, state and federal officials fined the company $600,000 for poor management procedures, PCB problems, and inadequate groundwater monitoring system at the site. The federal EPA temporarily suspended shipments of

Superfund wastes to the site after a March 1985 test sample showed possible contamination of the aquifer with industrial solvents. The ban was later lifted after further tests were made. Superfund wastes were again allowed to be dumped at the Emelle landfill even after EPA officials discovered that "one of the site's groundwater monitoring systems did not meet federal regulations and was incapable of detecting leaks."[53]

Opponents view the landfill as a "poison pill for Sumter County, a symbol of industrial profligacy, and a superficial Band-Aid over the nation's toxic waste cancer."[54] Local opposition to the waste operation has come mainly from two organizations: the Minority People's Council (MPC), a black grassroots community group that was founded to assist blacks who worked on the Tennessee-Tombigee Waterway, and Alabamians for a Clean Environment (ACE), a mostly white umbrella environmental group led by Kaye Kiker. Centuries of strained race relations and a "plantation" power arrangement have kept blacks and whites apart and limited communication channels between the races. It is important to note that it was the MPC who first raised the question of the potential threat posed by Chemwaste. Despite the numerous racial hurdles that limit coalition politics, there are a few signs of change.

The toxic-waste issue appears to be one area of agreement among local activists—black social justice advocates and white environmentalists—who would not ordinarily sit down together in the same room as "equals." Of course, there is not a ground swell of Sumter County residents poised to overrun Chemwaste nor is there a mass movement of color-coordinated grassroots activists waiting in line to join mainstream environmental organizations. There is, however, a small (but growing) segment of local community residents who are joining forces in challenging the nation's largest waste disposal company. More than anything else, this emergent coalition symbolizes a convergence of social justice and environmental goals and an erosion in the apartheid-type political and economic arrangements that typified the "Old South."[55] This is the first such alliance in Sumter County history.

Summary of Disputes and Resolutions

The five case studies have provided a detailed account of the problems and dispute-handling mechanisms used by black residents who were confronted with a threat from industrial facilities. The problems included risks from a secondary lead smelter, chemical manufacturing plant, hazardous-waste disposal facilities (landfill and incinerator), and a municipal landfill. Table 3.4 details the conflicts, tactics, and resolutions in the five study communities.

TABLE 3.4 Distribution of Environmental Conflict, Tactics, and Resolution in Five Black Communities

Assessment Dimension	Emelle	West Dallas	Alsen	Houston's Northwood Manor	Institute
Issue Crystallization					
Environment	X		X		X
Public health	X	X	X	X	X
Equity and social justice	X	X	X	X	X
Economic trade-off	X				
Type of Opposition Tactics					
Government administrative	X	X	X	X	X
Government legal action		X			
Private legal action		X	X	X	
Demonstration/protest	X	X	X	X	X
Petition/referenda	X	X	X	X	X
Press lobbying	X	X	X	X	X
Type of Leadership Group					
Mainstream environmental	X[a]		X[a]		X[a]
Grassroot environmental	X	X			X
Social action	X	X	X	X	X
Emergent coalition	X	X			
Resolution Mechanisms					
Legislation				X	
Government decision	X	X	X	X	X
Adjudication	X	X	X		
Private negotiation		X	X		X
Outcomes					
Closure		X			
Capacity reduction		X	X	X	X
Fine or compensation	X	X	X		X
Technical modification	X	X	X		X
Approved				X	

[a]Representatives from mainstream environmental organizations, though not providing a leadership role, did take part in the local environmental disputes.

We were especially interested in discovering how the community threat was defined by local opinion leaders. That is, was the threat viewed as an environmental or health issue or something else altogether? Four of the disputes involved existing industrial facilities, while the Houston landfill dispute involved a proposed facility. Only in Emelle and Institute did community leaders view the threat as an "environmental" problem. Opinion leaders were more likely to define the community threat in terms of a public health problem and an equity issue. The idea of economic trade-offs was a real issue in Emelle. This is not surprising since the Chemwaste facility is the largest employer in the county. Otherwise, economic-environment trade-offs were seen as having little or no bearing on the disputes—mainly because a small number of local black residents actually benefited (jobs or tax payments) directly from the physical location of the facilities.

What type of opposition tactics were used by the residents? Local citizen opposition to the unwanted facilities came in a number of forms. Although the tactics varied somewhat across communities, there were some common strategies used by opposition leaders in the affected areas. For example, all of the communities adopted action strategies that were instrumental in getting the various levels of government involved in the disputes. Opposition leaders in all five communities used direct action—including protests, demonstrations, and press lobbying—in tandem with petition drives. West Dallas, however, was the only study community that was successful in getting the city and state government to pursue legal action against the polluting industry. Three of the communities (West Dallas, Alsen, and Houston's Northwood Manor) filed class-action lawsuits against the unwanted industrial facilities using their own private attorneys.

Who spearheaded the local citizen opposition against the polluting industries? There is clear evidence that indigenous social action groups provided the leadership for the citizen opposition. As was expected, preexisting institutions and their leaders played a pivotal role in the beginning, planning, and mobilization stages of the movement.[56] There was some overlap among the leadership of the indigenous social action groups, neighborhood improvement associations, and the grassroots groups (usually organized around a single issue of equity or sense of unfair treatment). For example, several officers in Houston's Northeast Community Action Group (NECAG) held leadership positions in the Northwood Manor neighborhood association.

Community leaders in West Dallas were able to extend their influence beyond the neighborhood in convincing the Dallas mayor to appoint a government-sanctioned citywide study group (Dallas Alliance Environmental Task Force) to work on the lead contamination problem. Much of the impetus for creating the citywide task force emanated from the local lead pollution awareness group. Similarly, residents in Institute organized themselves into the People Concerned About MIC to protest the threat from the nearby Union Carbide plant.

In Emelle, the problem was initially attacked on two fronts, with race being the major divider. Whites were in one camp and blacks were in another. Blacks were the first to voice opposition to Chemwaste. Later, black civil rights activists and white environmentalists joined forces—but still maintaining their separate organizations—to work on the hazardous-waste problem. This is not a small point given the history of race relations in Alabama's blackbelt.

Overall, there were few whites among the citizen opposition groups. However, the attorneys for the West Dallas and Alsen residents were white. The attorney for the residents from Houston's Northwood Manor was black. Citizen protesters in Alsen, Institute, and Emelle were able to elicit some involvement from outside groups—mainly from national environmental groups, including Greenpeace, Citizen's Clearinghouse for Hazardous Waste, and the Sierra Club. Although these nationally connected environmentalists did not play a pivotal leadership role in the local dispute, they were effective in getting media attention focused on the local problem.

What were the dispute-resolution mechanisms used by citizen groups? The resolution mechanisms fell into four categories. Houston was the only area under study that dealt with the problem through legislation—with the passage of several ordinances dealing with dumping at the controversial landfill and spatial location of future landfill sites. Disputes resolution in all five communities called for some type of governmental decision. The government actions included improved monitoring systems, upgrading safety and emergency programs, compliance with zoning codes and emission standards, and adjudication.

Three of the communities (West Dallas, Alsen, and Houston) filed lawsuits against the companies. However, the Houston case was the only one that actually went to trial. The other two cases were settled out of court. Private negotiation and bargaining were used to address (though not resolve) the ongoing environmental disputes in Emelle, Alsen, and Institute.

By sitting down with the company representatives, community leaders were able to extract concessions as victims. On the other hand, these same concessions may be viewed by community residents as "selling-out." There are citizen winners in the case of the West Dallas neighborhood, the only study area that was successful in forcing the polluting industry to completely shut down—but not dismantle and clean up the site. Additionally, capacity reductions placed on the industries in Dallas (prior to it shutting down), Alsen, Houston, and Institute all can be viewed as movement in a positive direction.

The Reverend Leon White; Mrs. and Dr. Joseph Lowery, president of the Southern Christian Leadership Conference; Walter Fauntroy, a congressional delegate; Ken Ferruccio; and Dr. James Green lead a Warren County demonstration, 1982. (Photo by Jenny Labalme)

Warren County protesters line the highway in an attempt to block the dump trucks loaded with PCB-tainted dirt, 1982. (Photo by Jenny Labalme)

Houston's Northwood Manor residents protesting the construction of the Whispering Pines sanitary landfill, which was located near their homes and schools, 1980. (Photo by Robert D. Bullard)

Houston's Holmes Road municipal garbage incinerator located in the Sunnyside neighborhood, 1980. (Photo by Robert D. Bullard)

The Reverend Benjamin F. Chavis, Jr. (at podium), at the National Press Club in Washington, D.C., where he released the national study by the Commission for Racial Justice concerning toxic wastes and race, 1987. (Photo by Gene Young)

Crews begin cleanup of lead-tainted soil in West Dallas, Texas, neighborhood, 1992. (Photo by Luis D. Sepulveda, president of West Dallas Coalition for Environmental Justice)

A lone house stands in Reveilletown, Louisiana, after a buyout from a nearby industry, 1992. (Photo by Robert D. Bullard)

Residential property in Wallace that was rezoned for the proposed Formosa Chemical and Fiber Corporation plant, 1993. (Photo by Robert D. Bullard)

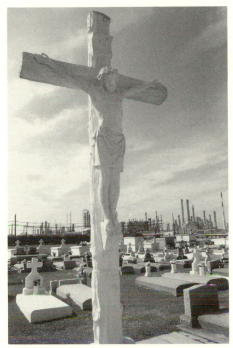

A cemetery and nearby petrochemical industries located along River Road, Hahnville, Louisiana, 1993. (Photo by Robert D. Bullard)

Atlanta school children participate in 1990 Earth Day tree-planting ceremony at the Martin Luther King, Jr., Community Center, 1990. (Photo by Sulaiman Mahdi)

Activists show solidarity at a rally on the nation's capitol during the meeting of the First National People of Color Environmental Leadership Summit, 1991. (Photo by Robert D. Bullard)

Participants at the Southern Organizing Committee for Economic and Social Justice's labor/environmental conference in New Orleans, 1992. (Photo by Adaora Lathan)

Litigation brought by citizens in West Dallas and Alsen resulted in multimillion dollar, out-of-court settlement agreements in favor of the plaintiffs. Fines were also imposed on the industries by governmental regulatory agencies. Government officials fined the Institute and Emelle facilities for safety violations. Although citizen groups were unsuccessful (with the exception of West Dallas residents) in closing the facilities, they were able to force the firms to make technical modifications in plant operations, update safety and pollution monitoring systems, and reduce emission levels. These outcomes amount to a compromise, benefits that accrue to both the community (concessions) and the industry (keeping the plant in operation).

Houston residents also won a number of concessions from the state and local government on solid waste. Many of these changes have benefits that extend beyond the local neighborhood. Nevertheless, the landfill was built. The judge ruled against the citizen plaintiffs in the lawsuit brought by the Northwood Manor residents. This was clearly a victory for the industry. Nevertheless, the concessions won by NECAG are historic. They mark a turning point in the way Houston allocates land use, with its antizoning, pro-development priority. Waste facility siting restrictions are tantamount to zoning—still a dirty word in Houston.[57] Moreover, the Texas Department of Health—the state permitting agency for solid-waste sites—in modifying its rules requiring socioeconomic, demographic, and land-use data be incorporated into future permit applications, tacitly admitted the utility of "nontechnical" data in site evaluation.

Finally, the results from these case histories clearly show that black community leaders are not only concerned about their physical environment but are willing to actively pursue strategies designed to improve the quality of their neighborhoods. These community leaders have not waited for "outsiders" to rush to their rescue—outside assistance has been slow in coming. Black community activists have taken on this fight largely as an extension of the human rights struggle. Dumping on the black communities is seen as environmental racism.

Pollution and environmental degradation in black communities pose a threat to life, health, and well-being. Many residents are trapped in polluted environments with no real hope of escape. Racism continues to limit mobility options available to black families. Because there are few places for them to run—compared with lower- and middle-income whites—it is not surprising that black activists have begun "drawing lines in the dirt" and resisting industrial polluters.

What factors motivate black community residents to take actions against these industrial giants? Are lessons learned from the mainstream civil rights movement readily adaptable to blacks' quest for environmental equity? These questions are addressed in the next chapter where the results of the household surveys are examined.

CHAPTER FOUR

◆

The Environmental Justice Movement: Survey Results

Public support for environmental reform has remained strong over the years. This has been the case even during the energy crisis, economic recession, tax revolts, and the Reagan era.[1] Numerous public opinion polls have clearly documented that "environmental protection, like issues such as health care and education, has become one of the lasting concerns of the public."[2] Moreover, minority and low-income groups have begun to organize against the toxic threat. Although this movement is in its infancy stage, it has the potential of snowballing into a larger force.

The literature is replete with surveys on environmental attitudes, organization membership, and citizen resistance. A growing body of studies now documents that minority and poor communities have been targets for unwanted land uses.[3] However, little is known about how minority residents are coping with environmental threats—whether from government or private industry. These problems did not spring up overnight, as many threats have been around for years. It is just recently that minority communities have begun to challenge the industrial firms.

In an attempt to assess the nature of the environmental dispute-resolution strategies used by black residents, a series of surveys were conducted with household heads in the five study areas. The household surveys were used to supplement the data gathered in interviews with local opinion leaders. The analysis is based on the responses of 523 residents who were randomly selected from black household heads in Emelle (Alabama), West Dallas and Houston (Texas), Alsen (Louisiana), and Institute (West Virginia). These data provide a comparative analysis of black residents' views on the local disputes and the actions taken to alleviate the problems.

Before I detail the way local household heads responded to the questions, I will describe the sample. A more detailed profile of the residential areas was presented in the preceding chapter. The respondents were primarily home owners from low- to middle-income neighborhoods (see Table 4.1). Seven of every ten households surveyed owned their home. This percentage is substantially higher than the 44 percent national black home ownership rate. Most of the households (75.3 percent) surveyed lived in single-family detached homes. A larger share of the West Dallas (41.3 percent) and Institute households (30.7 percent) lived in multifamily dwellings. The multifamily dwellings in West Dallas were largely public housing developments; while the multifamily units in Institute were mainly off-campus apartments located adjacent to West Virginia State College. The housing is used by students and faculty. Because of the rural and somewhat isolated nature of Emelle, over one-fourth (27 percent) of its residents lived in mobile homes. The population density in Sumter County is only 18.7 persons per square mile compared with 77.6 persons per square mile in the state of Alabama.

Six of every ten household heads surveyed were employed in blue collar occupations (occupations where polluting industries are more likely to be found), making them likely targets of environmental blackmail by manufacturing industries. More than 60 percent of the respondents had earned incomes less than $15,000. One out of every four individuals surveyed had at least one year of college. The household heads from West Dallas and Emelle were the least educated. Household heads from Houston's Northwood Manor neighborhood were the most affluent of all areas studied. The West Dallas residents were the most economically disadvantaged (based on home ownership, education, percentage in white-collar occupations, and income of household heads). The West Dallas neighborhood comes closest to the classic urban ghetto, an area dominated by a massive public housing project, widespread poverty, and a large underclass.

Given the background of community residents surveyed, how did these individuals rate their community in terms of environmental quality?

Rating of Environmental Problems

An effort was made to obtain the respondents' evaluation of the environmental quality in their respective communities. They were asked to rate the severity of selected environmental problems. Overall, air pollution,

TABLE 4.1 Selected Demographic Characteristics of the Study Subsamples (percent)

Characteristics	Total (N=523)	Emelle (N=100)	West Dallas (N=104)	Alsen (N=105)	Houston's Northwood Manor (N=113)	Institute (N=101)
Occupancy						
Own	71.1	79.0	42.3	91.4	94.7	48.5
Rent	28.3	21.0	57.7	8.6	5.3	51.5
Type Residence						
Detached	75.3	64.0	56.7	90.5	96.5	66.3
Mobile home	7.6	27.0	1.9	7.6	0.0	3.0
Multifamily	17.0	9.0	41.3	1.9	3.5	30.7
Education						
High school or less	74.7	86.0	92.3	75.2	64.6	55.4
Some college	25.3	14.0	7.7	24.8	35.4	44.6
Occupation						
White collar	40.0	23.5	18.1	40.2	54.4	62.8
Blue collar	60.0	76.5	81.9	59.8	45.6	37.2
Income						
<$15,000	62.1	83.2	87.5	63.8	23.0	51.7
$15,000+	37.9	16.8	12.5	36.2	77.0	48.3
Sex						
Male	38.6	15.0	44.2	41.9	34.5	57.4
Female	61.4	85.0	55.8	58.1	65.5	42.6
Age						
<40	46.8	46.5	51.0	39.0	41.6	57.0
40+	53.2	53.5	49.0	61.0	58.4	43.0

closeness of industry to homes (a form of industrial encroachment), and pollution of lakes and streams were rated the three most "severe" environmental problems (see Table 4.2). Nearly three-fourths (73.8 percent) of those sampled rated air pollution as a severe problem, 68.1 percent rated industry's proximity to their homes as a severe problem, and 61.6 percent indicated that they felt the pollution of local lakes and streams was a severe environmental problem. Air pollution and closeness of industry to homes were rated the top environmental problems by four of the five communities sampled.

TABLE 4.2 Rating of Local Environmental Problems by Study Area (percent)

Severe Problem[a]	Total (N=523)	Emelle (N=100)	West Dallas (N=104)	Alsen (N=105)	Houston's Northwood Manor (N=113)	Institute (N=101)
Pollution of lakes and streams	61.6	44.0	64.5	68.6	78.8	49.5
Air pollution	73.8	36.0	69.2	80.9	90.3	80.2
Noise in the area	42.3	22.0	64.3	31.4	67.3	22.8
Litter and solid waste	48.9	31.0	59.7	40.0	78.8	31.7
Hazardous waste	56.6	53.5	54.8	69.5	45.7	59.5
Toxic chemical leaks	56.6	52.0	47.2	55.2	39.8	81.1
Industry too close to homes	68.1	47.0	54.8	83.8	85.9	66.4

[a]The response categories for the above items included "no problem," "small problem," "somewhat severe," and "severe." The combined "somewhat severe" and "severe" categories are reported above.

The response pattern from the local residents did not turn up any surprises. For example, respondents from Houston's Northwood Manor neighborhood and the West Dallas neighborhood rated pollution of lakes and streams as one of the most severe environmental problems encountered by local residents. Respondents from Emelle and Alsen, on the other hand, rated hazardous waste as a major problem. The problem of toxic chemical leaks (emissions from the nearby chemical plant) was judged to be the most severe environmental threat in the Institute community. Although worlds apart economically, residents from Houston and West Dallas were the only groups where a majority listed solid waste and excessive noise as severe problems, a response pattern reflective of the urban, or big city, nature of the two neighborhoods.

The environmental ratings from the black community residents have been summarized below.

Emelle

The environmental rating in Emelle can be explained by the respondents' perception of a "threat" posed by the nearby Chemwaste hazardous-waste landfill, the nation's largest commercial hazardous-waste dump. Emelle respondents, thus, rated hazardous waste, toxic chemical leaks, and closeness of industry to their homes as the three most severe environmental problems in their community.

West Dallas

Residents in West Dallas, confronted with pollution from the nearby RSR lead smelter for more than five decades, rated air pollution, pollution of lakes and streams, and noise (associated with industry operation) as major environmental problems in their neighborhood.

Alsen

Pollution and emissions from the Rollins hazardous-waste disposal facilities have been a major sore point and contributor to this community's poor air quality. Residents also expressed the view that hazardous waste and toxics from the petrochemical industries that line the Mississippi River were severe environmental problems facing their community.

Houston's Northwood Manor

Respondents from the Northwood Manor neighborhood rated air pollution as the number one environmental problem; the situation is exacerbated by the heavy concentration of industry in the city's northeast sector. This problem was closely followed by residents' dissatisfaction with the location of industry near their homes (the siting of the Whispering Pines municipal landfill). The city does not have zoning, but has allowed a preponderance of industrial firms to locate in black and low-income residential areas. The litter and solid-waste problem and water pollution problem were assigned equal severity ratings by respondents from the Houston neighborhood. Both of these problems are tied to residents' fears associated with the municipal landfill—risks of contamination of ground water, illegal dumping, and neighborhood stigma as the "dumping grounds."

Institute

It is quite understandable why residents from this community rated toxic chemical leaks, air pollution, and closeness of industry to their homes as the most severe environmental problems. Institute and its residents are tucked away in the Kenawha River Valley along West Virginia's "chemical corridor." They live in the shadow of the nearby Union Carbide chemical plant and toxic emissions that routinely escape from the plant.

A rural-urban difference was detected in the environmental ratings. Noise and solid-waste problems were assigned higher severity ratings by residents who live in the two large cities (Houston and Dallas). Black neighborhoods, whether rural or urban, are not randomly scattered over the landscape. They are, however, a result of the interplay between wealth, real estate practices, and other institutional barriers. Conversely, environmental externalities (from landfills, garbage dumps, incinerators, or smelters) are not randomly scattered between poor and affluent citizens. David M. Smith observed:

> The location of every facility favours or disfavours those nearby, and thus redistributes well-being or ill-being. Any development of land has similar affects. How people in different areas establish differential claims on society's resources depends on the spatial exercise of political power. ... Ultimately, who gets what where and how must be viewed as a question of equity or fairness.[4]

Overall, air pollution appears to be a problem that was consistently given high severity ratings by the residents surveyed. All of the industries involved in the disputes are close to the residential areas; their location is not unrelated to the pollution problems identified by the local residents. It is safe to assume that few of these residents want to live near a toxic time bomb. The problem is not a "chicken or egg" argument—the question of which came first—because the neighborhoods were in place before the industries selected their sites. Minority and low-income neighborhoods, however, are especially vulnerable to industrial encroachment and the environmental risks associated with their operation.

Zoning, deed restrictions, and other "protectionist" land-use devices have been ineffective in segregating industrial uses from residential uses. especially in low-income, minority, and older areas. Rich neighborhoods routinely use lawsuits to block unwanted land uses that would sully their area, while the poor who cannot afford lawyers must put up with all kinds of nonresidential uses next to their homes.[5] Exclusionary zoning has been the major control of unwanted activities and undesirable land uses. Even so, black neighborhoods (poor and affluent) end up with a large share of unwanted land uses. Those living nearby are hurt most by these land uses since the adverse effects generally fall off with distance from the source.[6]

It is not unusual for land-use decisions to flow from zoning boards that are top-heavy with developer and real estate interests. Siting decisions may make more political sense than economic sense. Low-income and minority neighborhoods in many cases find themselves in the direct path of expanding industrial markets. More often than not these same neighborhoods lack the political clout to direct the expansion away from their residential areas.[7] For those residents whose property values are lowered and health threatened by such decisions, the issue amounts to one of equity. Do black community residents view these siting decisions as another form of discrimination?

Siting Conflict and the Question of Equity

Each of the communities surveyed was confronted with a major problem involving an industrial facility located in a residential area. How did residents feel about the industry being placed in their midst and close to their homes? An attempt was made to get the local residents' views on this very question. Without a doubt, this question goes to the heart of the fairness and equity issue. Three-fourths of the residents surveyed felt it was not fair for the industrial firms to locate the facilities in their neighborhoods (see Table 4.3). Residents from Institute, by far, gave a more favorable rating on the fairness question than any of the communities surveyed. Just under one-half (46.5 percent) of the residents felt it was fair for Union Carbide to locate the chemical plant in Institute. On the other hand, a little over one-fourth of the respondents in Emelle (28 percent) and West Dallas (26 percent) gave a similar favorable response to the industrial siting decision.

A majority (55 percent) of the households surveyed also felt that their community had been singled out, or targeted, to receive the industrial facility. The sentiments of environmental discrimination, disparate treatment, and deprivation were strongest among the Houston, Alsen, and Emelle residents. For example, 82 percent of Houston's Northwood

TABLE 4.3   Residents' Attitudes on Facility Siting Equity (percent)

Attitudinal Items	Total (N=523)	Emelle (N=100)	West Dallas (N=104)	Alsen (N=105)	Houston's Northwood Manor (N=113)	Institute (N=101)
Feel it was fair to locate facility in community						
Yes	24.9	28.0	26.0	15.2	6.2	46.5
No	76.1	72.0	74.0	84.8	93.8	53.5
Feel community was singled out to receive facility						
Yes	54.9	51.0	41.3	53.3	82.3	43.6
No	45.1	49.0	58.7	46.7	17.7	56.4
Feel angry to have facility in community						
Yes	73.6	57.0	76.0	83.8	95.6	52.5
No	26.4	43.0	24.0	16.2	4.4	47.5
Have become less angry over time						
Yes	41.7	22.6	61.6	46.2	36.6	34.5
No	58.3	77.4	38.4	53.8	63.4	65.5
Have come to accept the idea that the facility will likely be in the community for some time						
Yes	76.5	88.0	74.0	75.2	55.8	92.1
No	23.5	12.0	26.0	24.8	44.2	7.9

Manor residents felt their neighborhood was targeted for the municipal landfill. Discontent and anger were most pronounced among residents from Houston's Northwood Manor neighborhood, Alsen, and West Dallas. Residents from these three neighborhoods translated this anger into litigation against the polluting industries. On the other hand, residents from Institute and Emelle expressed markedly less anger than their counterparts.

The unequal sharing of benefit and burden engenders feelings of unfair treatment and reinforces racial and class distinctions. Michael Edelstein, in his book *Contaminated Communities*, addressed this very issue: "The fact the one is asked to bear the risks for others without sharing the benefits provides a sufficient basis for the perception of inequality. Given this, it is unlikely that siting of a facility will be seen as fair and just."[8]

Concern about equity appears to be the key to black community resistance to the industrial siting. There is always an imbalance between costs and benefits. Costs are more localized, while benefits are more dispersed. David Morell, a political scientist and expert on hazardous-waste facility siting, summarized this dilemma:

> The [industrial] facility's costs, are, without exception concentrated within the local area. Noise, odors, air emissions, groundwater leachate—whatever—all threaten the facility's immediate neighbors, not people hundreds of miles away who may well benefit from its daily operations.[9]

Anger does not necessarily translate into action. As most of us realize, anger alone will not close a garbage dump. There is never a guarantee that citizen opposition will result in changing the condition or problem. This is true for all social movements. Because of competing points of view, individuals may disagree about outcomes, whether a clear-cut victory or compromise. In the case of black community residents, an overwhelming majority expressed little hope of seeing an immediate solution to their environmental dilemma. Three-fourths of the residents had resigned themselves to the idea that the facility would probably remain in their respective areas in the foreseeable future. This sentiment was strongest in Institute and Emelle, the two communities where concessions were made without resolving the environmental disputes. This was even true in West Dallas where the RSR Corporation lead smelter was forced to close, and where residents won a multimillion dollar settlement against the company. West Dallas residents are able to stand on any neighborhood street and see the 300-foot-tall lead smelter smokestack as a reminder of the problem. The plant may be closed, but it is still in the neighborhood. More important, the plant site has yet to be cleaned up. In a sense, local residents have learned to live with the threat.

What is the root of these disparities? Both race and class are important elements in environmentally based disparities. Racial discrimination involves "behavioral processes aimed at maintaining the privileges of the dominant group."[10] By successfully defending their neighborhoods against the intrusion of unwanted facilities, whites have contributed to the environmental problems in minority areas. The results, whether intended or not, reflect the wishes of the larger community and promote action strategies reflective of the not-in-my-backyard (NIMBY) syndrome. It is impossible to go inside the heads of individuals making land-use decisions and determine their intentions. Whether intentional or not, the results of land-use decisions are quite revealing of status hierarchies (race and class) favoring whites and the affluent over the poor and people of color.

Racial discrimination is a real problem. Many of the overt forms of discrimination have disappeared, but the more subtle forms achieve the same results. There was agreement among a sizable share of residents that their communities had been "picked on" by polluting industries (see Table 4.4). Why were these communities chosen and not some other communities? This was one of the questions addressed in our survey. By far, residents saw race as the dominant factor. Nearly two-thirds (63.4 percent) of the residents who felt their neighborhood had been singled out said it was because their neighborhood was black. This view was strongest among the Institute, Houston, and Alsen residents.

Residents from West Dallas and Emelle, the two poorest communities, were less convinced of the racial dynamics involved in the industrial siting decisions. About 80 percent of those surveyed in West Dallas and 70 percent in Emelle gave nonracial explanations (e.g., poverty and need for jobs, lack of power and organization among community residents, and land values) for the decision to locate the facilities in their respective neighborhoods. Nearly one-third of the household heads from West Dallas and one-fourth of the Emelle respondents gave purely economic reasons—the need for jobs—as a major reason for the facility siting decision. Employment was viewed as a possible trade-off for having the industrial facility nearby. It should be noted that having an industry nearby does not automatically guarantee local residents jobs.

Economic Versus Environmental Trade-offs

The application of economic trade-offs in mitigating siting disputes and environmental conflict continues to generate a wide range of discussion. This is especially true for poor communities that are beset with rising unemployment, extreme poverty, a shrinking tax base, and decaying business infrastructure. Compensation, economic incentives, and monetary inducements have been proposed, for example, as an alternative strategy to minimize citizen opposition to hazardous-waste facility siting.[11] The endorsement of trade-offs usually emanates from city leaders rather than from local citizens.

How does compensation operate? Communities that agree to host hazardous-waste and other noxious facilities are promised compensation in an amount such that the perceived benefits outweigh the risks. The economic inducements are supposed to serve as equalizers to redress the im-

TABLE 4.4 Reasons Respondents Feel Their Community Was Singled Out in the Facility Siting Process (percent)

Reasons[a]	Total (N=279)	Emelle (N=47)	West Dallas (N=40)	Alsen (N=55)	Houston's Northwood Manor (N=93)	Institute (N=44)
Race of residents	63.4	29.8	20.0	78.2	78.5	88.6
Residents are poor and need jobs	12.2	23.4	30.0	3.6	7.5	4.6
Residents are powerless	6.8	8.5	10.0	9.1	6.5	-
Residents are unorganized	3.6	10.6	2.5	-	4.3	-
Land values and location	14.0	27.5	37.5	9.1	3.2	6.8

[a]The above categories represent the responses to an open-ended item asked only of those individuals who believed their community had been singled out for the facility.

balance. There are, however, risks and potential inequities associated with a policy of compensation. Moreover, the moral question surrounding compensation has not been adequately addressed. That is, should society pay those who are less fortunate to accept risks that others can afford to escape? Obviously, compensation taken to the extreme can only exacerbate existing environmental inequities. The Commission for Racial Justice cautions us on the use of compensation in environmental disputes: "To advance such a theory [compensation] in the absence of the consideration of the racial and socioeconomic characteristics of host communities and existing forms of institutionalized racism leaves room for potential discrimination."[12]

A voluminous body of research now exists on public concern about noxious facilities, risks, and mitigation strategies.[13] However, few of these studies have looked at this problem in minority and low-income communities. Given the nature of economic booster campaigns and "growth machine" politics, city leaders may endorse trade-offs, while local citizens who live nearby may object to the siting decision. Although citizen attitudes may have little impact on local decision making, they are important elements in defining disputes and structuring resolution strategies.

The issue of trade-offs was addressed by asking the residents an array of questions about health risks, jobs versus environment, employment opportunities, tax breaks, and overall benefit of having the industrial facility in their community. The data in Table 4.5 show that over half (56.3 percent) of the respondents believed that residents in their community were accepting health risks as a trade-off for jobs. This represented a kind of "environmental blackmail."[14] It is not just low-income neighborhoods that are paying a health price for nearby jobs; residents in the middle-income Houston neighborhood gave a similar response. Although these findings do not indicate citizen endorsement of health risks, they do underscore the dilemma confronting individuals who have employing (and polluting) industries as neighbors.

Given the economic conditions of the black community, is there an antienvironment bias among its residents? Overall, the data did not reveal such a bias. As a matter of fact, the opposite was true. Two-thirds of the households surveyed rated concern for the environment as more important than jobs. There was some variation in the way community residents responded to this issue. As expected, the greatest pro-jobs sentiment was registered by residents from West Dallas and Emelle, the two poorest communities. More than 67 percent of the household heads from West Dallas and 41 percent of those from Emelle rated jobs as more important than environmental concerns. West Dallas is an economically impoverished neighborhood located in the growth-driven Dallas–Fort Worth Metroplex. On the other hand, Emelle typifies the rural poverty found in the Alabama blackbelt. Requiring people to choose between jobs or the environment is inherently unfair. The solution to this dilemma lies in making workplaces safe for workers. Anything short of this goal places workers at an unfair disadvantage.

We were interested in the types of employment gains residents felt their community derived from the industrial facility. Was there an improvement in employment opportunities? Overall, some 62 percent of the household heads saw no improvement in employment of local residents as a direct result of the nearby industrial facility. Just under three-fourths (70.5 percent) of the residents in Institute and nearly one-half (49.5 percent) of the residents from Emelle saw their communities deriving employment from the nearby facilities. Residents in West Dallas, Alsen, and Houston's Northwood Manor were less inclined to view the industries as employment-generators for local neighborhood residents. This was especially the case for the Houston respondents, where only 9 percent of the residents felt that the Whispering Pines landfill would actually translate into jobs for Northwood Manor residents. Because the facilities under study are not labor-intensive industries, it was not surprising that few jobs actually "trickled down" to local community residents. Failure of industry to deliver on its promise of jobs appears to have hardened local citizen animosity toward the facilities.

TABLE 4.5 Distribution of Responses to Items Assessing Economic Versus Environmental Trade-offs (percent)

Items	Total (N=523)	Emelle (N=100)	West Dallas (N=104)	Alsen (N=105)	Houston's Northwood Manor (N=113)	Institute (N=101)
Individuals in this community accept health risks as a trade-off for jobs						
Agree	56.3	49.5	50.0	58.3	67.6	55.0
Disagree	43.7	50.5	50.0	41.7	32.4	45.0
We should think of jobs first and environment second						
Agree	33.3	41.0	67.3	19.0	23.0	16.9
Disagree	66.7	59.0	32.7	81.0	77.0	83.1
Employment opportunities for local residents have improved with the facility						
Agree	38.4	49.5	36.9	28.3	9.0	70.5
Disagree	61.6	50.5	63.1	71.7	91.0	29.5
The facility has generated needed tax dollars for the community						
Agree	49.9	61.6	64.1	23.1	59.2	44.8
Disagree	50.1	38.4	35.9	76.9	40.8	55.2
The benefits that the community derive from the facility far out-weigh the negatives						
Agree	30.4	38.2	49.0	13.2	18.8	35.9
Disagree	69.6	61.8	51.0	86.8	81.2	64.1

Industries sometimes use the potential for expanding the local tax base as a selling point and incentive to gain entry into a community. Few communities can afford to turn down money destined for their coffers, especially if tax revenues are shrinking. Who benefits from such arrangements? Residents had mixed feelings on the tax benefits derived from the local facility. For example, individuals from the two unincorporated areas (Institute and Alsen) felt that they were getting shortchanged in the form of taxes paid by the nearby industry. Nearly 77 percent of the Alsen residents indicated that the Rollins hazardous-waste facility had not generated needed tax dollars for the community; and 55 percent of the Institute residents gave a similar response regarding the local Union Carbide chemical plant's contribution to the local tax base. Unincorporated areas by nature offer industries the advantage and locational incentive of minimizing tax liabilities.

Conversely, a majority of the residents from the incorporated areas (Emelle, West Dallas, and Houston) felt they were at least receiving some tax benefits from having the industrial facilities in their communities and nearby. Whether the tax benefits outweigh the costs is a topic of considerable debate. Charles Streadit, president of Houston's Northeast Community Action Group, addressed the tax benefits and liabilities associated with the Whispering Pines landfill in his neighborhood:

> Sure, Browning Ferris Industries [owner of Whispering Pines landfill] pays taxes, but so do we. We need all the money we can get to upgrade our school system. But we shouldn't have to be poisoned to get improvements for our children. When my property values go down, that means less for the schools and my children's education. … A silent war is being waged against black neighborhoods. Slowly, we are being picked off by the industries that don't give a damn about polluting our neighborhood, contaminating our water, fouling our air, clogging our streets with big garbage trucks, and lowering our property values. It's hard enough for blacks to scrape and save enough money to buy a home, then you see your dream shattered by a garbage dump. That's a dirty trick. No amount of money can buy self respect.[15]

After all of the health, environmental, and economic factors associated with the industrial facilities were taken into account, residents were asked if they felt the "positives outweigh the negatives." An overwhelming majority (70 percent) of the residents saw the industrial facilities as more of a "burden" than a "benefit" to their communities. These findings underscore the uneven benefits and questionable economic rewards for communities that host noxious facilities. Local residents had little, if any, say in the facility siting process. In most cases (except Houston), black community residents became relevant actors after the fact. Residents seem to be saying that the minimum payoffs these companies could make is to hire local residents and pay tax revenues to improve local health, education, fire, and police services—all of which are underfunded in minority areas.

No doubt, compensation will continue to be used as a lure in the facility siting war, particularly in controversial siting proposals. Some communities are more amenable to accepting economic trade-offs, while others will aggressively resist such proposals. Compensation is not a panacea for mitigating public opposition and resistance to facilities that are perceived by local citizens to be a risk to their health and safety, community image, and economic investment (property values).

Environmental Activism

There is convincing evidence that black and low-income communities have borne a large burden of pollution and poor environmental quality.[16] The reason behind this disparity cannot be blamed on lack of environmental concern. Concern for the environment cuts across social and class strata[17] and in some cases is directly correlated with pollution levels. Minority and poor communities, with high levels of pollution, often exhibit higher levels of concerns than communities with low levels of pollution.[18] Concern about environmental pollution and participation in activities that are designed to change the problem are two distinct dimensions of environmentalism. Very little is known about the linkages between pollution levels and black environmental activism or about the factors that propel or impede black mobilization against environmental threats.

We do know that blacks have affiliated with a wide range of "expressive" and "instrumental" voluntary associations.[19] Black involvement in environmental activities can best be understood when their participation in other voluntary associations is explored. Although the residents polled in this study held membership in diverse organizations and groups, few of them were members of environmental organizations—only 16.3 percent were members of environmental groups (see Table 4.6). One-fourth of the respondents from Alsen belonged to an environmental organization, while less than one in ten household heads from West Dallas was a member of an environmental organization. As is true in the larger society, environmental organizations have not attracted a large following of black community residents. The households surveyed appear to mirror the underrepresentation of blacks in the mainstream environmental movement.

There are more than 3,000 environmental organizations in the United States. Some 250 of these organizations operate at the national or multi-state level. The nine largest environmental organizations have a combined membership of more than 4 million people.[20] Blacks and other minorities make up a small share of the membership in mainstream environmental

TABLE 4.6 Distribution of Membership in Voluntary Associations (percent)

Organization Membership	Total (N=523)	Emelle (N=100)	West Dallas (N=104)	Alsen (N=105)	Houston's Northwood Manor (N=113)	Institute (N=101)
Church	76.5	95.0	68.3	83.8	85.0	49.5
Service club or lodge	17.8	25.0	9.6	16.6	19.5	18.8
Parents group	23.1	30.0	15.4	30.5	28.3	10.9
Sports and leisure group	13.4	9.0	6.7	17.1	17.7	15.8
Labor union	11.5	4.0	8.7	9.5	21.2	11.5
Political group	13.2	12.0	5.8	5.7	21.2	20.8
Civic club	16.3	6.0	14.4	7.6	34.5	16.8
Civil rights group	19.9	13.0	12.5	15.2	21.2	37.6
Community improvement group	27.9	13.0	26.9	50.5	32.7	14.9
Environmental group	16.3	9.0	10.6	26.7	16.8	17.8

organizations. They are also severely underrepresented among the professional staff of these organizations. In 1984, there were just four blacks among the 200 professionals who worked for the ten major environmental groups in Washington, D.C.[21] Clearly, it is not enough to have environmental advocates *for* poor and minority communities. There need to be more of these individuals on the staffs and boards of the environmental organizations.

As was expected, voluntary association membership was concentrated in the black church; over 76 percent of the black household heads were church members. Church affiliation was followed by community improvement groups (28 percent) and parents groups (23 percent). About one-fifth of the respondents held membership in civil rights groups. The black church remains a solid cultural institution in these communities. Church leaders in black communities have a long tradition of meshing social and political issues in their religious services. Black churches served as the organizing cornerstone of the civil rights movement and appear to be a useful vehicle for black communities fighting toxics.

There are many organizational advantages associated with having an active environmental group within the black community. It is not, however, a prerequisite for mobilizing black citizens on the toxics issue. Preexisting organizations have moved in to fill the void by piggybacking the toxics issue onto the local social action agendas, including neighborhood associations, civic clubs, political groups, and labor unions. Organized labor has only been marginally involved in the local environmental issues as reflected by the low union participation rates among the residents. This low membership, only 11.5 percent, reflects the region's antiunion character and proliferation of "right-to-work" states in the South.

The residents were affiliated with a number of community-based organizations such as community improvement groups, civic clubs, civil rights organizations, and parents groups. Overlapping membership was the dominant pattern among the residents. Communication appears to be enhanced for those groups that had overlapping memberships and common goals, making mobilization a possibility. Mobilization goals become even more difficult to achieve when individuals have been kept in the dark. Valuable time is expended making the victims aware of their problem and the similarities they have with other minority and low-income neighborhoods.

What type of actions did local residents take in resisting the threat? The distribution of activities taken by the residents in opposition to the industrial facilities is presented in Table 4.7. The most commonly used opposition tactic involved signing petitions opposing the industrial firm. More than one-half (54 percent) of the respondents had signed a petition favoring closure of the polluting industry. Just under one-half (46.5 percent) of

TABLE 4.7 Participation in Opposition Activities Designed to Resolve the Local Environmental Problem (percent)

Environmental Activity	Total (N=523)	Emelle (N=100)	West Dallas (N=104)	Alsen (N=105)	Houston's Northwood Manor (N=113)	Institute (N=101)
Wrote a letter to an influential person	25.5	8.0	34.6	22.9	31.0	19.8
Telephoned an influential person	33.8	7.0	37.5	51.4	38.1	33.7
Signed a petition opposing the facility	53.9	26.0	51.9	65.7	69.0	54.5
Circulated or started a petition	23.9	5.0	39.4	28.6	34.5	9.9
Organized a meeting in own home	16.6	3.0	38.5	13.3	21.2	5.9
Attended a meeting in someone else's home	41.3	10.0	47.1	63.8	54.9	27.7
Discussed the matter at a church meeting	37.9	18.0	45.2	58.1	42.5	23.8
Went door-to-door to talk to neighbors	24.5	10.0	43.3	21.0	38.1	7.9
Prepared handouts, fliers, and leaflets	22.8	9.0	34.6	23.8	31.9	12.9
Marched in protest demonstration	21.2	7.0	32.7	16.2	36.3	11.9
Attended public hearing	46.5	22.0	42.3	67.6	48.7	50.5
Helped raise funds to fight the facility	30.2	9.0	37.5	31.4	55.8	13.9

the household heads had attended a public hearing, 41.3 percent had attended a meeting in someone else's home, and 38 percent had discussed the dispute at a church meeting.

It is this reliance on nonenvironmental organizations (for leadership and followers) that separates black environmental activism from mainstream environmentalism. The nonconventional nature of the citizen opposition groups may even serve as a deterrent in gaining the support and acceptance of these grassroots activists by mainstream environmental and resource conservation groups, which tend to be more traditional and conservative. Black community activists and environmentalists are worlds apart on nonenvironmental matters. Coalition politics has been used to bridge this gulf. No matter how much agreement is reached, racial and class barriers remain. For example, when the coalition meetings are over, blacks and whites return to their respective neighborhoods, which are usually separate.

Just how committed are black community activists to environmental reform? One way of determining commitment is willingness to support a cause with money, or "putting one's money where one's mouth is." Money becomes especially important when communities choose litigation as a resolution strategy. Civil lawsuits involving health and environmental disputes can by very costly and protracted. This fact alone may act as a deterrent to litigation initiated by communities of limited financial means. Corporations have deep pockets and can usually outspend and outlast grassroots organizations. Nevertheless, grassroots groups do challenge corporate polluters.

Participation in fund-raising activities was greatest among the households in communities where litigation was chosen as an opposition strategy. More than half (56 percent) of the respondents from Houston's Northwood Manor neighborhood (the most affluent of the five communities studied), 37.5 percent from West Dallas (the poorest area surveyed), and 31.4 percent from Alsen had engaged in some type of fund-raising activity in their efforts to resolve the dispute. Local citizen groups used a variety of fund drives, including bake sales, raffles, door-to-door soliciting, and collecting donations in church gatherings. Neighborhood churches were used extensively in eliciting donations. The practice of "passing the plate" for worthy causes is common among black churches. These local efforts were the major funding sources in support of the class-action lawsuits brought against the industrial firms. On the other hand, only 9 percent of the Emelle residents and 14 percent of the Institute residents had actually helped raise funds in opposition to the local hazardous-waste facility.

Residents of Emelle, the only rural community studied, exhibited the least participatory behavior on all twelve of the opposition activities.

Community organizing, never an easy task, is even more difficult when people are hard to reach. Emelle was typical of a community with low density and rural character. Community organizers ran into similar problems in mobilizing Sumter County residents during the height of the civil rights movement. Lingering political and economic arrangements of the Old South (i.e., white minority rule and a plantation economy) did little to promote black-white equity in Alabama's blackbelt. White racism has limited social and economic mobility options and environmental choices for Alabama's blackbelt residents. The much-touted progress of the New South has bypassed this area. The plight of Emelle and Sumter County residents is now being publicized by outside groups such as the United Church of Christ's Commission for Racial Justice, Southern Christian Leadership Conference (SCLC), Citizen's Clearinghouse for Hazardous Waste, and Greenpeace.

In light of the meager gains made by environmental groups in the black community, the greatest potential for legitimating equity concerns appears to lie within the preexisting social institutions (church groups, community improvement and neighborhood associations, civil rights groups, and other grassroots organizations). The question comes down to trust. Who can black community residents trust? These indigenous groups already have active members and an informed leadership.[22] Many of them have a long history of mobilizing their constituents against social injustice (as environmental inequities are now perceived) and institutional barriers in such areas as employment discrimination, housing and school segregation, redlining, exclusionary zoning, and other unfair land-use practices.

The task of mobilizing local citizens on an environmental issue is enhanced when the community has the leadership, knowledge, tactical skills, and communication networks to challenge the system of domination, including giant corporations. Skills are often acquired in institutions that are indigenous to the black community and where blacks are in decision-making positions.[23] The black church and community improvement groups typify this sort of training ground for black leadership. Few blacks are being trained in mainstream environmental organizations. Similarly, few blacks hold leadership positions in mainstream environmental organizations.

Black environmental activism is linked to feelings of deprivation—community residents equate their condition with institutionalized discrimination. This growing sense of environmental inequity (unfair treatment) contributes to the endorsement by many black community residents of collective actions (protests, lobbying, media attention, "equal protection" arguments, and litigation) that are closely aligned with the social justice movement. The environmental dispute becomes a unifying point around which individuals rally. Environmental equity, thus, becomes a compatible goal within the community's quest for social justice. Until environmentalists begin to link ecological and equity issues, black social justice activists will continue to view mainstream environmental organizations as elitist and suspect.

The offer of jobs, expanded tax revenues, and economic incentives (monetary and others) may on the surface appeal to individuals who are desperate to change their depressed economic state. However, there are limits to the risks that even poor people are willing to tolerate. Health risks are quite difficult to compensate. Moreover, there is a larger ethical issue involved. For many black community residents, the sort-term economic gains of having employing industries nearby do not outweigh the potential health and environmental threats from these industries.

Finally, the credit for mobilizing black residents around toxics issues rests with indigenous black community leaders, not outside elites. The resource mobilization theory emphasizes the importance of outside elites (e.g., governmental leaders, courts, liberals, and philanthropic foundations) in organizing and sustaining social movements in minority communities.[24] In the case of environmental conflicts involving minority communities, outside elites were drawn into the disputes later in the process—usually after the disputes were publicized in the media.

Black protest against environmental threats can be seen as rational collective action that emerged out of preexisting social structures and institutions within the racially segregated and politically oppressed black community. Overall, the actions taken by residents were planned and carried out by black activist leaders who have strong ties to indigenous community organizations. The battle for environmental equity has been waged by those who stand the most to gain from a victory—indigenous community residents themselves.

◆

CHAPTER FIVE

Environmental Racism Revisited

The South has always been thought of as a backward land, based on its social, economic, political, and environmental policies. By default, the region became a "sacrifice zone," a sump for the rest of the nation's toxic waste.[1] A colonial mentality exists in the South, where local government and big business take advantage of people who are politically and economically powerless. Many of these attitudes emerged from the region's marriage to slavery and the plantation system, which exploited both humans and the land.[2]

The Deep South is stuck with this unique legacy—the legacy of slavery, Jim Crow, and white resistance to equal justice for all. This legacy has also affected the region's ecology. Southerners, black and white, have less education, lower incomes, higher infant mortality rates, and lower life expectancy than Americans elsewhere. It should be no surprise that the environmental quality Southerners experience is markedly different from that of other regions of the country.

The South is characterized by "look-the-other-way environmental policies and giveaway tax breaks."[3] It is the U.S. Third World, where "political bosses encourage outsiders to buy the region's human and natural resources at bargain prices."[4] Lax enforcement of environmental regulations has left the region's air, water, and land the most industry befouled in the United States.

The Role of Racism

Many of the differences in environmental quality between black and white communities result from institutional racism, which influences local land use, enforcement of environmental regulations, industrial facility siting, and the locations in which people of color live, work, and play. The roots of institutional racism are deep and have been difficult to eliminate.[5] Discrimination is a manifestation of institutional racism and results in life being very different for whites and blacks. Historically, racism has been and continues to be a "conspicuous part of the American sociopolitical system, and as a result, black people in particular, and ethnic and racial minority groups of color, find themselves at a disadvantage in contemporary society."[6]

Environmental racism is real; it is not merely an invention of wild-eyed sociologists or radical environmental justice activists. It is just as real as the racism found in the housing industry, educational institutions, the employment arena, and the judicial system. What is environmental racism, and how does one recognize it? *Environmental racism* refers to any policy, practice, or directive that differentially affects or disadvantages (whether intended or unintended) individuals, groups, or communities based on race or color. Environmental racism combines with public policies and industry practices to provide *benefits* for whites while shifting industry *costs* to people of color.[7] It is reinforced by governmental, legal, economic, political, and military institutions. In a sense, "Every state institution is a racial institution."[8]

Environmental decision making and policies often mirror the power arrangements of the dominant society and its institutions. A form of illegal "exaction" forces people of color to pay the costs of environmental benefits for the public at large. The question of who pays for and who benefits from the current environmental and industrial policies is central to this analysis of environmental racism and other systems of domination and exploitation.

Racism influences the likelihood of exposure to environmental and health risks as well as of less access to health care.[9] Many U.S. environmental policies distribute the costs in a regressive pattern and provide disproportionate benefits for whites and individuals at the upper end of the education and income scales.[10] Numerous studies, dating back to the 1970s, reveal that people-of-color communities have borne greater health and environmental risk burdens than the society at large.[11]

Elevated public health risks are found in some populations even when social class is held constant. For example, race has been found to be independent of class in the distribution of air pollution,[12] contaminated fish consumption,[13] location of municipal landfills and incinerators,[14] abandoned toxic-waste dumps,[15] cleanup of Superfund sites,[16] and lead poisoning in children.[17]

Lead poisoning is a classic example of an environmental health problem that disproportionately affects African American children at every class level. Lead affects between 3 and 4 million children in the United States—most of whom are African Americans and Latinos who live in urban areas. Among children five years old and younger, the percentage of African American children who have excessive levels of lead in their blood far exceeds that of whites at all income levels.[18]

The federal Agency for Toxic Substances and Disease Registry (ATSDR) found that in families earning less than six thousand dollars a year, 68 percent of African American children had lead poisoning, compared with 36 percent of white children. In families with an annual income exceeding fifteen thousand dollars, more than 38 percent of African American children suffered from lead poisoning, compared with 12 percent of whites.[19] Even when income was held constant, African American children were two to three times more likely than their white counterparts to suffer from lead poisoning.

Virtually all of the studies of exposure to outdoor air pollution have found significant differences in exposure according to income and race. African Americans and Latinos are more likely than are whites to live in areas with reduced air quality. For example, National Argonne Laboratory researchers D. K. Wernette and L. A. Nieves found:

> In 1990, 437 of the 3,109 counties and independent cities failed to meet at least one of the EPA ambient air quality standards. ... Fifty-seven percent of whites, 65 percent of African Americans, and 80 percent of Hispanics live in 437 counties with substandard air quality. Out of the whole population, a total of 33 percent of whites, 50 percent of African Americans, and 60 percent of Hispanics live in the 136 counties in which two or more air pollutants exceed standards. The percentages living in the 29 counties designated as nonattainment areas for three or more pollutants are 12 percent of whites, 20 percent of African Americans, and 31 percent of Hispanics.[20]

The public health community has insufficient information to explain the magnitude of some of the air pollution–related health problems. However, we do know that persons suffering from asthma are particularly sensitive to the effects of carbon monoxide, sulfur dioxides, particulate matter, ozone, and nitrogen oxides.[21] African Americans, for example, have a significantly higher prevalence of asthma than the general population.[22] Environmental problems are endangering the health of communities all across the United States.

Unequal Protection

The nation's environmental laws, regulations, and policies are not applied uniformly; as a result, some individuals, neighborhoods, and communities are exposed to elevated health risks. A 1992 study by staff writers from the *National Law Journal* uncovered glaring inequities in the way the federal Environmental Protection Agency (EPA) enforces its laws:

> There is a racial divide in the way the U.S. government cleans up toxic waste sites and punishes polluters. White communities see faster action, better results and stiffer penalties than communities where blacks, Hispanics and other minorities live. This unequal protection often occurs whether the community is wealthy or poor.[23]

In their study, these writers examined census records, civil court dockets, and the EPA's own record of performance at 1,177 Superfund toxic-waste sites. The report revealed the following:

1. Penalties imposed under hazardous-waste laws at sites having the greatest percentage of whites were 500 percent higher than penalties in areas with the greatest minority populations, averaging $335,556 for white areas compared to $55,318 for minority areas.
2. The disparity under the toxic-waste law occurred by race alone, not by income. The average penalty in areas with the lowest income levels was $113,491, 3 percent more than the average penalty in areas with the highest median income.
3. When all of the federal environmental laws aimed at protecting citizens from air, water, and waste pollution were considered, penalties imposed in white communities were 46 percent higher than those in minority communities.
4. Under the giant Superfund cleanup program, it took 20 percent longer to place hazardous-waste sites in minority areas on the national priority list than it took for those in white areas to be placed on the list.
5. In more than half of the ten autonomous regions that administer EPA programs around the country, action on cleanup at Superfund sites took from 12 to 42 percent longer to initiate at minority sites than at white sites.
6. At minority sites, the EPA chose "containment," the capping or walling off of a hazardous-waste dump site, 7 percent more frequently than the cleanup method preferred under the law: permanent "treatment" to eliminate the waste or rid it of its toxins. At white sites, the EPA ordered treatment 22 percent more often than it did containment.[24]

These findings suggest that unequal protection is placing communities of color at special risk. The study also supplements the findings of earlier studies and reinforces what grassroots leaders have long been saying: Not only are people of color differentially affected by industrial pollution, but they can also expect different treatment from the government.

Environmental decision making operates at the juncture of science, economics, politics, special interests, and ethics. The current environmental model places communities of color at special risk. African American and other communities of color are often victims of land-use decision making that mirrors the power arrangements of the dominant society. Historically, exclusionary zoning (and rezoning) has been a subtle form of using government authority and power to foster and perpetuate discriminatory practices. Generally, planning and zoning commissions are not racially and ethnically diverse.

Exclusionary and restrictive practices that limit participation of African Americans and other people of color in decision-making boards, commissions, regulatory bodies, and management staff are all forms of environmental racism. The various governmental agencies charged with protecting the public are far from achieving a racially and ethnically diverse work force. The demonstration of a strong commitment to fostering diversity in the work force is essential to achieving the government's mission of protecting human health and the environment.

Limiting the access of African Americans, Latino Americans, Asian Americans, and native Americans to management positions has no doubt affected the outcomes of some important environmental decisions in at-risk communities. In order to get balanced and just decisions, the decision makers (managers) must reflect the diversity—cultural, racial, ethnic, and gender—of the United States.

At the federal EPA there are over eighteen thousand employees; one third are assigned to headquarters offices in the metropolitan Washington, D.C., area, and two thirds work in regional and laboratory offices scattered throughout the United States. The EPA work force is about evenly divided between men (51 percent) and women (49 percent), and just over one fourth (26 percent) are members of minority groups. However, women and minorities continue to be underrepresented in EPA's management staff. In 1992, women and minorities constituted 28 percent and 9.7 percent, respectively, of the management staff.[25]

Data from a 1992 EPA report, *Women, Minorities and People with Disabilities,* show that the agency missed numerous opportunities to further diversify its work force. In fiscal year 1991, for example, a total of 412 management hires were made, with only 33 positions (8 percent) going to minorities and 142 (34 percent) going to white women. In fiscal year 1992, 354 management hires were made, with 42 positions (11.9 percent) going to minorities and 126 (35.6 percent) going to white women.

EPA's 1991 Equal Employment Opportunity Commission (EEOC) report reveals that the agency lagged behind many other federal agencies in hiring and promoting racial and ethnic minorities to professional positions. Of the fifty-six federal agencies that have five hundred or more employees, the EPA ranked thirty-fifth in the percentage of African Americans in professional positions, twenty-second in the percentage of Latino Americans in professional positions, and thirty-ninth in the number of native Americans in professional positions. Clearly, work force diversity is an essential component in any strategy to combat environmental racism.

Environmental Apartheid

Apartheid-type housing, development, and environmental policies limit mobility, reduce neighborhood options, diminish job opportunities, and decrease choices for millions of Americans.[26] Race still plays a significant role in the distribution of public "benefits" and public "burdens" associated with economic growth. Why do some communities get dumped on and others do not? Why do some communities get cleaned up whereas others have to wait? Waste generation is directly correlated with per capita income; however, few waste facilities are proposed and actually built in the mostly white suburbs.

The Commission for Racial Justice's landmark study, *Toxic Wastes and Race*, found race to be the single most important factor (i.e., more important than income, the percentage of people who own their homes, and property values) in the location of abandoned toxic-waste sites.[27] The study also found that (1) three of five African Americans live in communities with abandoned toxic-waste sites; (2) 60 percent (15 million) of African Americans live in communities with one or more abandoned toxic-waste sites; (3) three of the five largest commercial hazardous-waste landfills are located in predominately African American or Latino communities, accounting for 40 percent of the nation's total estimated landfill capacity; and (4) African Americans are heavily overrepresented in the population of cities with the largest number of abandoned toxic-waste sites, which include Memphis, St. Louis, Houston, Cleveland, Chicago, and Atlanta.[28]

Communities with hazardous-waste incinerators generally have large minority populations, low incomes, and low property values. A 1990 Greenpeace report, *Playing with Fire*, found that (1) the minority portion of the population in communities with existing incinerators is 89 percent higher than the national average; (2) communities in which incinerators are proposed have ratios of minorities to whites that are 60 percent higher than the national average; (3) average annual income in communities with existing incinerators is 15 percent lower than the national average; (4)

property values in communities that have incinerators are 38 percent lower than the national average; and (5) in communities in which incinerators are proposed, average property values are 35 percent lower than the national average.[29]

Waste facility siting imbalances that were uncovered by the U.S. General Accounting Office (GAO) in 1983 have not disappeared.[30] The GAO discovered that three-quarters of the offsite commercial hazardous-waste landfills in Region IV (Alabama, Florida, Georgia, Kentucky, Mississippi, North Carolina, South Carolina, and Tennessee) were located in predominately African American communities. A decade later, African Americans still made up about one fifth of the population in EPA Region IV. In 1993, all of the offsite commercial hazardous-waste landfills in the region were located in two mostly African American communities.

Some residents of the region suspect that their communities are rapidly becoming "sacrifice zones" because of the placement there of garbage dumps, landfills, incinerators, and petrochemical plants. Nowhere is this more apparent than in southeast Louisiana, where unincorporated African American communities are especially vulnerable to industrial pollution.

Louisiana as "Paradise" Lost

African Americans have always constituted a sizable share of the population of southern states, where the plantation economy was dominant—as in Louisiana. Louisiana has tagged itself a "sportsman's paradise." The state's economy slowly began to change in the early 1900s from an agricultural and fishing economy—based on its cypress swamps, waterways, and fertile soil—to one based on oil. Oil exploration led to the construction of a refinery in Baton Rouge. The Mississippi River served as a magnet for petrochemical companies because of its capacity for carrying barges and its access to disposal of chemical waste.

With the collapse of the sugar plantation system after World War II, Louisiana became a prime location for the petrochemical industry. In the 1940s, the state's population shifted in the direction of jobs created by this new oil-based economy, and by 1956, some 87,200 residents were directly employed by the petrochemical industry. Growth in the 1960s was related to a generous tax exemption and other inducements offered by then Governor John McKeithen. By the 1970s, the Louisiana industrial corridor along the Mississippi River was producing 60 percent of the U.S. vinyl chloride and nitrogen fertilizer and 26 percent of its chlorine.

In 1990, African Americans constituted nearly 31 percent of Louisiana's population. How has this group fared under the system in which the petrochemical industry is king? Amos Favorite, a World War II and civil rights veteran and resident of Geismer, Louisiana, agrees that the petro-chemical industries are the new masters: "We are the victims. ... We are all victimized by a system that puts dollars before everything else. That's the way it was in the old days when the dogs and whips were masters, and that's the way it is today when we got stuff in the water and air we can't even see that can kill us deader than we ever thought we could die."[31]

A May 1993 report by the EPA focused on the Lower Mississippi River industrial corridor—the eighty-five-mile stretch from Baton Rouge to New Orleans. The study confirmed what many environmental activists and local residents already knew:

1. Many of the facilities emitting large amounts of TRI (toxic release inventory) chemicals are located in areas with predominately minority populations.
2. Populations within two miles of facilities releasing 90 percent of total indus-trial corridor air releases feature a higher proportion of minorities than the state average; facilities releasing 88 percent [of TRI] have a higher propor-tion [of minorities] than the Industrial Corridor parishes' average.
3. Although no connection between TRI emission and health risks has been clearly demonstrated, numerous studies and media reports have high-lighted the potential for significant risks to these populations from chemical releases.
4. Several historically black rural communities have been bought out by chem-ical or petroleum refining facilities as plant buffers.[32]

Louisiana Department of Environmental Quality (LDEQ) officials re-sponded to the findings of the EPA report as an "image" and "attitude" problem. In a review of the EPA report, Gary Johnson of the LDEQ wrote:

I feel that if the data is published as presented this would place a negative connotation on the state of Louisiana regarding our on-going efforts toward toxics reductions in [the] Baton Rouge–New Orleans corridor. Reporting data without applying a positive connotation would not be beneficial to what is planned to change perception and attitudes. ...

I want to clearly point out that how regulatory agencies present data in the future will clearly impact the cooperation we receive in return from industry and industry associations. Industry is seeking and expects "fairness" from the regulatory community. Anyone working in the environmental field today should be extremely cautious in publishing information regarding "environ-mental equity" and specific geographic regions, specifically the Lower Mis-sissippi Corridor.[33]

LDEQ officials need only visit the unincorporated African American communities (the ones that are left) along River Road to discover that these residents are more concerned about pollution prevention than about public relations. The current and former residents of Geismer, St. Gabriel, Lions, Good Hope, Morrisonville, Reveilletown, and Sunrise also deserve "fair" treatment from regulatory agencies. However, Johnson's letter to the federal EPA questions "environmental equity" and also demands "fair" treatment of industry along the Baton Rouge–New Orleans corridor.

Many of the polluting industries are located next to African American communities that were settled by former slaves—areas that were unincorporated and in which the land was cheap. Local residents had few political rights (most blacks were denied the right to vote or to hold public office). Although the promise of jobs was the selling point for industries coming to towns along the Mississippi River, only a few jobs were offered to African American residents—and these were usually the lowest-paying and the dirtiest jobs.

Louisiana is a poor state. However, many of the giant corporations that operate there get special tax breaks. For example, thirty large corporations—many of which are major polluters—received $2.5 billion in Louisiana property-tax exemptions in the 1980s. Only a few permanent new jobs resulted from these exemptions.[34]

In 1992, the Institute for Southern Studies' *Green Index* ranked Louisiana forty-ninth of the fifty states in overall environmental quality. The *Green Index* is based on seventy-seven federal and state policy indicators.[35] Louisiana ranked fiftieth in toxic release to surface water, high-risk cancer facilities, per capita toxic underground injection, and oil spills into state waters. In the areas of community and work force health, it also ranked near the bottom: rate of infant mortality (forty-ninth), number of households without plumbing (forty-third), number of households with just septic tanks (forty-fourth), number of doctors delivering patient care (forty-first), and number of workers in high-risk jobs (fortieth). Toxic-waste discharge and industrial pollution are correlated with poorer economic conditions. The state could improve its general welfare by enacting and enforcing regulations to protect the environment.[36]

Nearly three fourths of Louisiana's population—more than 3 million people—get their drinking water from underground aquifers. Dozens of these aquifers are threatened by contamination from polluting industries, the three biggest of which are Dow Chemical, Vulcan, and PPG.[37] Some of the state's residents fear they will ultimately be forced to depend upon bottled drinking water, which would be cost-prohibitive for many low-income and moderate-income households.

The Lower Mississippi River industrial corridor contains some 125 companies that manufacture a range of products, including fertilizers, gasoline, paints, and plastics. More than 2 billion pounds of toxic chemicals were emitted from these plants between 1987 and 1989. This corridor has been dubbed "cancer alley" by environmentalists and local residents.[38] Linda King of the Environmental Health Network, a grassroots group based in Louisiana, described the area as follows: "We don't live in areas that spew out only copper, only benzene. ... We live in chemical stews."[39] Free-lance writer Conger Beasley, writing in *Buzzworm*, described some of the health threats posed by the petrochemical industry in "cancer alley."

> People living within a mile of the plants have a 4.5 percent greater chance of contracting lung cancer than those who live one to three miles away. They are [the] least knowledgeable about hazardous waste effects. A quarter-century after enactment of major civil rights laws, they remain distrustful of politicians, black and white, who historically have manipulated the system for their own benefit.[40]

Ascension Parish typifies what many people refer to as a toxic "sacrifice zone." The rural, mostly African American parish lies ten miles south of Baton Rouge. In two parish towns of Geismer and St. Gabriel, eighteen petrochemical plants are crammed into a nine and a half square mile area. Companies such as BASF, Vulcan, Triad, CF Industries, Liquid Airbonic, Bordon Chemical, Shell, Uniroyal, Rubicon, Ciba-Geigy, and others discharge 196 million pounds of pollutants annually into the water and air.[41] Discharges include the carcinogens vinyl chloride and benzene, mercury (which is harmful to the nervous system), chloroform, toluene, and carbon tetrachloride (which can cause birth defects).

Amos Favorite described the hellish nightmare in his hometown of Geismer—a small, mostly African American river town. "You ought to see this place at night. ... When these companies burn off their waste the air lights up like a battlefield. I'm telling you it's scary. Nighttime around here is like an evil dream."[42] Favorite is convinced that government officials have written off entire communities along the river. In his view, public policy makers appear to feel the lives of black people and poor people are expendable.

Government has often cooperated with industry in disenfranchising African American communities. A prime example of this practice is seen in Wallace, a small community located on the east bank of the Mississippi River in St. John the Baptist Parish. The town is 95 percent African American. As an unincorporated area, the community does not have a governing body but relies upon the St. John the Baptist Parish Council to protect its health, welfare, and environment. The white parish officials have not provided equal protection for all citizens. (See Figure 5.1.)

Wallace is a close-knit community of home owners whose land holdings have been in their families for several generations. The community had always been zoned as residential—until the Parish Council voted to make

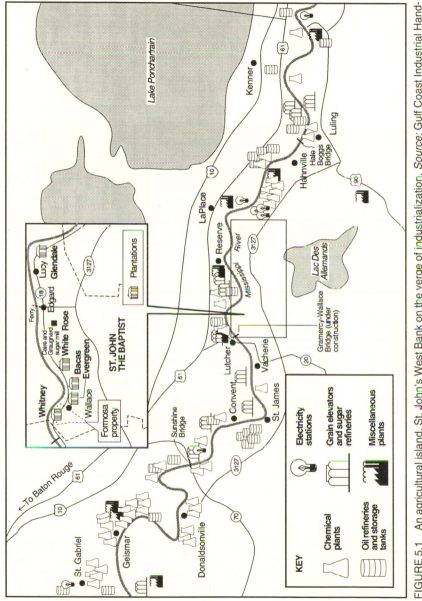

FIGURE 5.1 An agricultural island, St. John's West Bank on the verge of industrialization. *Source:* Gulf Coast Industrial Handbook, Port of South Louisiana, Illinois Central Railroad, *Times Picayune.* Reprinted by permission.

way for a proposed industrial plant. In 1990, Formosa Plastics Corporation asked the Parish Council to rezone 1,800 acres of land (which included Wallace) from residential to industrial.[43] Wallace residents were surprised and angered by the Parish Council decision. Kelly Colquette and Elizabeth Robertson, writing in the *Tulane Environmental Law Journal*, voiced suspicion of the parish officials' decision:

> First, residential property usually receives the utmost protection from parish zoning commissions. ... Second, because other industrially zoned properties already existed on the west bank [of the Mississippi River], the Parish Council could have allowed Formosa to use the industrial land already available. ... Third, and most offensive, it is widely known that Formosa has a well-earned reputation as a world class environmental outlaw.[44]

After intense grassroots organizing by the Gulf Coast Tenants Organization (GCTO)—an alliance of grassroots environmental and social justice groups in Alabama, Mississippi, and Louisiana—and a lawsuit filed by the Sierra Club Legal Defense Fund, Formosa was forced to withdraw its proposal in 1992, and the plant was not built. This represented a victory for the local organizers. Wallace residents refused to trade their health and the life of their community for a few unsafe, low-paying jobs.

Important organizing work is underway in southern Louisiana's river communities, some of which are under siege from nearby industries. Many of these threatened communities existed long before the petrochemical industry came to the region. A number of chemical companies have begun to take aggressive steps to limit their liability by buying out nearby communities; several such buyouts have occurred in recent years. For example, Reveilletown was bought out by Georgia Gulf, Morrisonville by Dow Chemical, and Sunrise by Placid Refining Company.

Reveilletown. This sleepy little African American community, located on the Mississippi River, dates back to the plantation era. After traces of vinyl chloride were found in the blood of local children in 1987, thirteen Reveilletown property owners filed a lawsuit against Georgia Gulf. The case was later settled out of court. Twenty other families subsequently agreed to sell their land and homes to Georgia Gulf for a reported $1.2 million. In 1990 the company completed a program to move fifty Reveilletown families away from its vinyl chloride plant.[45]

Morrisonville. Morrisonville was founded in the 1870s by former slaves. The town's founder, Robert Morrison, was a minister who struggled to create this community around the church he led, the Nazarene Baptist Church. The community survived Mississippi River flooding and Jim Crow, but it could not survive Dow Chemical. Some Morrisonville residents can still recall when the land Dow stands on was part of a huge sugarcane empire owned by the Mayflower and Union Plantation. The plantation house is still standing and can be seen inside the fence owned by Dow. In 1959, the community sold some land to Dow. Many of the residents now see this transaction as the mistake that marked the beginning of their community's demise. The land that was sold to Dow created a greenbelt, but Dow expanded and built on the land—up to the property lines of some Morrisonville residents.[46]

The Morrisonville chemical plant is Dow's largest facility in Louisiana. "Dow built right out to the fence until they were on top of us," says Jack Martin, a longtime Morrisonville resident. The buyout has brought sadness to the community; Doretha Thompson sums up its demise. "It's like a big death taking place. ... I always thought I'd spend the rest of my life in Morrisonville with my relatives. But it seems like what Dow wants, Dow gets."[47]

The chemical conglomerate spent more than $10 million in a voluntary buyout of the town's 250 home owners—the first of its kind without a lawsuit. Dow compensated people for their homes, but the "community" is lost forever. The town's residents have moved upriver, downriver, and to Baton Rouge. Many of them return every Sunday to worship in the Nazarene Baptist Church—the only surviving symbol of the Morrisonville community.

Sunrise. The community of Sunrise was purchased in 1874 from a white landowner by Alexander Banes, a former slave. In 1904, Banes sold the property to Benjamin Mayer, a white businessman from Baton Rouge. Mayer subsequently subdivided the land and sold parcels to individuals. In the 1930s, Sunrise was inhabited by mostly white residents; in 1970, the community was 17 percent white and 83 percent black. Sunrise is the home of Placid Refining Company, an independent oil refining and marketing company. Placid takes crude oil and material resources produced in Louisiana and converts these products into gasoline and diesel and jet fuels. In the area closest to the Placid refinery, 48 percent of the residents are white and 52 percent are black.[48]

In 1979, Placid initiated a program to purchase the property of Sunrise refining company employees, through which Placid acquired more than one hundred parcels of land—about one third of the lots in Sunrise. By 1985, the company had purchased $947,000 worth of property in the community. However, the town's African American residents were not offered the same opportunities for being bought out that were given to their white counterparts. White residents who lived closest to the plant at the time of the buyout and other white residents were bought out first. In 1990, the remaining residents of the community filed a lawsuit against the company. The suit listed 241 individuals who owned thirty-six houses and 89 residents who were renters as plaintiffs. In response to the lawsuit, in March 1991 Placid initiated its Sunrise program, under which it offered to buy the homes of any nonplaintiff home owners in Sunrise. In addition to the purchase price, owners were given five thousand dollars per household.

Under this program, Placid acquired more than 90 percent of the homes of the nonplaintiff owners. Plaintiffs in the lawsuit were not eligible, nor did they want to participate in the Sunrise program. Placid and the plaintiffs finally reached an out-of-court settlement under which Placid would purchase all property of the plaintiffs.

From American Dream to Nightmare

Texarkana is a twin city that straddles the Texas-Arkansas state line. In 1990, the population of the Texas side of the city was 31,656, of which about one third were African Americans. Residential patterns were shaped by Jim Crow. Carver Terrace was one of the few neighborhoods where upwardly mobile middle-income African Americans could own homes in racially segregated Texarkana. The all-black Carver Terrace neighborhood was built in a one hundred–year flood plain and on an old wood-treating site—with the full knowledge of city officials.

Koppers Company, a wood-treating firm, operated on the site until 1961. Carver Terrace was built in the 1960s and served as "strivers row" (a residential enclave for upwardly mobile middle-class families) for the seventy-nine African American home owners, who included teachers, ministers, mail carriers, and factory workers. Over the years, residents' homes have been flooded repeatedly. In 1980, the state of Texas discovered that the soil and groundwater were contaminated with chemicals commonly used in wood preserving: pentachlorophenol (PCP), arsenic, and creosote. The neighborhood became a Superfund site in 1984,[49] and a health assessment was conducted at the site that same year. The EPA concluded that the Koppers Superfund site posed a "potential risk to human health resulting from possible exposure to hazardous substances at concentrations that may result in adverse health effects."[50]

Clean soil and sod were placed on some of the yards. A Record of Decision (ROD) was made by the EPA in 1988 that called for a cleanup of the community. Residents were instructed not to let their children play outside and not to dig in their yards or eat food from their gardens. Some of the residents were not satisfied with the EPA's handling of the contamination problem and turned to their local congresspersons. In fact, it took an act of Congress for Carver Terrace residents to be heard. The EPA was mandated by Congress to amend its 1988 ROD on the site and to buy out and relocate the affected residents.

The EPA contracted with the Army Corps of Engineers (COE) to handle the $5 million federal buyout. On April 23, 1991, COE official Richard O. Murray, chief of the Real Estate Division, mailed letters to Carver Terrace residents informing them of the buyout. Some residents were confused and many were intimidated by the content and tone of the letters and by subsequent visits from COE officials who explained the property appraisals. For example, one paragraph in Murray's letter was especially troubling to home owners:

> Your property is being acquired on behalf of the EPA. If we are unable to negotiate a direct purchase from you, it will be necessary to acquire the property through condemnation proceedings. This information is not to be considered a threat, but in our opinion, it is necessary that we provide it to you so that you are fully informed of the laws and procedure applicable to this acquisition program. Please be assured that we will make every effort to negotiate a fair settlement with you. Should it be necessary to acquire your property through condemnation proceedings, the property will by reappraised. The Department of Justice, who will represent the United States, has directed that the reappraisal be based on the value of the property in its actual condition, which would necessitate consideration of the fact that the property is located within an environmentally unsafe area. This, in all probability, would lower the appraised value of your property.[51]

In a June 25, 1992, "citizen accountability hearing," sponsored by the Southwest Network for Environmental and Economic Justice in Dallas, EPA and COE officials were queried about the language and origin of the controversial statement in the letter. The hearing panel was made up of representatives from the Southwest Organizing Project, the National Association for the Advancement of Colored People's Legal Defense Fund, the Panos Institute, and the Texas Network. A COE representative informed the panel that "an official from the Justice Department" insisted that the paragraph be included. To date, the government representatives have been unable to determine which Justice Department official authorized the statement.

In addition to being threatening, insensitive, and, some residents felt, racist, the COE letter failed to grasp the socio-historical significance of a community like Carver Terrace. Because of institutional racism, housing and residential options are more restrictive for Texarkana's African American residents than for their white counterparts.

These problems are compounded by the fact that many of the Carver Terrace residents are elderly, retired, disabled, or living on fixed incomes. After enjoying nearly three decades of home ownership, which is still an integral part of the American dream, many Carver Terrace residents are being involuntarily uprooted from their homes, social institutions, and community and dispersed throughout the greater Texarkana area.

Some of the residents asked to be relocated as a community. This proposal was rejected by the COE. The $5 million government buyout had no provisions for compensating the residents for the "loss of community." The federal buyout will likely turn some of the owners into renters, push some of the residents back into Texarkana's ghetto, and otherwise worsen the economic conditions and overall quality of life (mental health and psychological well-being) for some individuals who thought they had planned for their retirement in a safe, quiet neighborhood near family and friends.

The last residents in Carver Terrace signed an agreement to sell their homes on August 6, 1992.[52] Once the residents are relocated from the contaminated community, the COE and the EPA have no further contact with them. However, the trauma of the move may manifest itself six months, a year, or even longer after COE and EPA officials have closed the files on the Koppers Superfund site.

The federal government is mandated to provide a resident with "comparable" housing under the Uniform Relocation Act. Since Carver Terrace was the premier African American neighborhood in the city, in which neighborhoods will the residents be able to secure comparable housing? How will they cope with the move and with their new physical surroundings?

A community is more than merely houses and yards; it is made up of homes, families, neighbors, friends, churches, civic clubs, and other social institutions. What government body will protect residents of unincorporated communities, many of whom are often members of the most vulnerable groups in society—namely, the elderly, the disabled, and persons living on fixed incomes? Will these individuals and families become environmental refugees? It is fairly safe to assume that neither government nor industry buyouts should worsen residents' situations after their move. The results (and mistakes) from these buyouts will likely have broad implications for future grassroots organizing and environmental education campaigns in the South and in other regions of the country.

Clearly, the time is long overdue for the United States to provide equal protection for all of its people—in their homes, workplaces, and playgrounds—and places (e.g., rural, urban, suburban, reservations, and similar locales). Environmental justice and pollution prevention must become overarching principles of environmental protection if we are to eliminate existing inequities.

◆

CHAPTER SIX

Environmental Justice as a Working Model

Communities all across the United States have come to realize that the environmental protection apparatus is broken and needs to be fixed. Many of these same communities are engaged in life-and-death struggles; consequently, they cannot wait another two decades for the federal Environmental Protection Agency (EPA) or some other governmental agency to develop a new environmental protection arrangement. In this chapter I explore the current environmental protection model and offer an alternative framework for addressing the needs and concerns of disenfranchised communities.

Waiting for Government Action

Environmental decision making reflects the imperfections found in the larger U.S. society. The federal EPA only took action on environmental justice concerns in 1990 after some prodding from both people-of-color academics and grassroots activists. Many of these activists are convinced that waiting for the EPA to act has endangered the health and welfare of their communities. Unlike the EPA, communities of color did not discover environmental inequities in 1990. African Americans and other people of color have known about, and have been living with, inequitable environmental quality for decades—most without the protection of the federal EPA or state and local government agencies.

Current government practices reinforce a system in which environmental protection is a privilege and not a right. White communities receive special benefits and privileges by virtue of their residents' skin color. The dominant environmental protection paradigm emphasizes probability of fatality as the model for decision making. However, environmental stressors often result in health effects that fall short of death—including developmental, reproductive, respiratory, neurotoxic, and psychological effects.

As a consequence, the assignment of "acceptable" risk and the use of "averages" often result from value judgments that legitimate existing inequities. A case in point is the impact of cultural, class, and geographic differences in fish consumption in the United States.[1] Some subpopulations—people living along waterways, persons who depend upon fish for their subsistence, Asian Americans, native Americans, and African Americans—consume more fish than does the general population. The EPA's definition of an "average" fish consumer and its current water quality standards for dioxin fail to reflect the exposure of subpopulations that consume large quantities of fish.

The dominant environmental protection paradigm reinforces rather than challenges the stratification of *people* (race, ethnicity, status, power), *place* (central cities, suburbs, rural areas, unincorporated areas, native American reservations), and *work* (e.g., office workers are afforded greater protection than farm workers). The paradigm exists to manage, regulate, and distribute risks. As a result, the dominant paradigm has (1) institutionalized unequal enforcement; (2) traded human health for profit; (3) placed the burden of proof on the "victims" and not on the polluting industry; (4) legitimated human exposure to harmful chemicals, pesticides, and hazardous substances; (5) promoted risky technologies, such as incinerators; (6) exploited the vulnerability of economically and politically disenfranchised communities; (7) subsidized ecological destruction; (8) created an industry around risk assessment; (9) delayed cleanup actions; and (10) failed to develop pollution prevention as the overarching and dominant strategy.[2]

The mission of the federal EPA was never designed to address environmental policies and practices that result in unfair, unjust, and inequitable outcomes. EPA and other government officials are not likely to ask the questions that go to the heart of environmental injustice: Who is most affected? Why are they affected? Who created the problem? What can be done to remedy the problem? How can the problem be prevented?

Impetus for Changing the System

The impetus for changing the dominant environmental protection paradigm has *not* come from within regulatory agencies, the polluting industry, or the "industry" that has been built around risk management. The environmental justice movement is led by a loose alliance of grassroots and national environmental and civil rights leaders who question the foundation of the current environmental protection paradigm.

Environmental justice activists have targeted disparate enforcement, compliance, and policy formulations as they affect public health decision making. Several events in the 1990s have brought environmental justice concerns into the national public policy debate. They include the following.

1. A dialogue on disparate impact was initiated in 1990 among social scientists, social justice leaders, national environmental groups, the federal EPA, and the Agency for Toxic Substances and Disease Registry (ATSDR).

2. In January 1990, the Gulf Coast Tenants Organization, the Southwest Organizing Project, the Commission for Racial Justice, the Southern Organizing Committee for Economic and Social Justice, and several dozen other grassroots groups wrote letters to the "big ten" environmental groups challenging them to end their racism and elitism.

3. Letters from the Michigan Coalition in 1991 prompted the federal EPA to form a Work Group on Environmental Equity. The agency later created an Office of Environmental Equity and an Environmental Equity Cluster (coordinated by an assistant administrator for enforcement), issued an *Environmental Equity* report,[3] and agreed to meet with environmental leaders on a quarterly basis.

4. ATSDR established a minority health initiative (after some prodding from environmental, health, and social justice advocates), held a Minority Environmental Health Conference in 1991, and initiated a study of minority communities that are located near National Priority List (NPL) hazardous-waste sites.

5. The First National People of Color Environmental Leadership Summit was held in Washington, D.C., in 1991, with over 650 delegates from all fifty states (including Alaska and Hawaii), Puerto Rico, Mexico, Canada, and as far away as the Marshall Islands. This summit galvanized grassroots and national support for strategies to combat environmental racism.[4]

6. The EPA, ATSDR, and the National Institute for Environmental Health Sciences jointly sponsored the workshop Equity in Environmental Health: Research Issues and Needs at Research Triangle, North Carolina, in 1992.

7. The Environmental Justice Act of 1992 was introduced into Congress by Congressman John Lewis (D-Georgia) and Senator Albert Gore (D-Tennessee); the act was redrafted and reintroduced in 1993 by Lewis and Senator Max Baucus (D-Montana).

8. The Southern Organizing Committee for Economic and Social Justice held its 1992 post-summit labor-environment conference in New Orleans; over two thousand persons attended.
9. The 1993 EPA cabinet bill introduced into Congress contains environmental justice provisions.
10. The National Association for the Advancement of Colored People (NAACP) selected Dr. Benjamin F. Chavis, Jr., one of the nation's leading environmental justice advocates, to head the nation's oldest African American civil rights organization.
11. I was selected to serve as a member of Bill Clinton's Transition Team in the Natural Resources and Environment Cluster. This cluster included the Departments of the Interior, Agriculture, and Energy and the Environmental Protection Agency.

In recent years, much attention has been devoted to environmental justice and equity. Equity can be distilled into three broad categories: procedural, geographic, and social equity.

Procedural equity refers to the "fairness" question: the extent to which governing rules and regulations, evaluation criteria, and enforcement are applied in a nondiscriminatory manner. Unequal protection results from nonscientific and undemocratic decisions, such as exclusionary practices, conflicts of interest, public hearings held in remote locations and at inconvenient times, and use of English-only material as the language to communicate with and conduct hearings for non-English-speaking publics.

Geographic equity refers to the location and spatial configuration of communities and their proximity to environmental hazards, noxious facilities, and locally unwanted land uses (LULUs), such as landfills, incinerators, sewer-treatment plants, lead smelters, refineries, and other noxious facilities. For example, hazardous-waste incinerators are not randomly scattered across the landscape.

Social equity assesses the role of sociological factors (race, ethnicity, class, culture, life-styles, political power, and similar factors) on environmental decision making. Poor people and people of color often work in the most dangerous jobs and live in the most polluted neighborhoods, and their children are exposed to many kinds of environmental toxins on the playgrounds and in their homes.

Unequal protection may result from land-use decisions that determine the location of residential amenities and disamenities. Unincorporated and poor communities and communities of color often suffer a triple vulnerability in noxious facility siting, as occurred in the rezoning of Wallace, Louisiana.

Remedying Past Inequities

The use (although unsuccessful) by states of the "fair share" argument to stem the interstate transport of municipal and hazardous wastes is an equity issue. Millions of Americans live in physical environments that are overburdened with a multitude of environmental problems, including older housing that contains lead-based paint, congested freeways that crisscross neighborhoods, and industries that emit dangerous pollutants. Environmental justice advocates have sought to persuade the various levels of government (federal, state, and local) to adopt a framework that addresses distributive impacts and issues of concentration, enforcement, and compliance.

In 1990, New York City adopted a "fair share" legislative model designed to ensure that every borough bears its fair share of noxious facilities. Public hearings have begun to address risk burdens in New York City's boroughs. Proceedings from a hearing on environmental disparities in the Bronx point to concerns raised by African Americans and Puerto Ricans, who see their neighborhoods being threatened by garbage transfer stations, salvage yards, and recycling centers.

In 1992, Chicago Congresswoman Cardiss Collins offered an amendment to the bill that reauthorized the Resource Conservation and Recovery Act (RCRA), which would require "community information statements" that would assess the demographic makeup of the proposed waste site areas and the cumulative impact a new facility would have on the existing environmental burden. Congressman John Conyers's (D-Michigan) Department of Environmental Protection Act and Congressman Lewis's Environmental Justice Act, both currently before Congress, contain strong provisions that address unequal protection, differential exposures, and siting inequities. Both would require the EPA to collect and publish a list, in rank order, of the total weight of toxic chemicals present in designated environmental high-impact areas (EHIAs). State environmental-equity bills have been introduced in New York, South Carolina, and Georgia.

In 1993, the Texas Air Control Board and the Texas Water Commission established a statewide Task Force on Environmental Equity and Justice, the first state panel to examine the politically explosive environmental racism issue. The task force will review the following areas:

1. Factors that have traditionally tended to cause risk to be concentrated in lower-income and minority communities in Texas
2. Statutes, policies, and procedures used by the Texas Water Commis-

sion and the Texas Air Control Board that relate to the location of facilities that pose environmental risk

3. Data and methodologies by which the state might become more specifically aware of situations in which neighborhoods are at particularly high risk and might incorporate environmental-equity considerations into the risk-assessment process

4. Enforcement practices to determine if alternative methods of allocating resources would more equitably serve minority or other high-risk communities, as well as outcomes to identify any tendencies toward more lenient policies in communities of color

5. The role played by local government in influencing siting and location decisions, which often pose significant elements of risk

6. The efforts of the agencies in ensuring equitable representation of people of color in their own work forces and in helping minority youth to learn about career opportunities in the environmental field

7. Methods by which the state environmental agency communicates with communities of color and can become more "user friendly" to persons of color

8. Approaches to institutionalizing a focus on lower-income and minority communities when formulating and implementing policies, procedures, and legislation.[5]

Historically, the impetus for social change has come from outside the government. Discrimination in housing, employment, education, public accommodations, and municipal service delivery had to be attacked through legislative mandates after considerable agitation from civil rights organizations. Unequal environmental protection and environmental racism cannot likely be addressed without special initiatives undertaken to enforce the current laws and regulations and the enactment of new laws and regulations that target unequal environmental protection.

A Model Environmental Justice Framework

Urban environmental inequities were identified in a 1971 Council on Environmental Quality (CEQ) report. However, it took more than two decades for environmental-equity and environmental justice issues to be resurrected by a coalition of people-of-color academicians and activists. The question of environmental justice is not anchored in a debate about whether decision makers should tinker with risk-based management. The environmental justice framework rests upon an ethical analysis of strategies to eliminate unfair, unjust, and inequitable conditions and decisions. The framework seeks to prevent the threat before it occurs.[6]

The environmental justice framework incorporates other social movements that seek to eliminate harmful practices (discrimination harms the victim) in housing, land use, industrial planning, health care, and sanitation services. The impacts of redlining, economic disinvestment, infrastructure decline, housing deterioration, lead poisoning, industrial pollution, poverty, and unemployment are not unrelated if one lives in an urban ghetto or barrio, a rural hamlet, or a reservation.

The environmental justice framework attempts to uncover the underlying assumptions that may contribute to and produce unequal protection. This framework brings to the surface the *ethical* and *political* questions of "who gets what, why, and how much." Some general characteristics of the framework include the following.

1. *The environmental justice framework incorporates the principle of the* right *of all individuals to be protected from environmental degradation.* This will require legislation creating a Fair Environmental Protection Act modeled after the various federal civil rights acts that promote nondiscrimination (with the ultimate goal of achieving a zero-tolerance threshold) in such areas as housing, education, and employment. This act would need to address both the *intended* and the *unintended* effects of public policies, land-use decisions, and industry practices that have disparate impacts on racial and ethnic minorities and other vulnerable groups. The purpose of this act is to prohibit environmental discrimination based on race. The precedents for this framework are the Civil Rights Act of 1964, which attempted to address—both de jure and de facto—school segregation, the Fair Housing Act of 1968 and as amended in 1988, and the Voting Rights Act of 1965.

2. *The environmental justice framework adopts a public health model of prevention (elimination of the threat before harm occurs) as the preferred strategy.* Affected communities should not have to wait until causation or conclusive "proof" is established before preventive action is taken. For example, the framework offers a solution to the lead problem by shifting the primary focus from *treatment* (after children have been poisoned) to *prevention* (elimination of the threat by abating the incidence of lead in houses).

Overwhelming scientific evidence exists on the ill effects of lead on the human body. However, little action has been taken to rid the nation of lead poisoning caused by housing—a preventable disease. Former Health and Human Services Secretary Louis Sullivan tagged it the "number one environmental health threat to children."[7]

There are a few signs that the environmental justice framework is taking shape among broad coalitions of environmental, social justice, and civil libertarian groups. The Natural Resources Defense Council, the NAACP Legal Defense and Education Fund, the American Civil Liberties Union, and the Legal Aid Society of Alameda County joined forces in 1991 and won a $15–20 million out-of-court settlement for a blood-lead testing program in California. The *Matthews v. Coye* lawsuit involved the state of California not providing the federally mandated testing of some 557,000 Medicaid children for lead. This historic agreement will likely trigger similar actions in other states that have failed to provide federally mandated screening.[8]

Lead screening is an important element in this problem, but it is *not* the solution. Prevention is the solution. New government-mandated lead abatement and enforcement initiatives are needed. For example, an aggressive lead cleanup program is needed under Title X housing legislation (provisions of the Affordable Housing Act). To be successful, this federal legislation will require a coordinated working relationship among governmental agencies (e.g., the EPA, Housing and Urban Development, and Health and Human Services). In 1993, the federal EPA did not have in place the mandated safety standards for lead dust in homes.

If termite inspections can be mandated to protect individual home investments, a lead-free home can surely be mandated to protect public health. Ultimately, the lead abatement debate—public health (who is affected) versus property rights (who pays for cleanup)—is a value conflict that will not be resolved by the scientific community.

3. *The environmental justice framework shifts the burden of proof to polluters and dischargers who do harm, discriminate, or do not give equal protection to racial and ethnic minorities and other "protected" classes.* Under the current system, individuals who challenge polluters must "prove" that they have been harmed, discriminated against, or disproportionately impacted. Few affected communities have the resources to hire the lawyers, expert witnesses, and doctors needed to sustain such a challenge. The environmental justice strategy would require the parties that are applying for operating permits (for landfills, incinerators, smelters, refineries, chemical plants, and similar structures) to "prove" that their operations are not harmful to human health, will not disproportionately affect racial and ethnic minorities and other protected groups, and are nondiscriminatory.

4. *The environmental justice framework would allow disparate impact and statistical weight, as opposed to "intent," to infer discrimination.* Proving intentional or purposeful discrimination in a court of law is nearly impossible, as demonstrated in *Bean v. Southwestern Waste Management* (discussed previously). Since this case, not a single landfill or incinerator has been sited in an African American neighborhood in Houston.

It took nearly a decade after *Bean v. Southwestern Waste Management* for environmental discrimination to resurface in the courts. A number of recent cases have challenged siting decisions using the environmental discrimination argument: *East Bibb Twiggs Neighborhood Assoc. v. Macon-Bibb County Planning & Zoning Commission* (1989), *Bordeaux Action Comm. v.*

Metro Gov't of Nashville (1990), *R.I.S.E. v. Kay* (1991), and *El Pueblo para El Aire y Agua Limpio v. Chemical Waste Management, Inc.* (1991). To date, no environmental discrimination lawsuit using civil rights laws has prevailed because of the "intent" test. Proving "purposeful" discrimination in waste facility siting cases has been next to impossible.

5. *The environmental justice framework redresses disproportionate impact through "targeted" action and resources.* This strategy would target resources in which environmental and health problems are greatest (as determined by some ranking scheme but not limited to risk assessment). Reliance solely on "objective" science disguises the exploitative way the polluting industries have operated in some communities and condones a passive acceptance of the status quo.[9] The EPA already has geographic targeting that involves:

(a) selecting a physical area, often a naturally defined area such as a hydrologic watershed, (b) assessing the condition of the natural resources and range of environmental threat—including risks to public health, (c) formulating and implementing integrated, holistic strategies for restoring or protecting living resources and their habitats within that area, and (d) evaluating the progress of those strategies toward their objectives.[10]

In the 1992 EPA report *Securing Our Legacy,* the agency describes geographic initiatives as "protecting what we love."[11] Again, human *values* are involved in determining *which* geographic areas deserve public investments. The strategy emphasizes "pollution prevention, multimedia enforcement, research into causes and cures of environmental stress, stopping habitat loss, education, and constituency building."[12] Geographic initiatives are underway in the Chesapeake Bay, the Great Lakes, the Gulf of Mexico, and the Mexican border regions.

Environmental justice targeting would channel resources to the "hot spots," communities that are burdened with more than their fair share of environmental problems. For example, EPA's Region VI has developed a Geographic Information System and comparative risk methodologies to evaluate environmental-equity concerns in the region. The methodology combines susceptibility factors (e.g., age, pregnancy, race, income, preexisting disease, and life-styles) with chemical release data (e.g., the Toxic Release Inventory and monitoring information), geographic and demographic data (e.g., site-specific areas around hazardous-waste sites, census tracts, zip codes, cities, and states), and state health department vital statistics data in developing a regional equity assessment.

Regions VI's Gulf Coast Toxics Initiatives project, developed in 1992, is an outgrowth of the equity assessment. The project targets facilities on the Texas and Louisiana coasts, a "sensitive … ecoregion where most of the releases in the five-state region occur." Inspectors will spend 38 percent (I do not know how this percentage was determined) of their time in this "multi-media enforcement effort."[13] In order for this project to move beyond the first-step phase and begin to address real inequities, it will need to channel *most* of its resources (not just inspectors) to the areas where *most* of the problems occur.

By using the EPA's Region VI Gulf Coast Toxics Initiatives equity assessment, it comes as no surprise that communities along the Houston ship channel and petrochemical corridor to the Louisiana communities that line the eighty-five-mile stretch of the Mississippi River from Baton Rouge to New Orleans were ranked at or near the top in terms of health risks from industrial pollution. Similar rankings would likely be achieved using the environmental justice framework. However, the question that remains is one of resource allocation—the level of resources Region VI will channel into solving the pollution problem in communities that have a disproportionately large share of poor people, working-class people, and people of color. Health concerns raised by residents and grassroots activists who live in Louisiana communities such as Alsen, St. Gabriel, Geismer, and Lions—all of which are located in close proximity to polluting industries—have not been adequately addressed by local parish supervisors, state environmental and health officials, and the federal and regional offices of the EPA or ATSDR.[14]

Winning at the Grassroots

There is clear evidence that institutional barriers severely limit access to clean environments. Despite the attempts made by the government to level the playing field, all communities are still not created equal. Environmental inequities are created and maintained by institutional arrangements—policies that favor one group over another. Such environmental policies are unjust, unfair, and in many cases racist in their application. Studies of differential impacts and exposures are studies of justice.

Environmental justice leaders are now challenging the policies and practices that force individuals, workers, and communities to accept environmental risks others can avoid by "voting with their feet." In addition, they are questioning the practice of dominating the natural world, rather than respecting and nurturing it. They are demanding that the problems of pesticides and farm workers, of workers in "sweat shops" (mostly women and immigrants in the garment industry, in poultry and catfish processing plants, and in computer assembly operations), and of lead and inner-city children be elevated to the national environmental action agenda.

Environmental justice activists have not limited their focus to toxics or racism. Their movement is inclusive, cutting across race, ethnicity, class, region, and political affiliation. Environmental justice leaders are demanding justice for everyone. The same guiding principles that challenge the ecological destruction and threat to public health in West Dallas also apply in Appalachia, on native American reservations, in our urban centers, and on both sides of the U.S.-Mexican border.

Some activists question the ethical implications of the North American Free Trade Agreement (NAFTA). More than twenty years of experience with the twin plants in the maquiladora zone located along the U.S.-Mexican border, in which workers—the majority of whom are young women—are paying a high price in terms of their health in exchange for low-paying jobs and unsafe working conditions, serves as a prelude to NAFTA. Texas occupies a nine-hundred-mile border with Mexico. This zone is home to the manufacturing and assembly plants of many large U.S. and Japanese corporations.

People-of-color groups were the ones who endured hardship and struggle in order to bring environmental justice issues to the forefront; these groups now deserve to be recognized and supported. The 1992 *People of Color Environmental Groups Directory* profiled more than 205 groups from thirty-five states, the District of Columbia, Puerto Rico, and Canada.[15] People-of-color groups in the South and other regions of the country continue to provide the leadership in struggles to address problems of sustainable development, economic blackmail, industrial policy, land rights and sovereignty, occupational health and safety, grassroots empowerment, urban land use, equal protection laws, environmental paradigm shifts, and ethics and values in science.

A dilemma has emerged on how to prioritize grants needed by grassroots organizations that serve communities of color. The needs of the national foundations of these groups have a long track record of funding. Clearly, strengthening the capacity of people-of-color organizations and indigenous institutions is the preferred strategy for empowering these people's communities.

There are clear signs that a "new" environmental movement is alive and well in the United States. Grassroots groups in communities of color are making their voices heard in the halls of Congress, the state houses, and city halls. Some groups have begun to form working relationships with national environmental and social justice organizations. The First National People of Color Environmental Leadership Summit, discussed under "Impetus for Changing the System" earlier in this chapter, is an example of this heightened activism.

Grassroots activism increased in communities of color following the summit. Many delegates left Washington, D.C., with the goal of changing conditions when they returned to their respective communities. For example, black and white residents in Sumter County, Alabama, have continued their struggle against Chemical Waste Management's hazardous-waste landfill. Local grassroots groups have had some success in getting state officials to use the "fairness," or equity, argument in Alabama's attempt to address the out-of-state hazardous-waste issue.

Institute, West Virginia, residents are still concerned about emissions from the nearby chemical plant. These fears were not allayed by the sale of the Institute Union Carbide plant to the French chemical conglomerate Rhone Poulenc. Local grassroots groups have had some success in having their story told in a film on the chemical industry in the Kanawha River Valley.[16] Local groups have also enlisted the support of several national environmental groups, including Greenpeace, the Citizens' Clearinghouse for Hazardous Waste, and the National Toxics Campaign (NTC).

Alsen, Louisiana, residents have continued to monitor air emissions from the Rollins Environmental Services hazardous-waste incinerator. In addition to the incinerator problem, the grassroots group in Alsen has focused its attention of a Superfund site near Devils Swamp. The Alsen environmental group recently received a technical assistance grant (TAG) from the federal EPA in recognition of the public input in the site cleanup.

Several historically black colleges and universities (HBCUs) have begun to conduct research and to work with Alsen residents and other affected African American communities along the Mississippi River. For example, professors from Southern University in Baton Rouge and from Xavier University collaborated on a research project that examined community buyouts. In 1992, Xavier University, under the leadership of sociology professor Beverly H. Wright, became the leader of an environmental justice consortium of New Orleans–area universities (including Xavier University, Southern University in New Orleans, Dillard University, and the University of New Orleans). A year later, Xavier University created the Deep South Center for Environmental Justice, which works closely with the Gulf Coast Tenants Organization in building a community-university partnership to work on environmental issues in "cancer alley."

In 1991, Luis Sepulveda and his grassroots group in West Dallas, Texas, forced the lead issue back onto the city and federal environmental agendas. New discoveries of lead-tainted soil as high as ninety-nine thousand parts per million (ppm) triggered protests at city hall and at the EPA Region VI headquarters—a high-rise office building tagged the "Emerald City" because of its green coloring. (The EPA considers two hundred and fifty ppm of lead in soil to be dangerous to humans.) The West Dallas group formed alliances with other groups, such as the Texas Network, the Southwest Organizing Project, the Southwest Network for Environmental and Economic Justice, and Texans United.

West Dallas activists were not successful in getting the neighborhood declared a federal Superfund site. However, in December 1991—twenty years after the first government study was issued on the West Dallas smelter—the federal EPA ordered a comprehensive cleanup of the West Dallas neighborhood. The cleanup called for the removal of thirty thousand to forty thousand cubic yards (roughly eighteen hundred truckloads) of lead-contaminated soil from several neighborhood sites, including school yards and about 140 private homes. The project cost the EPA around $4 million.

The Houston case points to the long-lasting impact of a community saying "no" to waste facility siting. Not a single landfill, incinerator, or waste facility has been sited in Houston since the Whispering Pines landfill was built in 1979. Residents of Northwood Manor and other Houston neighborhoods remember the long city hall sessions, the protests, and the litigation involved in that case.

As a concession to the residents of Northwood Manor, and as a way to redress some of the injustices detailed in the *Bean v. Southwestern Waste* lawsuit, in the early 1980s the Houston city council passed an ordinance regulating solid-waste facility siting. This action was a prelude to zoning, in a city that takes pride in being the only major U.S. city without zoning. The memories of past siting battles were rekindled by a 1992 proposal by the Ohio-based WPF Corporation to build a garbage composting plant in a mostly African American Houston neighborhood. The company applied for a permit to build a $15 million Type V (composting) municipal solid-waste facility on a 31.6-acre site, which would service about 120 trucks and receive 750 tons of household garbage a day.[17]

The proposed site lies within a mostly African American neighborhood that has a long history of landfills dating back to the disputes surrounding the notorious Holmes Road dump and its poorly operating incinerator. The home owners who live near the southeast Houston waste facilities are predominantly African American.

Dolores Sandling, a retired school principal, along with the Austin-based chapter of the Environmental Defense Fund (EDF), organized the opposition that derailed the composting proposal.[18] Mrs. Sandling's church, Blueridge United Methodist Church, is building a new structure just a mile from the proposed composting facility.

A number of civic club representatives joined in the protest to block the composting facility—including the Sugar Valley Civic Club, the Central City Civic Club, and the Meridith Manor Civic Club. In an unexpected twist, local residents got a boost from a business ally. Officials from Houston's AstroWorld—a popular amusement park and major tourist attraction—voiced their strong opposition to the proposed municipal composting facility operating just a mile from their gates.[19] The broad coalition of civic, environmental, and business leaders defeated the composting proposal.

Conclusion

Institutional research and environmental decision making have failed to address the "justice" questions of who gets help and who does not, who can afford help and who cannot, why some contaminated communities get studied and others are left off the research agenda, why industry poisons some communities and not others, why some contaminated communities get cleaned up and others do not, and why some communities are protected and others are not. The solution to the problem of unequal protection lies in the realm of environmental justice for all Americans. No community—rich or poor, black or white, urban or suburban—should be allowed to become a sacrifice zone. The lessons learned from the civil rights struggles over housing, employment, education, and public accommodations over the past four decades suggest that environmental justice will need to have a legislative foundation. It is not enough to demonstrate the existence of unjust and unfair conditions: The practices that caused the conditions must be made illegal—and ultimately be eliminated.

How can environmental justice be incorporated into decision making? First, the environmental justice framework demands that the current laws be enforced in a nondiscriminatory manner. Second, a legislative initiative is needed. Unequal protection must be attacked through a federal Fair Environmental Protection Act that makes protection a right rather than a privilege. Third, legislative initiatives will also need to be directed at states. Since many of the decisions and problems lie with state actions, states will need to model their legislative initiatives (or develop stronger initiatives) on the federal legislation.

Noxious facility siting, permitting, and cleanup decisions involve more politics than science. Federal, state, and local initiatives are needed to target resources into the areas with the greatest environmental and public health problems. States that are initiating "fair share" plans to address *interstate* waste conflicts (siting equity) need also to begin to address *intrastate* siting equity concerns being raised by affected communities.

Benefits and burdens are not randomly distributed. Sole reliance on "objective" science for environmental decision making in a world shaped largely by power politics and special interests often masks institutional racism. A national environmental justice framework is needed to begin addressing environmental inequities that result from procedural, geographic, and societal imbalances.

◆

Action Strategies
for the 1990s

In this brief concluding chapter I hope to summarize the major findings on black environmentalism and delineate some action strategies that are needed to enhance the larger environmental movement in the areas of social justice and equity. The recommendations outlined in this section are not meant to be exhaustive. Although the nation's black communities are extremely diverse and may differ on a number of socioeconomic or class dimensions, they still have a great deal in common and may find these action plans easily adaptable.

Lessons Learned

Black Environmentalism

It is now time for people to stop asking the question, Do minorities care about the environment? The evidence is clear and irrefutable that white middle-class communities do not have a monopoly on environmental concern nor are they the only groups moved to action when confronted with the threat of pollution. Although a "concern and action gap"[1] may still exist between blacks and whites, black communities are no longer being bullied into submission by industrial polluters and government regulators.

Clearly, a "new" form of environmentalism has taken root in America and in the black community. Since the late 1970s, a new grassroots social movement emerged around the toxics threat. Citizens mobilized around the antiwaste theme. These social activists acquired new skills in areas where they had little or no prior experience. They soon became resident "experts" on the toxics issue.[2] The new grassroots environmentalists burst on the scene as "toxic busters." They, however, did not limit their attacks to well-publicized toxic contamination issues, but sought remedial actions on problems like "housing, transportation, air quality, and even economic development—issues the traditional environmental agenda had largely ignored."[3] Robert Gottlieb and Helen Ingram described the grassroots environmental movement as having the following traits:

- Focuses on equity and the urban industrial complex
- Challenges the mainstream environmental movement for its conservative tactics but not its goals
- Emphasizes the needs of the community and workplace as primary agenda items
- Uses its own self-taught "experts" and citizen lawsuits instead of relying on legislation and lobbying
- Takes a "populist" stance on environmental issues relying on active members rather than dues-payers from mailing lists
- Embraces a democratic ideology akin to the civil rights and women's movements of the 1960s.[4]

Environmentalism, concern and action, has been too narrowly defined. Concern has been incorrectly equated with check-writing, dues-paying, and membership in environmental organizations. These biases no doubt have contributed to the misunderstanding of the grassroots environmental movement in minority communities.

Black community activists in this new movement focused their attention on toxics and the notion of deprivation.[5] When black community residents compared their environmental quality with that of the larger society, a sense of deprivation or unequal treatment emerged. Once again, institutional racism and discriminatory land-use policies and practices of government—at all levels—influenced the creation and perpetuation of racially separate and unequal residential areas for blacks and whites.[6]

Institutional barriers have locked millions of blacks in polluted neighborhoods and hazardous, low-paying jobs, making it difficult for them to "vote with their feet" and escape these health-threatening environments. Mainstream environmentalists have been slow in recognizing these grassroots social activists as "environmentalists," mainly because of the way the problems are framed. Conversely, few black activists see themselves as environmentalists. Local problems are generally defined along equity lines as blacks see themselves fighting another form of institutional discrimination.

The environmental-equity movement is an extension of the social justice movement. Environmentalists may be concerned about clean air, but may have opposing views on the construction of low-income housing in white, middle-class, suburban neighborhoods. Black residents have come to understand that environmentalists are no more enlightened than nonenvironmentalists when it comes to minority communities. But then, why should they be more enlightened? After all, we are all products of socialization and reflect the various biases and prejudices of this process. It is not surprising that mainstream environmental organizations have not been active on issues that disproportionately impact minority communities, as in the case of toxics, workplace hazards, urban and rural housing needs, and the myriad of problems resulting from the strains in the urban industrial complex. Yet, minorities are the ones accused of being ill-informed, unconcerned, and inactive on environmental issues.

Job Blackmail

Why were black organizations late in challenging the environmental imbalance that exists in the United States? There is enough blame to go around. Black organizations and their leaders have not been as sensitive to the environmental threat to minorities as they have been to problems in education, housing, jobs, drugs, and more recently the AIDS epidemic. In some cases, black leaders have operated out of fear of erosion of hard-fought economic gains by some environmental reform proposals. Black Congressional Caucus staffer Paul Ruffins addressed this issue:

> Many civil-rights groups have longstanding relationships with unions and corporations. [Benjamin] Hooks [of the NAACP] is not likely to forget that United Auto Worker Walter P. Reuther marched with Martin Luther King Jr. long before Earth Day was invented. On the other hand, most environmental groups have done little to reach out to minorities, making it easy for industry to portray them as elitist.[7]

Grassroots groups in black communities are beginning to take a stand against threatened plant closure and job loss as a trade-off for environmental risks. Job blackmail has lost some of its appeal, especially in those areas where the economic incentives (jobs, taxes, monetary contributions, etc.) flow outside of the black community. People can hardly be blackmailed over benefits they never receive from local polluting industry. Because of the potential to exacerbate existing environmental inequities, black community residents and their leaders are now questioning the underlying assumptions behind "risk compensation" as applied in minority and poor areas.

In their push to become acceptable and credible, many mainstream environmental organizations adopted a corporate model in their structure, demeanor, and outlook. This metamorphosis has had a down side. These corporatelike environmental organizations have alienated many grassroots leaders and community organizers (both black and white) from the larger movement—a complaint not unlike that of constituents who feel apart from their locally elected representatives in Washington.

Compensation and Victims

Local community groups may be turned off by the idea of sitting around a table with a waste disposal giant, a government regulator, and an environmentalist to negotiate the siting of a toxic waste incinerator in their community. The lines become blurred in terms of the parties representing the interests of the community and those of business. Negotiations of this type fuel residents' perception of an "unholy trinity" where the battle lines are drawn along an "us versus them" power arrangement. Moreover, overdependence on and blind acceptance of risk-assessment analysis and "the best available technology" for policy-setting serves to intimidate, confuse, and overwhelm individuals at the grassroots level.

Talk of risk compensation for a host community raises a series of moral dilemmas, especially where environmental imbalances already exist. Should risks be borne by a smaller group to spare the larger groups?[8] Past discriminatory waste siting practices should not guide future policy decisions. For example, a "community saturated with facilities may have less impact sensitivity to a proposed project than might an area having few facilities."[9] Any saturation policy derived from past siting practices perpetuates equity impacts. Facility siting becomes a "modern ritual for selecting victims for sacrifice."[10]

Mobilizing the Grassroots

It is unlikely that the grassroots environmental movement will ever become a mass movement in the black community. However, there are clear signs that a small cadre of dedicated activists have taken up the "cause" of environmental justice. Few social movements can count on total support and involvement of their constituent groups. All social movements have "free riders," individuals who benefit from the efforts of a few.[11] Blacks in the grassroots environmental movement have been and will probably remain wedded to their established social action organizations. After all, American society has yet to achieve a race-neutral state where these organizations are no longer needed. Black institutions still serve a special niche in society. Although the color barrier has been breached in most professional groups around the country, blacks still find it useful to have their own organizations. The predominately black National Bar Association (NBA), National Medical Association (NMA), National Association of Black Social Workers (NABSW), Association of Black Psychologists (ABP), and Association of Black Sociologists (ABS) are examples of race-based professional organizations. The chances are slim of having a mass movement of blacks flooding the ranks of mainstream environmental and conservation organizations.

Grassroots environmental organizations, whether in black or white communities, have the advantage of being closer to the people they serve and the problems they address. Future growth in the environmental movement is likely to come from the bottom up, grassroots environmental groups linking up with social action groups for expanded spheres of influence and focus.

Dispute Handling Mechanisms

Black communities do not have a long track record in challenging government decisions and private industries that threaten the health of their residents. Many of the organizations and institutions were formed as a reaction to racism and dealt primarily with social justice issues. The NAACP, Urban League, Southern Christian Leadership Conference, Commission for Racial Justice, and National Black United Front are some examples of these organizations. These organizations operated at the multistate level and had affiliates in cities across the nation. With the exception of Reverend Joseph Lowery of the Southern Christian Leadership Conference and Benjamin F. Chavis, Jr., of the United Church of Christ's Commission for Racial Justice, few national civil rights leaders and organizations embraced an ideology that linked environmental disparities with racism. It was not until the 1980s that national civil rights organizations began to make such links. This linking of institutional racism with the structure of resource allocation (clean environments) has led black social action groups to adopt environmental justice as a civil rights issue, an issue well worth "taking to the street." The 1993 selection of Chavis—a longtime civil rights and environmental justice activist—to head the NAACP is an example of this trend.

NIMBY has operated to insulate many white communities from the localized environmental impacts of solid waste facilities while providing them the benefits of garbage disposal. NIMBY, like white racism, creates and perpetuates privileges for whites at the expense of people of color. Citizens see the siting question as an all-out war. Those communities that can mobilize political influence improve their chance of "winning" this war.[12] Because blacks and other people of color remain underrepresented in elected and appointed offices, they most often must rely on indirect representation, usually white officials who may or may not understand the nature and severity of the community problem. Citizen redress often becomes a political issue.

The Frontline Warriors

Who are the frontline leaders in this quest for environmental justice? What role do outside elites play? The war against toxics in black communities has been waged largely by individuals indigenous to those black communities. Black grassroots community groups received some moral support from outside elites, but few elites were down in the trenches fighting alongside the toxic warriors. On the other hand, it was the ministers from the black churches and the activist leaders from the social action organizations (e.g., civic clubs, neighborhood associations, parents groups, etc.) who mobilized black community residents against the toxics threat. Few of these leaders identified themselves as environmentalists or saw their struggle solely as an environmental problem. Their struggle embraced larger issues of equity, social justice, and resource distribution. Black leaders and their constituents questioned the fairness of the decision-making process surrounding facility siting. People's perceptions are important factors in dispute handling. Gail Bingham noted:

> Although people's strategies for resolving environmental disputes may vary depending on their views about social conflict and the characteristics of a particular dispute, individuals and groups care about similar factors. They care about the outcomes and the extent to which it satisfies the real issues in disputes, as they see them. They care about the process—its fairness, its efficiency, and the opportunities it provides them for influencing a decision.[13]

Most environmental disputes revolve around siting issues, involving government or private industry. Proposals for future sites are more likely to attract environmentalists' support than are existing sites.[14] It is much easier to get outside assistance in fighting a noxious facility that is on paper than one that is in operation. Again, plant closure means economic dislocation. Because minority communities are burdened with a greater share of existing facilities—many of which have been in operation for decades—it is an uphill battle of convincing outside environmental groups to support efforts to close such facilities.

Toward the Politics of Inclusion

Diversification

It makes a lot of sense for the organized environmental movement in the United States to broaden its base to include people of color, low-income, and working-class individuals and issues. Why diversify? As a participant in a Minority Roundtable of the Conservation Leadership Project held in the summer of 1989 in Seattle, I observed a host of reasons given by blacks, Hispanics, native Americans, and native Hawaiians for diversification. Some the responses included:

- Minority voter blocs are forming convincingly in many regions of the country.
- The voting record of the Congressional Black Caucus is the most solid environmental record in Congress.
- The demographic shift toward more women and minorities in the workplace makes diversification both desirable and inevitable.
- Reacting positively to that demographic shift will demand and increase the sophistication of the mainstream environmental organizations.
- Diversity is ecologically and biologically correct.
- Diversity is ethically and morally correct.
- America's greatest asset is its human diversity, its multicultural heritage.
- Diversity broadens the perspective.[15]

Diversification makes good economic and political sense for the long-range survival of the environmental movement. However, it is not about selfishness or "quota-filling." Diversification can go a long way in enhancing the national environmental movement's worldwide credibility and legitimacy in dealing with global environmental and development issues, especially in Third World nations.

No More Excuses

The nation's major environmental organizations mirror the national picture of a severe underrepresentation of people-of-color professionals at all levels. A 1991 survey of 110 people-of-color environmental groups revealed that these groups tend to be small and understaffed. Around one third of the groups had operating budgets under ten thousand dollars, and just over half had paid staffs.[16] The Center for Environment, Commerce and Energy (CE²), based in the nation's capital, is just one of the few national black environmental organizations. Norris McDonald, the president of CE², charged environmental organizations with making the same excuses as American corporations. Corporate recruiters' fallback position has been "they can't find blacks and other minorities."[17] Or they halt their search after finding one minority—the we-have-one-minority (WHOM) syndrome—a malady commonly observed in corporate America and academia. However, McDonald has found something altogether different when advertising for minority interns. His office is routinely inundated with minority applicants vying for the few environmental internship positions he has in his organization.

Recruitment of Minority Professionals

Why should environmental organizations recruit minority professionals? The Human Environment Center's 1981 report *Minority Education for Environmental and Natural Resources Professions: Higher Education* offered a timely reply to the diversification query:

> There are some obvious reasons for people and institutions in environmental and resource fields to cultivate minorities' interest: equal opportunity commitment and concerns, a desire to recruit talent from sources largely untapped, the chance to expand public understanding of these professions' purposes and worth. Those who teach, advocate, or employ in these fields will elicit more minority interest if they are versed in the relevance of environment and resources to the well-being of minority people.[18]

Inclusion of more minority professionals among the ranks of environmental, occupational, and health and safety organizations would have far-reaching benefits beyond the organizations and groups served. Such an inclusion strategy would infuse egalitarian principles into the larger environmental movement—something it has lacked up to the present time. In addressing the egalitarian issue, the Human Environment Center reported that:

> Again, only economic justice can bring environmental justice, but minority professionals rising through the management ranks of government and industry can give impetus to the process. ... Given the fact that race and racism today, and the lingering presence of some exclusionary "environmentalism," racial and ethnic integration of these professions is vital to their integrity and to their commitment to serve all. Minority professionals can help environmental and natural resource management serve and draw participation from many kinds of people who do not now perceive the fields' policies and processes as relevant, much less responsive, to their communities and concerns. Surely, equitable sharing of resource benefits and protection of our common environment are worthy life goals for any person.[19]

The 1990s have seen a few encouraging signs pointing to a shift in the approach mainstream environmental organizations are using to diversify their constituency. The Environmental Consortium for Minority Outreach (TEC) was established by representatives from the Trust for Public Land, Human Environment Center, and the Group of Ten (i.e., the ten largest environmental organizations). Black environmentalist Gerry Stover of TEC and a participant in the Minority Roundtable in Seattle addressed the shortage of minorities in the environmental movement and the need for affirmative action:

> A major problem faced by all of the major environmental and conservation organizations in the United States today is the recruitment and retention of minorities for middle, senior, and executive level positions. Through the years there has been repeated verbal commitment to increased Affirmative Action efforts within our ranks, yet, for the most part, the results have been dismal. ... The most commonly heard reasons for this situation are: (1) "The pool of qualified candidates is almost nonexistent." Or (2) "Recruiting takes time under normal circumstances. Recruiting minorities can be an endless task with limited or no results." Or (3) "Good minority candidates usually turn us down because of our salary levels or because of a lack of understanding of career potential within our organization."[20]

A consortium of this type is long overdue. TEC had the lofty mission of enfranchising minority populations that will further enhance the existing environmental movement. The specific objectives of this environmental-sponsored consortium were:

- Establish a focused minority recruitment program for staff and board positions within participating organizations
- Establish a coordinated minority internship program to expose minority youth to environmental and conservation issues and concerns and to promote future interest in environmental careers
- Establish and/or enhance human resource training programs to increase career development and retention for minorities in particular and for all of our staffs in general
- Develop curricula and materials for education at all levels within our minority communities that will enhance general knowledge for our industry, of issues, and of the career opportunities available
- Reach out to and conduct projects in conjunction with organizations and agencies serving minority communities
- Sponsor conferences, symposia, and workshops to identify and address issues of common concern to both the environmental and minority communities
- Encourage, promote, and coordinate support to and for grassroots environmental activities within minority communities
- Promote issue papers and other publications that focus on increasing minority involvement in efforts to improve at local, national, and global levels[21]

To be successful, TEC and any other consortium of this type must be accountable to the people they set out to serve—low-income, working-class, and people-of-color communities. Unfortunately, TEC was not accountable, and it failed. TEC and its parent organization, the Human Environment Center, are no longer players in the environmental justice arena.

Nearly everyone can agree on the need for more people-of-color leaders in the environmental and conservation movement. Enlarging this pool is not likely to be an easy or overnight task. TEC, however, cannot solve this acute shortage alone. Other institutions must pitch in and carry their share of the work, especially colleges and universities.

American colleges and universities have a miserable track record in recruiting and turning out minorities in the environmental fields. There are, however, some signs of stepped-up college recruitment efforts across all disciplines. One visible program is Vanderbilt University's Student Environmental Health Project (STEHP), founded in 1983. STEHP offers internships for students to work with community groups trying to understand environmental laws, regulations, and agencies; reviews technical documents; prepares public hearings; and draws water and soil samples for testing. Since 1986, STEHP has targeted minority students, mainly in the South, in an attempt to get them to "choose natural resources and environmental health as professions, increase the awareness of toxic waste problems throughout the South, and establish a closer link between historically black colleges and universities and surrounding communities."[22]

Vanderbilt University recently instituted an enhancement of STEHP, its Black Environmental Advancement Program (BEAP), designed to attract young black activists to community-based environmental fields. The advantage of BEAP is its recognition of the overlap between civil rights activities that organize against poverty, racism, and more recently toxics, and those that build on the strengths of this earlier movement.

Organizing Neighborhoods

The environmental equity movement has elements of the three dominant approaches to organizing neighborhoods: social work, political activism, and neighborhood maintenance.[23] First, the *social work approach* uses "enablers" and "advocates' to secure needed community services. Environmental protection is a public service not unlike fire and police protection or garbage collection. Second, the *political activist approach* views the organizing of communities as a means of empowering local residents to defend their space and develop a political power base to influence decision making. Policy makers and government officials seldom respond to environmental complaints from an individual, but complaints originating from organizations generally receive a more favorable response. Third, the *neighborhood maintenance approach,* usually associated with middle-class and upper-class neighborhoods, organizes around improving and maintaining residential areas while opposing external and internal threats from hostile forces. The toxics war is a classic example of community residents drawing closer together in their defense of "turf" and struggle against encroachment from noxious facilities and unwanted land uses.

Grassroots organizing within communities of color will likely continue to blossom as communities become aware of health and environmental threats. As an aid in future organization of neighborhoods, however, there is a clear need to:

- Link minority, working-class, and middle-class environmental activists on issues that cut across geographic boundaries and political jurisdictions
- Create organizing channels that cut across the political spectrum
- Develop leader exchange programs designed to break down the legacy of mistrust and artificial barriers that separate people and hinder mobilization
- Design training and leadership development programs for emergent grassroots environmental justice groups
- Institute "adopt-a-community" programs at historically black colleges and universities (HBCUs) around environmental justice and resource allocation areas—targeting minority communities threatened by toxics
- Develop new inter-organizational linkages and organizations that cut across racial and class boundaries

Communication Networks

It is important for the victims of the toxics wars to know that there have been citizen victories. For grassroots groups, especially underdog groups, knowing that others in similar circumstances have triumphed gives them an added incentive to keep up the struggle. Ghetto residents, for example, are routinely bombarded with messages reinforcing their powerlessness and marginal status. Positive feedback is needed as a counteractive measure. Grassroots communication networks can maximize output when they are channeled into a larger information system (e.g., Southern Organizing Committee for Economic and Social Justice and Gulf Coast Tenants Organization). Some strategies for enhancing the communication networks include:

- Disseminating information that highlights the community's strength and power (potential) base. Minority groups should not be timid or shy when it comes to the use of their power

- Exposing the impact of NIMBY by having policy makers deal with this phenomenon not as an exaggerated or irrational fear
- Instilling self-confidence in community leaders and residents
- Communicating environmentalism as a universal equity issue
- Teaching people when they have won—the opposition will seldom admit defeat as a way of diminishing citizen victories
- Getting environmental organizations to accept social justice and urban industrial issues as legitimate environmental agenda items
- Dispelling prevailing myths and stereotypes on both sides (environmentalists and social justice activists) with interorganizational communication
- Helping minority, working-class, and poor persons understand they have a stake or vested interest in wilderness and conservation programs, while not jeopardizing their support and credibility on urban and industrial policy areas

Conclusion

The environmental movement has proven that it can make a difference in the quality of life we enjoy in the United States. Environmentalists and conservationists alike wield substantial power and influence from city halls to the United States Congress. They also have a significant role in shaping the nation's development patterns, particularly when it comes to environmental impacts and land use.

The 1990s offer some challenging opportunities for the environmental movement to embrace social justice and other minority concerns. There can be no environmental justice without social justice. Population shifts and demographic trends all point to a more diverse America. It is time for the environmental movement to diversify and reach out to the "other" America—communities that have borne a disproportionate burden of the nation's pollution problem.

In the early 1990s, some progress was made in getting the environmental justice message to a broader audience, especially to colleges and universities. For example, environmental justice leaders have participated in conferences and seminars held at a number of southern law schools, including the University of Virginia, Tulane University, the University of Maryland, and the University of Georgia. Environmental career conferences have been held in major urban centers with large African American student populations (e.g., Atlanta and New Orleans). The NAACP Legal Defense and Educational Fund held a national conference of scholars, practitioners, and grassroots environmental justice leaders at Howard University Law School to map out legal strategies to address environmental inequities and unequal protection.

In 1993, Xavier University's Center for Environmental Programs coordinated an environmental justice symposium that attracted students from the other New Orleans–based schools, such as Dillard University, Southern University in New Orleans, the University of New Orleans, and Tulane University. Xavier University also hosted the Southern Organizing Committee for Economic and Social Justice labor/environment conference. Also in 1993, Clark-Atlanta University spearheaded an EPA Region IV environmental justice and equity conference, whose participants included academics, activists, and policy makers. Environmental justice leaders have called for similar conferences to be held in the EPA's other nine regions.

No segment of the population should have to bear the brunt of the nation's industrial pollution problem. Yet, institutional barriers still limit residential choices and mobility options for millions of working-class persons, poor community residents, and people of color. Although much progress had been made in bringing blacks and other minority groups into the mainstream, all Americans do not have the same opportunities to escape the ravages of environmental toxins. Consequently, those communities that have the least economic means—people-of-color communities are overrepresented in this group—have become victims of the toxic wars.

Environmental discrimination is difficult to prove—as is the case of other forms of discrimination—in a court of law. Nevertheless, there is mounting empirical evidence that people-of-color and low-income communities suffer disproportionately from facility siting decisions involving municipal landfills, incinerators, and hazardous-waste disposal facilities. Since risks generally increase with proximity to the noxious facilities, it is the poor and minority communities who are paying a high price in terms of their health.

Environmental justice issues are now being raised in this country and around the world. In keeping the narrowly defined concept of environmentalism, the larger movement is doomed to the charge of being an elitist movement that cares more about "protecting the environment from humans" than about "protecting humans from the environment."

NOTES

◆

Chapter One

1. See Frederick R. Buttel and William L. Flinn, "Social Class and Mass Environmental Beliefs: A Reconsideration," *Environment and Behavior* 10 (September 1978): 433–450; Kenneth M. Bachrach and Alex J. Zautra, "Coping with Community Stress: The Threat of a Hazardous Waste Landfill," *Journal of Health and Social Behavior* 26 (June 1985): 127–141; Paul Mohai, "Public Concern and Elite Involvement in Environmental-Conservation Issues," *Social Science Quarterly* 66 (December 1985): 820–838.

2. Denton E. Morrison, "The Soft Cutting Edge of Environmentalism: Why and How the Appropriate Technology Notion Is Changing the Movement," *Natural Resources Journal* 20 (April 1980): 275–298.

3. Allan Schnaiberg, *The Environment: From Surplus to Scarcity* (New York: Oxford University Press, 1980), pp. 366–377.

4. See Morris E. Davis, "The Impact of Workplace Health and Safety on Black Workers: Assessment and Prognosis," *Labor Studies Journal* 4 (Spring 1981): 29–40; Richard Kazis and Richard Grossman, *Fear at Work: Job Blackmail, Labor, and the Environment* (New York: Pilgrim Press, 1983), Chapter 1; W. J. Kruvant, "People, Energy, and Pollution," in Dorothy K. Newman and Dawn Day, eds., *The American Energy Consumer* (Cambridge, Mass.: Ballinger, 1975), pp. 125–167; Robert D. Bullard, "Solid Waste Sites and the Black Houston Community," *Sociological Inquiry* 53 (Spring 1983): 273–288; Robert D. Bullard, "Endangered Environs: The Price of Unplanned Growth in Boomtown Houston," *California Sociologist* 7 (Summer 1984): 85–101; Robert D. Bullard and Beverly H. Wright, "Dumping Grounds in a Sunbelt City," *Urban Resources* 2 (Winter 1985): 37–39.

5. James E. Blackwell, *The Black Community: Diversity and Unity* (New York: Harper and Row, 1985), p. xiii.

6. Richard E. Lazarus and Raymond Launier, "Stress-Related Transactions Between Persons and Environment," in Lawrence A. Pervin and Michael Lewis, eds., *Perspectives in International Psychology* (New York: Plenum, 1978), pp. 297–327; Bachrach and Zautra, "Coping with Community Stress," pp. 127–129.

7. See Anthony M. Orum, "On Participation in Political Movements," *Journal of Applied Behavioral Science* 10 (April/June 1974): 181–207; Daniel L. Collins, Andrew Baum, and Jerome E. Singer, "Coping with Chronic Stress at Three Mile Island: Psychological and Biological Evidence," *Health Psychology* 2 (1983): 149–166; Mohai, "Public Concern and Elite Involvement," p. 832.

8. Robert D. Bullard and Beverly H. Wright, "Environmentalism and the Politics of Equity: Emergent Trends in the Black Community," *Mid-American Review of Sociology* 12 (Winter 1987): 21–37.

9. Aldon D. Morris, *The Origins of the Civil Rights Movement: Black Communities Organizing for Change* (New York: Free Press, 1984), p. x.

10. See Robert D. Bullard and Beverly H. Wright, "Blacks and the Environment," *Humboldt Journal of Social Relations* 14 (Summer 1987): 165–184; Bullard, "Solid Waste Sites and the Black Houston Community," pp. 273–288; Bullard, "Endangered Environs," pp. 84–102.

11. Riley E. Dunlap, "Public Opinion on the Environment in the Reagan Era: Polls, Pollution, and Politics Revisited," *Environment* 29 (July/August 1987): 6–11, 32–37.

12. Brian J. L. Berry, ed., *The Social Burden of Environmental Pollution: A Comparative Metropolitan Data Source* (Cambridge, Mass.: Ballinger, 1977); Sam Love, "Ecology and Social Justice: Is There a Conflict," *Environmental Action* 4 (1972): 3–6; Julian McCaull, "Discriminatory Air Pollution: If the Poor Don't Breathe," *Environment* 19 (March 1976): 26–32; Vernon Jordan, "Sins of Omission," *Environmental Action* 11 (April 1980): 26–30.

13. Denton E. Morrison, "How and Why Environmental Consciousness Has Trickled Down," in Allan Schnaiberg, Nicholas Watts, and Klaus Zimmermann, eds., *Distributional Conflict in Environmental-Resource Policy* (New York: St. Martin's Press, 1986), pp. 187–220.

14. Robert D. Bullard and Beverly H. Wright, "The Politics of Pollution: Implications for the Black Community," *Phylon* 47 (March 1986): 71–78.

15. Bullard and Wright, "Environmentalism and the Politics of Equity," p. 28.

16. Richard P. Gale, "The Environmental Movement and the Left: Antagonists or Allies?" *Sociological Inquiry* 53 (Spring 1983): 179–199.

17. Craig R. Humphrey and Frederick R. Buttel, *Environment, Energy, and Society* (Belmont, Calif.: Wadsworth Publishing Co., 1982), p. 253.

18. Ibid.

19. Arthur P. Jacoby and Nicholas Babchuk, "Instrumental Versus Expressive Voluntary Associations," *Sociology and Social Research* 47 (1973): 461–471.

20. Gale, "The Environmental Movement and the Left," p. 191.

21. Morris, *The Origins of the Civil Rights Movement*, p. xii.

22. Charles V. Willie, *The Caste and Class Controversy* (Bayside, N.Y.: General Hall, Inc., 1979), pp. 43–44; also Robert D. Bullard, ed., *In Search of the New South: The Black Urban Experience in the 1970s and 1980s* (Tuscaloosa: University of Alabama Press, 1989).

23. See Robert D. Bullard, *Invisible Houston: The Black Experience in Boom and Bust* (College Station: Texas A & M University Press, 1987), pp. 14–31.

24. Robert D. Bullard, "Blacks and the American Dream of Housing," in Jamshid A. Momeni, ed., *Race, Ethnicity, and Minority Housing in the United States* (Westport, Conn.: Greenwood Press, 1986), pp. 53–63; Bullard and Wright, "Environmentalism and the Politics of Equity," pp. 21–37.

25. Robert L. Lineberry, *Equity and Urban Policy: The Distribution of Municipal Public Services* (Beverly Hills: Sage, 1977), pp. 174–175.

26. Karl Taeuber and Alma K. Taeuber, *Negroes in Cities: Residential Segregation and Neighborhood Change* (Chicago: Aldine Publishing Co., 1965); Karl Taeuber, "Racial Segregation: The Persisting Dilemma," *Annals of the American Academy of Political and Social Sciences* 442 (November 1978): 87–96; Karl Taeuber, "Racial Residential Segregation, 28 Cities, 1970–1980," CDE Working Paper, University of Wisconsin, Madison (March 1983), p. 3; Robert D. Bullard, "The Black Family: Housing Alternatives in the 80s," *Journal of Black Studies* 14 (Spring 1984): 341–351.

27. Larry Ford and Ernst Griffin, "The Ghettoization of Paradise," *Geographical Review* 69 (April 1979): 140–158; J. A. Kushner, *Apartheid in America: An Historical and Legal Analysis of Contemporary Racial Segregation in the United States* (Arlington, Va.: Carrolton Press, Inc., 1980), p. 130.

28. Robert P. Burden, "The Forgotten Environment," in Lawrence E. Hinkle and William C. Loring, eds., *The Effects of the Man-Made Environment on Health and Behavior* (Washington, D.C.: U.S. Government Printing Office, 1977), p. 249.

29. Daniel Zwerdling, "Poverty and Pollution," *Progressive* 37 (January 1973): 25–29.

30. Kruvant, "People, Energy, and Pollution," p. 125–167.

31. Douglas Lee and H. K. Lee, "Conclusions and Reservations," in Douglas Lee, ed., *Environmental Factors in Respiratory Disease* (New York: Academic Press, 1972), pp. 250–251; Ronald Brownstein, "The Toxic Tragedy," in Ralph Nader, Ronald Brownstein, and John Richard, eds., *Who's Poisoning America: Corporate Polluters and Their Victims in the Chemical Age* (San Francisco: Sierra Club Books, 1982), pp. 1–52.

32. Kruvant, "People, Energy, and Pollution," p. 166.

33. Kazis and Grossman, *Fear at Work*, p. 48.

34. Barbara Blum, *Cities: An Environmental Wilderness* (Washington, D.C.: Environmental Protection Agency, 1978), p. 3.

35. Bullard and Wright, "Blacks and the Environment," pp. 170–171.

36. Zwerdling, "Poverty and Pollution," p. 27; Bullard and Wright, "The Politics of Pollution," pp. 71–78.

37. Bullard and Wright, "Blacks and the Environment," pp. 168–171; Bullard, "Endangered Environs," pp. 85–86.

38. See Constance Perrin, *Everything in Its Place: Social Order and Land Use in America* (Princeton, N.J.: Princeton University Press, 1977).

39. John R. Logan and Harvey L. Molotch, *Urban Fortunes: The Political Economy of Place* (Berkeley: University of California Press, 1987), p. 158.

40. See Harvey L. Molotch, "The City as a Growth Machine: Toward a Political Economy of Place," *American Journal of Sociology* 82 (1976): 309–330; John R. Logan, "Growth, Politics and Stratification of Places," *American Journal of Sociology* 84 (1978): 404–416; Ann B. Shlay and Peter Rossi, "Keeping up the Neighborhood: Estimating the Effect of Zoning," *American Sociology Review* 46 (December 1981): 703–719; Bullard and Wright, "Blacks and the Environment," pp. 168–171.

41. Humphrey and Buttel, *Environment, Energy, and Society*, pp. 11–136; Gale, "The Environmental Movement and the Left," pp. 179–199.

42. Samuel P. Hays, *Beauty, Health, and Permanence: Environmental Politics in the United States, 1955–1985* (Cambridge, Mass.: Cambridge University Press, 1987), p. 269.

43. David L. Sills, "The Environmental Movement and Its Critics," *Human Ecology* 13 (1975): 1–41; Morrison, "The Soft Cutting Edge of Environmentalism," pp. 275–298; Allan Schnaiberg, "Redistributive Goals Versus Distributive Politics: Social Equity Limits in Environmentalism and Appropriate Technology Movements," *Sociological Inquiry* 53 (Spring 1983): 200–219.

44. Denton E. Morrison and Riley E. Dunlap, "Environmentalism and Elitism: A Conceptual and Empirical Analysis," *Environmental Management* 10 (1986): 581–589.

45. Logan and Molotch, *Urban Fortunes,* pp. 50–98.

46. Kazis and Grossman, *Fear at Work,* p. 37.

47. Alan S. Miller, "Toward an Environment/Labor Coalition," *Environment* 22 (June 1980): 32–39.

48. See Barry Bluestone and Bennett Harrison, *The Deindustrialization of America* (New York: Basic Books, 1982). p. 90.

49. Buttel and Flinn, "Social Class and Mass Environmental Beliefs," pp. 433–450; Robert Cameron Mitchell, "Silent Spring/Solid Majorities," *Public Opinion* 2 (August/September 1979): 16–20; Robert Cameron Mitchell, "Public Opinion and Environmental Politics," in N. J. Vig and M. E. Kraft, eds., *Environmental Policy in the 1980's: Reagan's New Agenda* (Washington, D.C.: Congressional Quarterly Press, 1984), pp. 51–73; Mohai, "Public Concern and Elite Involvement," p. 821; Dorceta E. Taylor, "Blacks and the Environment: Toward an Explanation of the Concern and Action Gap Between Blacks and Whites," *Environment and Behavior* 21 (March 1989): 175–205.

50. See Ron E. Roberts and Robert Marsh Kloss, *Social Movements: Between the Balcony and the Barricade,* 2nd ed. (St. Louis: C. V. Mosby, 1979); James L. Wood and Maurice Jackson, eds., *Social Movements: Development, Participation and Dynamics* (Belmont, Calif.: Wadsworth, 1982).

51. For a detailed discussion of the resource mobilization model, see Anthony Oberschall, *Social Conflict and Social Movement* (Englewood, Cliffs, N.J.: Prentice-Hall, 1973); John D. McCarthy and Mayer Zald, *The Trend of Social Movements in America: Professionalism and Resource Mobilization* (Morristown, N.J.: General Learning Press, 1979); William Gamson, *The Study of Social Protest* (Homewood, Ill.: Dorsey Press, 1975); Charles Tilly, *From Mobilization to Revolution* (Reading, Mass.: Addison-Wesley, 1978); Craig J. Jenkins, "Resource Mobilization Theory and the Study of Social Movements," *Annual Review of Sociology* 9 (1983): 27–53.

52. Edward J. Walsh and Rex Warland, "Social Movement Involvement in the Wake of a Nuclear Accident: Activists and Free-Riders in the TMI Area," *American Sociological Review* 48 (December 1983): 764–780; Mohai, "Public Concern and Elite Involvement," pp. 822–823.

53. The discussion of issues that are likely to attract blacks to the environmental movement was adapted from Gale, "The Environmental Movement and the Left," pp. 182–186.

54. Ibid., p. 184.

55. See Ronald A. Taylor, "Do Environmentalists Care About Poor People?" *U.S. News and World Report* 96 (April 2, 1982): 51–55; Bullard, "Endangered Environs," p. 98; Bullard and Wright, "The Politics of Pollution," pp. 71–78.

56. Morris, *The Origins of the Civil Rights Movement,* p. 282.

57. Miller, "Toward an Environment/Labor Coalition," pp. 32–39; Sue Pollack and JoAnn Grozuczak, *Reagan, Toxics and Minorities* (Washington, D.C.: Urban Environmental Conference, Inc., 1984), Chapter 1; Kazis and Grossman, *Fear at Work,* pp. 3–35.

58. Andrew Porterfield and David Weir, "The Export of Hazardous Waste," *Nation* 245 (October 3, 1987): 340–344; Jim Vallette, *The International Trade in Wastes: A Greenpeace Inventory* (Washington, D.C.: Greenpeace, 1989), pp. 7–16.

59. Jack Bloom, *Class, Race and the Civil Rights Movement* (Bloomington: Indiana University Press, 1987), p. 18.

60. Bullard and Wright, "Environmentalism and the Politics of Equity," p. 32.

61. Urban Environment Conference, Inc., *Taking Back Our Health: An Institute on Surviving the Toxic Threat to Minority Communities* (Washington, D.C.: Urban Environment Conference, Inc., 1985), p. 29.

62. Bullard and Wright, "Environmentalism and the Politics of Equity," pp. 32–33.

63. Commission for Racial Justice, *Toxic Wastes and Race: A National Report on the Racial and Socioeconomic Characteristics of Communities with Hazardous Waste Sites* (New York: United Church of Christ, 1987), p. x.

64. Taylor, "Do Environmentalists Care About Poor People?" pp. 51–52.

65. Barbara Reynolds, "Triana, Alabama: The Unhealthiest Town in America," *National Wildlife* 18 (August 1980): 33; Bullard and Wright, "The Politics of Pollution," p. 75.

66. Michael Haggerty, "Crisis at Indian Creek," *Atlanta Journal and Constitution Magazine* (January 20, 1980): 14–25.

67. Ibid.

Chapter Two

1. U.S. Department of Housing and Urban Development, *Report of the President's Commission for a National Agenda for the Eighties* (Washington, D.C.: U.S. Government Printing Office, 1980), pp. 165–169; John D. Kasarda, "Implications of Contemporary Distribution Trends for National Urban Policy," *Social Science Quarterly* 61 (December 1980): 373–400.

2. John D. Kasarda, Michael D. Irwin, and Holly L. Hughes, "The South Is Still Rising," *American Demographics* 8 (June 1986): 34.

3. G. William Domhoff, "The Growth Machine and the Power Elite: A Challenge to Pluralists and Marxists Alike," in Robert J. Waste, ed., *Community Power: Directions for Future Research* (Newbury Park, Calif.: Sage, 1986), p. 58.

4. Harvey L. Molotch, "The City as a Growth Machine: Toward a Political Economy of Place," *American Journal of Sociology* 82 (September 1976): 320.

5. Domhoff, "The Growth Machine and the Power Elite," p. 61.

6. U.S. Bureau of the Census, *State and Metropolitan Area Data Book 1982* (Washington, D.C.: U.S. Government Printing Office, 1982), p. 2.

7. Robert D. Bullard, "Blacks and the New South: Challenges of the Eighties," *Journal of Intergroup Relations* 15 (Summer 1987): 25.

8. David C. Perry and Alfred J. Watkins, eds., *The Rise of the Sunbelt Cities* (Beverly Hills: Sage, 1977), p. 77; Robert D. Bullard, ed., *In Search of the New South: The Black Urban Experience in the 1970s and 1980s* (Tuscaloosa: University of Alabama Press, 1989), Chapter 1.

9. William W. Falk and Thomas A. Lyson, *High Tech, Low Tech, No Tech: Recent Industrial and Occupational Change in the South* (Albany: State University of New York Press, 1988), pp. 2–3.

10. Ibid., p. 55.

11. Chet Fuller, "I Hear Them Call It the New South," *Black Enterprise* 12 (November 1981): 41.

12. Ibid., pp. 41–44.

13. Joe R. Feagin and Clairece Booher Feagin, *Discrimination American Style: Institutional Racism and Sexism* (Malabar, Fla.: Robert E. Krueger Publishing, 1986), p. 9.

14. William C. Matney and Dwight L. Johnson, *America's Black Population: A Statistical View 1970–1982* (Washington, D.C.: U.S. Government Printing Office, 1983), p. 1.

15. Ibid., p. 2; Isaac Robinson, "Blacks Move Back to the South," *American Demographics* 9 (June 1986): 40–43.

16. Kasarda et al., "The South Is Still Rising," p. 32.

17. Gurney Breckenfeld, "Refilling the Metropolitan Doughnut," in David C. Perry and Alfred J. Watkins, eds., *The Rise of the Sunbelt Cities* (Beverly Hills: Sage, 1977), p. 238.

18. See Robert D. Bullard, *Invisible Houston: The Black Experience in Boom and Bust* (College Station: Texas A & M University Press, 1987), pp. 2–13; William J. Wilson, *The Truly Disadvantaged: The Inner City, the Underclass, and Public Policy* (Chicago: University of Chicago Press, 1987), pp. 180–181; John D. Kasarda, "Caught in the Web of Change," *Society* 21 (1983): 41–47; William J. Wilson, "The Black Underclass," *Wilson Quarterly* (Spring 1984): 88–99; David Beers and Diana Hembree, "The New Atlanta: A Tale of Two Cities," *Nation* 244 (March 1987): 347, 357–360; Margaret Edds, *Free at Last: What Really Happened When Civil Rights Came to Southern Politics* (Bethesda: Adler and Adler, 1987), pp. 51–76; Bradley R. Rice, "Atlanta: If Dixie Were Atlanta," in Richard M. Bernard and Bradley R. Rice, eds., *Sunbelt Cities: Politics and Growth Since World War II* (Austin: University of Texas Press, 1984), pp. 31–57; Art Harris, "Too Busy to Hate," *Esquire* 103 (June 1985): 129–133; Charles Jaret, "Black Migration and Socioeconomic Inequality in Atlanta and the Urban South," *Humboldt Journal of Social Relations* 14 (Summer 1987): 62–105; Nathan McCall, "Atlanta: City of the Next Generation," *Black Enterprise* 17 (May 1987): 56–58.

19. Joint Center for Political Studies, *Black Elected Officials: A National Roster* (New York: UNIPUB, 1984), p. 61.

20. Michael Preston, Lenneal J. Henderson, Jr., and Paul Puryear, eds., *The New Black Politics: The Search for Political Power* (New York: Longman, 1987), p. vii.

21. Chandler Davidson, ed., *Minority Vote Dilution* (Washington, D.C.: Howard University Press, 1984), pp. 1–26.

22. Bullard, *Invisible Houston*, pp. 2–13.

23. Robert D. Bullard and Beverly H. Wright, "Environmentalism and the Politics of Equity: Emergent Trends in the Black Community," *Mid-American Review of Sociology* 12 (Winter 1987): 32–33.

24. Kasarda, "The Implications of Contemporary Trends for National Urban Policy," pp. 373–400; Bullard, *Invisible Houston*, p. 2.

25. David R. Goldfield, *Promised Land: The South Since 1945* (Arlington Heights, Ill.: Harlan Davidson, 1987), p. 197.

26. Will Collette, "Somewhere Else USA: Fighting Back Against Chemical Dumpers," *Southern Neighborhoods* 9 (September 1985): 1–3.

27. Bullard and Wright, "Environmentalism and the Politics of Equity," pp. 22–24.

28. John R. Logan and Harvey L. Molotch, *Urban Fortunes: The Political Economy of Place* (Berkeley: University of California Press, 1988), p. 138.

29. Goldfield, *Promised Land*, pp. 211–212.

30. Ibid.

31. Michael H. Brown, *The Toxic Cloud: The Poisoning of America's Air* (New York: Harper and Row, 1987), p. 161.

32. Public Data Access, Inc., *Mortality and Toxics Along the Mississippi River* (New York: Greenpeace, 1988), p. 7.

33. Goldfield, *Promised Land*, p. 197.

34. Max Neiman and Ronald O. Loveridge, "Environmentalism and Local Growth Control: A Probe into the Class Bias Thesis," *Environment and Behavior* 13 (1981): 759–772.

35. Quoted in Goldfield, *Promised Land*, p. 197.

36. Ben A. Franklin, "In the Shadow of the Valley," *Sierra* 71 (May/June 1986): 40–41; Jane Slaughter, "Valley of the Shadow of Death," *Progressive* 49 (March 1985): 50; David Maraniss and Michael Weisskopf, "Jobs and Illness in Petrochemical Corridor," *Washington Post*, December 22, 1987, p. 1; Brown, *The Toxic Cloud*, pp. 152–161.

37. Bullard and Wright, "Environmentalism and the Politics of Equity," pp. 32–33.

38. Susan Pollack and JoAnn Grozuczak, *Reagan, Toxics and Minorities* (Washington, D.C.: Urban Environment Conference, Inc., 1984), p. 20.

39. Ken Geiser and Gerry Waneck, "PCBs and Warren County," *Science for the People* 15 (July/August 1983): 17; Kimberly French, "A Community Unites Against Toxic Waste," *Whole Life Times* (January/February 1983), p. 25.

40. Warren County Economic Development Commission, "Warren County Demographic Profile," (March 1984), pp. 1–14.

41. Geiser and Waneck, "PCBs and Warren County," p. 17.

42. Quoted in Urban Environment Conference, Inc., *Taking Back Our Health: An Institute on Surviving the Toxic Threat to Minority Communities* (Washington, D.C.: Urban Environment Conference, Inc., 1985), p. 38.

43. See *Winston-Salem Sentinel*, September 15, 1982, p. 13; *Durham Morning Herald*, September 30, 1982, p. 1B; *Winston-Salem Journal*, September 27, 1982, p. 7.

44. Quoted in *Winston-Salem Sentinel*, September 27, 1982, p. 7.

45. Ibid.

46. U.S. General Accounting Office, *Siting of Hazardous Waste Landfills and Their Correlation with Racial and Economic Status of Surrounding Communities* (Washington, D.C.: General Accounting Office, 1983), p. 1.

47. Ibid., p. 3.

48. Commission for Racial Justice, *Toxic Wastes and Race in the United States: A National Report on the Racial and Socioeconomic Characteristics of Communities with Hazardous Wastes Sites* (New York: United Church of Christ, 1987), p. xi.

49. Ibid., p. 16.

50. Ibid., p. 66.

51. Ibid., pp. 15–16.

52. Michael R. Greenberg and Richard F. Anderson, *Hazardous Waste Sites: The Credibility Gap* (New Brunswick, N.J.: Rutgers University Center for Urban Policy Research, 1984), p. 158.

53. Commission for Racial Justice, *Toxic Wastes and Race*, p. 3.

54. U.S. General Accounting Office, *Siting of Hazardous Waste Landfills*, p. 2; Samuel S. Epstein, Lester O. Brown, and Carl Pope, *Hazardous Waste in America* (San Francisco: Sierra Club Books, 1983), pp. 33–39; See Adeline Levine, *Love Canal: Science, Politics, and People* (Lexington, Mass.: Lexington Books, 1982), Chapter 1; Office of Technology Assessment, *Technologies and Management Strategies for Hazardous Waste Control* (Washington, D.C.: U.S. Government Printing Office, 1983), p. 3. Epstein et al., *Hazardous Waste in America*, pp. 6–11. Michael H. Brown, *Laying Waste: The Poisoning of America by Toxic Chemicals* (New York: Pantheon Books, 1980), p. 267.

55. Quoted in *New York Times*, November 19, 1983.

Chapter Three

1. Frank J. Popper, "The Environmentalist and the LULU," *Environment* 27 (March 1985): 7.

2. For a detailed discussion of national trends on locational conflict, see Thomas N. Gladwin, "Patterns of Environmental Conflict over Industrial Facilities in the United States, 1970–78," *Natural Resources Journal* 20 (April 1980): 243–274.

3. Robert D. Bullard, *Invisible Houston: The Black Experience in Boom and Bust* (College Station: Texas A & M University Press, 1987), Chapter 2.

4. See Robert D. Bullard, "Endangered Environs: The Price of Unplanned Growth in Boomtown Houston," *California Sociologist* 7 (Summer 1984): 84–102; Richard Babcock, "Houston: Unzoned, Unfettered, and Mostly Unrepentent," *Planning* 48 (1982): 21–23; Joe R. Feagin, "The Global Context of Metropolitan Growth: Houston and the Oil Industry," *American Journal of Sociology* 90 (May 1985): 1204–1230.

5. Robert D. Bullard, "Solid Waste Sites and the Black Houston Community," *Sociological Inquiry* 53 (Spring 1983): 273–288.

6. For a detailed account of this dispute, see Bullard, *Invisible Houston*, Chapter 6; *Houston Chronicle*, November 8, 11, 15, 22, 1979, December 15, 22, 1979, June 19, 1980; *Houston Post*, December 15, 1981.

7. City of Dallas, *1987 Census Tract Book* (Dallas: Dallas Department of Housing and Neighborhood Services, 1987), pp. 4–10.

8. The Enterprise Foundation, *Dallas: A Survey of Poverty and Housing* (Dallas: Meadows Foundation, 1983), pp. 43–45.

9. *Dallas Morning News*, December 7, 1986, p. 1A.

10. Ibid.; Dallas Alliance Environmental Task Force, *Final Report* (Dallas, Tex.: Dallas Alliance, June 29, 1983), p. 6; *Dallas Morning News*, June 1, 1981; K. W. Brown, J. W. Mullins, E. P. Richitt, G. T. Flatman, and S. C. Black, "Assessing Soil Lead Contamination in Dallas, Texas," *Environmental Monitoring and Assessment* 5 (1985): 137–154.

11. Dallas Alliance Environmental Task Force, *Final Report*, p. 3.

12. *Dallas Morning News*, October 2, 1981, p. 1A.

13. Quoted in *Dallas Morning News*, April 27, 1983, p. 1A. Interviews conducted on May 27, 1988, with Mattie Nash, a West Dallas neighborhood representative to the Dallas Alliance Environmental Task Force, and Reverend R. T. Conley, a West Dallas minister, yielded views similar to those of Patricia Spears. Local community leaders expressed the opinion that the government was dragging its feet because West Dallas was a poor black neighborhood.

14. U.S. Environmental Protection Agency, "Report of the Dallas Area Lead Assessment Study" (Dallas, Tex.: U.S. Environmental Protection Agency Region VI, 1983), p. 8.

15. See Jonathan Lash, Katherine Gillman, and David Sheridan, *A Season of Spoils: The Reagan Administration's Attack on the Environment* (New York: Pantheon Books, 1984), pp. 135–136.

16. Ibid., p. 131.

17. See *Dallas Morning News*, October 18, 1983, p. 1A; December 7, 1986, p. 31A.

18. Dallas Alliance Environmental Task Force, *Final Report*, p. i.

19. *Dallas Times-Herald*, July 17, 1983.

20. U.S. Bureau of the Census, *Number of Inhabitants: West Virginia* (Washington, D.C.: U.S. Government Printing Office, 1982), p. 8.

21. Arlene R. Thorn, "West Virginia State College: A Brief History"(March 30, 1977), p. 1.

22. Ben A. Franklin, "In the Shadow of the Valley," *Sierra* 71 (May/June 1986): p. 39.

23. Ibid., p. 41.

24. Jane Slaughter, "Valley of the Shadow of Death," *Progressive* 49 (March 1985): 50.

25. Franklin, "In the Shadow of the Valley," p. 40.

26. Mark Starr, Mary Hager, William J. Cook, and Carolyn Friday, "America's Toxic Tremors," *Newsweek* August 26, 1985, pp. 18–19.

27. See *Charleston Daily Mail*, August 23, 1985, pp. 1A, 6A; *Charleston Gazette*, August 24, 1985, pp. 1A, 16A; Sharon Beegley, Mary Hager, and Susan Agrest, "Maybe It Could Happen Here," *Newsweek* 105 (February 4, 1985), p. 24; *Houston Chronicle*, February 17, 1986, pp. 1A, 13A; Ann Page, "The Union Carbide Institute Plant: The Perception of Risk," paper presented at the Annual Meeting of the Society for the Study of Social Problems, New York (August 27–30, 1986), p. 10.

28. Beegley et al., "Maybe It Could Happen Here," p. 24; Franklin, "In the Shadow of Death," p. 42; Michael Brown, *The Toxic Cloud: The Poisoning of America's Air* (New York: Harper and Row, 1987), p. 225.

29. Franklin, "In the Shadow of the Valley," pp. 40–41.

30. Mark Starr, Mary Hager, William J. Cook, and Carolyn Friday, "America's Toxic Tremors," *Newsweek*, August 26, 1985, p. 18.

31. See Bill Dawson, "W. Va. Valley under Cloud of Distrust," *Houston Chronicle*, February 17, 1986, p. 13.

32. U.S. Bureau of the Census, *Neighborhood Statistics Program: Narrative Profile of Neighborhoods in Baton Rouge and East Baton Rouge, LA* (Washington, D.C.: U.S. Government Printing Office, 1982), pp. 2–4.

33. David Maraniss and Michael Weisskopf, "Jobs and Illness in Petrochemical Corridor," *Washington Post*, December 22, 1987, p. 1; Brown, *The Toxic Cloud*, pp. 152–161.

34. Bob Anderson, Mike Dunn, and Sonny Alabarado, "Prosperity in Paradise: Louisiana's Chemical Legacy," *Morning Advocate*, April 25, 1985, p. 3.

35. Brown, *The Toxic Cloud*, p. 157.

36. Commission for Racial Justice, *Toxic Wastes and Race in the United States*, p. 66.

37. Interview with Mary McCastle, June 23, 1988, Alsen, Louisiana.

38. Interview with Annie Bowdry, June 23, 1988, Alsen, Louisiana.

39. Interview with Admon McCastle, June 23, 1988, Alsen Louisiana.

40. Ibid.

41. Interview with Annie Bowdry.

42. U.S. General Accounting Office, *Siting of Hazardous Waste Landfills*, p. 1.

43. Andre Carothers, "The Coming of Age of Sumter County," *Greenpeace* 12 (1987): 13.

44. Booth Gunter and Mike Williams, "The Cadillac of Dumps," *Sierra* 71 (January/February 1986): 19.

45. Ibid.

46. Interview with Wendell Paris, April 18, 1988, Livingston, Alabama.

47. Interview with Sumter County Commissioner Obadiah Threadgill, May 21, 1988, Livingston, Alabama.

48. See *Sumter County Record*, May 29, 1977.

49. Carothers, "The Coming of Age of Sumter County," p. 12.

50. Gunter and Williams, "The Cadillac of Dumps," p. 20.

51. Interview with Wendell Paris.

52. Ibid.

53. Gunter and Williams, "The Cadillac of Dumps," pp. 19–20.

54. Carothers, "The Coming of Age of Sumter County," p. 12.

55. Ibid.

56. Aldon D. Morris, *The Origins of the Civil Rights Movement: Black Communities Organizing for Change* (New York: Free Press, 1984), p. 278.

57. Bullard, *Invisible Houston*, pp. 60–75.

Chapter Four

1. See Robert Cameron Mitchell, ed., "Public Opinion on Environmental Issues," in *Council on Environmental Quality: The Eleventh Annual Report of the Council on Environmental Quality* (Washington, D.C.: U.S. Government Printing Office,

1980), pp. 401–425; E. C. Ladd, "Clearing the Air: Public Opinion and Public Policy on the Environment," *Public Opinion* (February/March 1982): 16–20; Riley E. Dunlap, "Public Opinion on the Environment in the Reagan Era: Polls, Pollution, and Politics Revisited," *Environment* 29 (July/August 1987): 1.

2. Richard P. Anthony, "Polls, Pollution and Politics: Trends in Public Opinion on the Environment," *Environment* 24 (May 1982): 19.

3. Robert D. Bullard, "Endangered Environs: The Price of Unplanned Growth in Boomtown Houston," *California Sociologist* 7 (Summer 1984): 84; Richard Babcock, "Houston: Unzoned, Unfettered, and Mostly Unrepentent," *Planning* 48 (1982): 21–23; Joe R. Feagin, "The Global Context of Metropolitan Growth: Houston and the Oil Industry," *American Journal of Sociology* 90 (May 1985): 1204–1230; Robert L. Lineberry, *Equity and Urban Policy: The Distribution of Municipal Services* (Beverly Hills: Sage, 1977), p. 11.

4. David M. Smith, "Who Gets What Where and How: A Welfare Focus for Human Geography," *Geography* 59 (November 1974): 294.

5. John R. Logan and Harvey L. Molotch, *Urban Fortunes: The Political Economy of Place* (Berkeley: University of California Press, 1987), p. 158.

6. J. N. Smith, *Environmental Quality and Social Justice in Urban America* (Washington, D.C.: The Conservation Foundation, 1974), pp. 521–522.

7. Robert D. Bullard, "Solid Waste Sites and the Black Houston Community," *Sociological Inquiry* 53 (Spring 1983): 274–275.

8. Michael Edelstein, *Contaminated Communities: The Social and Psychological Impacts of Residential Toxic Exposure* (Boulder, Colo.: Westview Press, 1987), p. 185.

9. David Morell, "Siting and the Politics of Equity," in Robert W. Lake, ed., *Resolving Locational Conflict* (New Brunswick, N.J.: Rutgers University for Urban Policy Research, 1987), pp. 120–121.

10. Joe R. Feagin and Clairece Booher Feagin, *Discrimination American Style: Institutional Racism and Sexism* (Malabar, Fla.: Robert E. Krueger Publishing, 1986), p. 9.

11. See David Morell, "Siting and the Politics of Equity," pp. 117–136; Michael O'Hare, Lawrence Bacow, and Debra Sanderson, *Facility Siting and Public Opposition* (New York: Van Nostrand Reinhold, 1983); Howard Kunreuther, "A New Way to Site Hazardous Facilities," *Wall Street Journal,* December 27, 1985, p. 8; Kent E. Portney, "The Potential of the Theory of Compensation for Mitigating Public Opposition to Hazardous Waste Siting: Some Evidence from Five Massachusetts Communities," *Policy Studies Journal* 14 (1985): 81–89.

12. Commission for Racial Justice, *Toxic Wastes and Race in the United States: A National Report on the Racial and Socioeconomic Characteristics of Communities with Hazardous Waste Sites* (New York: United Church of Christ, 1987), p. 7.

13. David Morell and Christopher Magorian, "Risk, Fear, and Local Opposition: 'Not in My Back Yard,'" in David Morell and Christopher Magorian, eds., *Siting Hazardous Waste Facilities: Local Opposition and the Myth of Preemption* (Cambridge, Mass.: Ballinger Publishing Co., 1982), pp. 21–46; David Morell, "Siting and the Politics of Equity," pp. 117–136; Robert Cameron Mitchell and Richard T. Carson, "Protest, Property Rights, and Hazardous Waste," *Resources* 85 (Fall 1986): 6–9; Owen J. Furuseth and Mark S. Johnson, "Neighborhood Attitudes Toward a Sanitary Landfill: A North Carolina Study," *Applied Geography* 8 (1988): 135–145.

14. Richard Kazis and Richard Grossman, *Fear at Work: Job Blackmail, Labor, and the Environment* (New York: Pilgrim Press, 1983), pp. 15–16; Robert D. Bullard and Beverly H. Wright, "Environmentalism and the Politics of Equity: Emergent Trends in the Black Community," *Mid-American Review of Sociology* 12 (Winter 1987), p. 23.

15. Interview with Charles Streadit, president of Houston's Northeast Community Action Group, May 30, 1988.

16. W. J. Kruvant, "People, Energy, and Politics," in Dorothy K. Newman and Dawn Day, eds., *The American Energy Consumer*, p. 166; Julian McCaull, "Discriminatory Air Pollution: If the Poor Don't Breathe," *Environment* 19 (March 1976): 26–31; Peter Asch and Joseph J. Seneca, "Some Evidence on the Distribution of Air Quality," *Land Economics* 54 (August 1978): 278–297; Peter Dorman, "The Distributional Effect of the Uniform Air Pollution Policy in the United States," *Review of Radical Political Economy* 16 (Winter 1984): 151–164.

17. Kent Van Liere and Riley E. Dunlap, "The Social Bases of Environmental Concern: A Review of Hypotheses, Explanations, and Empirical Evidence," *Public Opinion Quarterly* 44 (Summer 1980): 181–197; Robert Cameron Mitchell, "Public Opinion and Environmental Politics in the 1970s and 1980s," in N. J. Vig and M. E. Kraft, eds., *Environmental Policy in the 1980s: Reagan's New Agenda* (Washington, D.C.: Congressional Quarterly Press, 1984), pp. 51–73.

18. Susan C. Cutter, "Community Concern for Pollution: Social and Environmental Influences," *Environment and Behavior* 13 (1981): 112.

19. Arthur P. Jacoby and Nicholas Babchuk, "Instrumental and Expressive Voluntary Associations," *Sociology and Social Research* 47 (1973): 461–471.

20. Craig R. Humphrey and Frederick R. Buttel, *Environment, Energy and Society* (Belmont, Calif.: Wadsworth, 1982), pp. 127–128.

21. Ronald L. Taylor, "Do Environmentalists Care About Poor People?" *U.S. News and World Report* 96 (April 2, 1982): 51.

22. Aldon D. Morris, *The Origins of the Civil Rights Movement: Black Communities Organizing for Change* (New York: Free Press, 1984), p. 278.

23. Ibid., p. 282.

24. Ibid., p. 280.

Chapter Five

1. Donald Schueler, "Southern Exposure," *Sierra* 77 (November/December 1992): 45.

2. Robert D. Bullard, "Ecological Inequities and the New South: Black Communities Under Siege," *Journal of Ethnic Studies* 17 (Winter 1990): 101–115.

3. Schueler, "Southern Exposure," p. 46.

4. Ibid., pp. 46–47.

5. See Joe R. Feagin and Clairece Booher Feagin, *Discrimination American Style: Institutional Racism and Sexism* (Malabar, Fla.: Krueger 1986); Robert D. Bullard and Joe R. Feagin, "Racism and the City," in M. Gottdiener and C. V. Pickvance, eds., *Urban Life in Transition* (Newbury Park, Calif.: Sage, 1991), pp. 55–76.

6. J. M. Jones, "The Concept of Racism and Its Changing Reality," in Benjamin P. Bowser and Raymond G. Hunt, eds., *Impact of Racism on White Americans* (Beverly Hills: Sage, 1981), p. 47.

7. See Robert D. Bullard, ed., *Confronting Environmental Racism: Voices from the Grassroots* (Boston: South End Press, 1993); Robert D. Bullard, "The Threat of Environmental Racism," *Natural Resources & Environment* 7 (Winter 1993): 23–26; Bunyan Bryant and Paul Mohai, eds., *Race and the Incidence of Environmental Hazards* (Boulder, Colo.: Westview Press, 1992); Regina Austin and Michael Schill, "Black, Brown, Poor, and Poisoned: Minority Grassroots Environmentalism and the Quest for Eco-Justice," *Kansas Journal of Law and Public Policy* 1, no. 1 (1991): 69–82; Kelly C. Colquette and Elizabeth A. Henry Robertson, "Environmental Racism: The Causes, Consequences, and Commendations," *Tulane Environmental Law Journal* 5, no. 1 (1991): 153–207; Rachel D. Godsil, "Remedying Environmental Racism," *Michigan Law Review* 90, no. 394 (1991): 394–427.

8. Michael Omi and Howard Winant, *Racial Formation in the United States: From the 1960's to the 1980's* (New York: Routledge and Kegan Paul, 1986), pp. 76–78.

9. See Bullard and Feagin, "Racism and the City," pp. 55–76; Robert D. Bullard, "Urban Infrastructure: Social, Environmental, and Health Risks to African Americans," in Billy J. Tidwell, ed., *The State of Black America 1992* (New York: National Urban League, 1992), pp. 183–196.

10. See R. B. Stewart, "Paradoxes of Liberty, Integrity, and Fraternity: The Collective Nature of Environmental Quality and Judicial Review of Administrative Action," *Environmental Law* 7, no. 3 (1977): 474–476; Leonard Gianessi, H. M. Peskin, and E. Wolff, "The Distributional Effects of Uniform Air Pollution Policy in the U.S.," *Quarterly Journal of Economics* 56, no. 1 (May 1979): 281–301.

11. See W. J. Kruvant, "People, Energy, and Pollution," in Dorothy K. Newman and Dawn Day, eds., *American Energy Consumer* (Cambridge, Mass.: Ballinger, 1975), pp. 125–167; Robert D. Bullard, "Solid Waste Sites and the Black Houston Community," *Sociological Inquiry* 53 (Spring 1983): 273–288; United Church of Christ Commission for Racial Justice, *Toxic Wastes and Race in the United States: A National Report on the Racial and Socioeconomic Characteristics of Communities with Hazardous Waste Sites* (New York: United Church of Christ, 1987); Dick Russell, "Environmental Racism," *Amicus Journal* 11 (Spring 1989): 22–32; Paul Ong and Evelyn Blumenberg, "Race and Environmentalism," Graduate School of Architecture and Urban Planning, UCLA (March 1990); Eric Mann, *L.A.'s Lethal Air: New Strategies for Policy, Organizing, and Action* (Los Angeles: Labor/Community Strategy Center, 1991); Leslie A. Nieves, "Not in Whose Backyard? Minority Population Concentrations and Noxious Facility Sites," paper presented at the Annual Meeting of the American Association for the Advancement of Science, Chicago (February 9, 1992); D. R. Wernette and L. A. Nieves, "Breathing Polluted Air: Minorities Are Disproportionately Exposed," *EPA Journal* 18 (March/April 1992): 16–17; Robert D. Bullard, "In Our Backyards: Minority Communities Get Most of the Dumps," *EPA Journal* 18 (March/April 1992): 11–12; Bryant and Mohai, *Race and the Incidence of Environmental Hazards*.

12. See Myrick A. Freeman, "The Distribution of Environmental Quality," in Allen V. Kneese and Blair T. Bower, eds., *Environmental Quality Analysis* (Baltimore: Johns Hopkins University Press for Resources for the Future, 1972); Michel

Gelobter, "The Distribution of Air Pollution by Income and Race," paper presented at the Second Symposium on Social Science in Resource Management, Urbana, Illinois (June 1988); Gianessi, Peskin, and Wolff, "The Distributional Effects of Uniform Air Pollution Policy in the U.S.," pp. 281–301.

13. Patrick C. West, J. Mark Fly, Frances Larkin, and Robert Marans, "Minority Anglers and Toxic Fish Consumption: Evidence from a State-Wide Survey in Michigan," in Bryant and Mohai, *Race and the Incidence of Environmental Hazards*.

14. Bullard, "Solid Waste Sites and the Black Houston Community," pp. 273–288; Robert D. Bullard, *Invisible Houston: The Black Experience in Boom and Bust* (College Station: Texas A & M University Press, 1987), chapter 6; Robert D. Bullard, "Environmental Racism and Land Use," *Land Use Forum: A Journal of Law, Policy & Practice* 2 (Spring 1993): 6–11.

15. United Church of Christ Commission for Racial Justice, *Toxic Wastes and Race*; Paul Mohai and Bunyan Bryant, "Environmental Racism: Reviewing the Evidence," in Bryant and Mohai, *Race and the Incidence of Environmental Hazards*.

16. Marianne Lavelle and Marcia Coyle, "Unequal Protection: The Racial Divide in Environmental Law," *National Law Journal* (September 21, 1992): 1–2.

17. Agency for Toxic Substances and Disease Registry, *The Nature and Extent of Lead Poisoning in Children in the United States: A Report to Congress* (Atlanta: U.S. Department of Health and Human Resources, 1988), pp. 1–12.

18. Ibid.

19. Ibid.

20. Wernette and Nieves, "Breathing Polluted Air," pp. 16–17.

21. See Mann, *L.A.'s Lethal Air*.

22. See H. P. Mak, H. Abbey, and R. C. Talamo, "Prevalence of Asthma and Health Service Utilization of Asthmatic Children in an Inner City," *Journal of Allergy and Clinical Immunology* 70 (1982): 367–372; I. F. Goldstein and A. L. Weinstein, "Air Pollution and Asthma: Effects of Exposure to Short-Term Sulfur Dioxide Peaks," *Environmental Research* 40 (1986): 332–345; J. Schwartz, D. Gold, D. W. Dockey, S. T. Weiss, and F. E. Speizer, "Predictors of Asthma and Persistent Wheeze in a National Sample of Children in the United States," *American Review of Respiratory Disease* 142 (1990): 555–562.

23. Lavelle and Coyle, "Unequal Protection," pp. S1–S2.

24. Ibid., p. 2.

25. See U.S. Environmental Protection Agency, *Women, Minorities and People with Disabilities* (Washington, D.C.: Environmental Protection Agency, 1992); U.S. Environmental Protection Agency, *EPA Headquarters Cultural Diversity Survey: Draft Final Report* (Washington, D.C.: Environmental Protection Agency Cultural Diversity Task Force, 1992).

26. Bullard, *Confronting Environmental Racism*, chapter 1; Robert D. Bullard, "Waste and Racism: A Stacked Deck?" *Forum for Applied Research and Public Policy* 8 (Spring 1993): 29–35; Robert D. Bullard, ed., *In Search of the New South: The Black Urban Experience in the 1970s and 1980s* (Tuscaloosa: University of Alabama Press, 1989).

27. Commission for Racial Justice, *Toxic Wastes and Race in the United States*, pp. xiii–xiv.

28. Ibid., pp. 18–19.

29. Pat Costner and Joe Thornton, *Playing with Fire* (Washington, D.C.: Greenpeace, 1990), pp. 48–49.

30. See U.S. General Accounting Office, *Siting of Hazardous Waste Landfills and Their Correlation with Racial and Economic Status of Surrounding Communities* (Washington, D.C.: General Accounting Office, 1983), p. 1.

31. See Conger Beasley, "Of Pollution and Poverty: Keeping Watch in Cancer Alley," *Buzzworm* 2, no. 4 (July/August 1990): 39.

32. U.S. Environmental Protection Agency, *Toxic Release Inventory & Emission Reductions 1987–1990 in the Lower Mississippi River Industrial Corridor* (Washington, D.C.: Environmental Protection Agency, Office of Pollution Prevention and Toxics, May 13, 1993), p. 25.

33. Letter from Gary Johnson, State of Louisiana, Department of Environmental Quality, "Review of Toxic Release Inventory … Lower Mississippi River Industrial Corridor," to EPA official Jeany Anderson-LaBar, November 18, 1992.

34. Schueler, "Southern Exposure," p. 46.

35. See Institute for Southern Studies, *1991–1992 Green Index: A State-by-State Guide to the Nation's Environmental Health* (Durham, N.C.: Institute for Southern Studies, 1992).

36. For a discussion of Louisiana's environmental and economic problems, see Paul H. Templet and Stephen Farber, *The Complementarity Between Environmental and Economic Risk: An Empirical Analysis* (Baton Rouge: Louisiana State University Institute for Environmental Studies, 1992).

37. James O'Byrne and Mark Schleifstein, "Drinking Water in Danger," *Times Picayune*, February 19, 1991, p. A5.

38. Pat Bryant, "Toxics and Racial Justice," *Social Policy* 20 (Summer 1989): 48–52; Beasley, "Of Pollution and Poverty: Keeping Watch in Cancer Alley," pp. 39–45.

39. Quoted in Ginny Carroll, "When Pollution Hits Home," *National Wildlife* 29 (August/September 1991): 35.

40. Beasley, "Of Pollution and Poverty: Keeping Watch in Cancer Alley," p. 41.

41. Ibid.

42. Ibid., p. 39.

43. Daniel Mandell, Sanford J. Lewis, and National Toxics Campaign Fund, *The Formosa Plastics Story: A Report to the People of St. John the Baptist Parish* (Boston: National Toxics Campaign, 1990).

44. Colquette and Robertson, "Environmental Racism," p. 176.

45. See Beverly H. Wright and Florence Robinson, "Voluntary Buy-Outs as an Alternative Damage Claims Arrangement: A Comparative Analysis of Three Impacted Communities" (Baton Rouge: Southern University Institute for Environmental Issues and Policy Assessment, December 15, 1992), pp. 10–11.

46. Ibid., pp. 8–10.

47. Quoted in James O'Byrne, "The Death of a Town: A Chemical Plant Closes In," *Times Picayune*, February 20, 1991, p. A12.

48. Wright and Robinson, "Voluntary Buy-Outs," pp. 11–13.

49. See Agency for Toxic Substances and Disease Registry, *Health Assessment, Koppers Superfund Site* (Texarkana, Tex.: U.S. Environmental Protection Agency, April 1989); U.S. Environmental Protection Agency, "Koppers Site Update: EPA Announces Amended Record of Decision for Site," *EPA Update* (March 5, 1992).

50. Agency for Toxic Substances and Disease Registry, *Health Assessment, Koppers Superfund Site*, p. 2.

51. Letter from Richard O. Murray, Department of Army, Fort Worth District, Corps of Engineers, to Mr. and Mrs. Nathaniel B. Oliver (April 23, 1991).

52. Site visit made to Texarkana to conduct interviews with residents for the NAACP Legal Defense and Educational Fund, August 4–11, 1992.

Chapter Six

1. See Pat C. West, J. M. Fly, F. Larkin, and R. Marans, "Minority Anglers and Toxic Fish Consumption: Evidence of the State-Wide Survey of Michigan," in Bunyan Bryant and Paul Mohai, eds., *Race and the Incidence of Environmental Hazards* (Boulder, Colo.: Westview Press, 1993), pp. 110–113.

2. Robert D. Bullard, "The Environmental Justice Framework: A Strategy for Addressing Unequal Protection," paper presented at the Resources for the Future Conference on Risk Management, Annapolis, Md. (November 1992).

3. U.S. Environmental Protection Agency, *Environmental Equity: Reducing Risk for All Communities* (Washington, D.C.: Environmental Protection Agency, 1992).

4. See United Church of Christ Commission for Racial Justice, *Proceedings: The First National People of Color Environmental Leadership Summit* (New York: Commission for Racial Justice, 1992).

5. Texas Air Control Board, "Task Force on Environmental Equity and Justice," press release, undated.

6. Robert D. Bullard, "Race and Environmental Justice in the United States," *Yale Journal of International Law* 18 (Winter 1993): 319–335; Robert D. Bullard, "The Threat of Environmental Racism," *Natural Resources & Environment* 7 (Winter 1993): 23–26, 55–56.

7. Louis Sullivan, "Remarks at the First Annual Conference on Childhood Lead Poisoning," in Alliance to End Childhood Lead Poisoning, *Preventing Child Lead Poisoning: Final Report* (Washington, D.C.: Alliance to End Childhood Lead Poisoning, 1991), p. A-2.

8. See Bill Lann Lee, "Environmental Litigation on Behalf of Poor, Minority Children: Matthews v. Coye: A Case Study," paper presented at the Annual Meeting of the American Association for the Advancement of Science, Chicago (February 9, 1992).

9. K. S. Shrader-Frechette, *Risk and Rationality: Philosophical Foundations for Populist Reforms* (Berkeley: University of California Press, 1992), p. 98.

10. U.S. Environmental Protection Agency, "Geographic Initiatives: Protecting What We Love," *Securing Our Legacy: An EPA Progress Report 1989–1991* (Washington, D.C.: Environmental Protection Agency, 1992), p. 12.

11. Ibid., p. 32.

12. Ibid.

13. U.S. EPA, *Environmental Equity*, p. 60.

14. Sanford Lewis, Brian Keating, and Dick Russell, *Inconclusive by Design: Waste, Fraud and Abuse in Federal Environmental Health Research* (Boston: National Toxics Campaign and Environmental Health Network, 1992).

15. Robert D. Bullard, *People of Color Environmental Groups Directory 1992* (Flint, Mich.: Charles Stewart Mott Foundation, 1992).

16. See "Chemical Valley," Appalshop Film and Video, Whitesburg, Kentucky, 1991.

17. See Gaynell Terrell, "AstroWorld Criticizes Proposed Composting Plant," *Houston Post*, June 10, 1992, p. A-16.

18. Bill Dawson, "Minorities Unite to Fight for Environmental Justice," *Houston Chronicle*, July 13, 1992, pp. A1, A17.

19. Terrell, "AstroWorld Criticizes Proposed Composting Plant," p. A16.

Chapter Seven

1. Dorceta E. Taylor, "Blacks and the Environment: Toward an Explanation of the Concern and Action Gap Between Blacks and Whites," *Environment and Behavior* 21 (March 1989): 175–205.

2. Lawrence Hamilton, "Concern About Toxic Waste: Three Demographic Predictors," *Sociological Perspective* 28 (1985): 463–486.

3. Robert Gottlieb and Helen Ingram, "The New Environmentalists," *Progressive* (August 1988): 14.

4. Ibid., pp. 14–15.

5. Robert D. Bullard and Beverly H. Wright, "Environmentalism and the Politics of Equity: Emergent Trends in the Black Community," *Mid-American Review of Sociology* 12 (Winter 1987): 22.

6. Yale Rabin, "The Roots of Segregation in the Eighties: The Role of Local Government," in Gary A. Tobin, ed., *Divided Neighborhoods: Changing Patterns of Racial Segregation* (Newbury Park, Calif.: Sage, 1987), p. 211.

7. Paul Ruffins, "Blacks Suffer Health Hazards Yet Remain Inactive on Environment," *Los Angeles Times*, August 28, 1989, p. 3.

8. John Seley and Julian Wolpert, "Equity and Location," in Roger E. Kasperson, ed., *Equity Issues in Radioactive Waste Management* (Cambridge, Mass.: Oelgeschlager Gunn, and Hain, 1983), p. 85.

9. Michael R. Edelstein, *Contaminated Communities: The Social and Psychological Impacts of Residential Toxic Exposure* (Boulder, Colo.: Westview Press, 1988), p. 186.

10. Ibid., p. 195.

11. Edward J. Walsh and Rex Warland, "Social Movement Involvement in the Wake of a Nuclear Accident: Activists and Free Riders in the TMI Area," *American Sociological Review* 48 (December 1983): 764–780.

12. Edelstein, *Contaminated Communities*, p. 188.

13. Gail Bingham, "Resolving Environmental Disputes: A Decade of Experience," in Robert W. Lake, ed., *Resolving Locational Conflict* (New Brunswick, N.J.: Rutgers University Center for Urban Policy Research, 1987), p. 316.

14. Thomas Gladwin, "Patterns of Environmental Conflict over Industrial Facilities in the United States, 1970–1978," in Lake, *Resolving Locational Conflict*, pp. 14–44.

15. Conservation Leadership Project Minority Roundtable, "Minutes," Seattle, Washington (August 25–26, 1989), p. 5.

16. See Robert D. Bullard, "Environmental Conflict and Dispute Resolution in Minority and Nonminority Communities: A Focus on the Grassroots," report submitted to the Fund for Research on Dispute Resolution, Washington, D.C. (August 1992), p. 82.

17. Quoted in Paul Ruffins, "Blacks Suffer Health Hazards," *Los Angeles Times,* August 28, 1989, p. 3.

18. Human Environment Center, *Minority Education for Environmental and Natural Resources Professions: Higher Education* (Washington, D.C.: Human Environment Center, 1981), p. iii.

19. Ibid., p. v.

20. Gerry Stover, "The Environmental Consortium for Minority Outreach (TEC)," (Washington, D.C.: The Environmental Consortium for Minority Outreach, 1989), p. 1.

21. Ibid., p. 5.

22. Charles Stewart Mott Foundation, *Our Good Earth: Are We Living on Borrowed Time?* (Flint, Mich.: Charles Stewart Mott Foundation, 1987), p. 39.

23. Robert Fisher, *Let the People Decide: Neighborhood Organizing in America* (Boston: Twayne Publishers, 1984), pp. 155–156.

SELECTED
BIBLIOGRAPHY

◆

Agency for Toxic Substances and Disease Registry. *The Nature and Extent of Lead Poisoning in Children in the United States: A Report to Congress.* Atlanta: U.S. Department of Health and Human Resources, 1988.

Agency for Toxic Substances and Disease Registry. *Health Assessment, Koppers Superfund Site.* Texarkana, Tex.: U.S. Environmental Protection Agency, April 1989.

Ambler, Marjane. "The Lands the Feds Forgot." *Sierra* (May/June), 44–48.

Anderson, Richard F., and Michael R. Greenberg. "Hazardous Waste Facility Siting: A Role of Planners." *Journal of the American Planning Association* 48 (Spring 1983), 204–218.

Anthony, Richard P. "Polls, Pollution and Politics: Trends in Public Opinion on the Environment." *Environment* 24 (May 1982), 14–20.

Asch, Peter, and Joseph J. Seneca. "Some Evidence on the Distribution of Air Quality." *Land Economics* 54 (August 1978), 278–297.

Austin, Regina, and Michael Schill. "Black, Brown, Poor, and Poisoned: Minority Grassroots Environmentalism and the Quest for Eco-Justice." *Kansas Journal of Law and Public Policy* 1, no. 1 (1991), 69–82.

Babcock, Richard. "Houston: Unzoned, Unfettered, and Mostly Unrepentent." *Planning* 48 (1982), 21–23.

Bachrach, Kenneth M., and Alex J. Zautra. "Coping with Community Stress: The Threat of a Hazardous Waste Landfull." *Journal of Health and Social Behavior* 26 (June 1985), 127–141.

Beasley, Conger. "Of Pollution and Poverty: Keeping Watch in Cancer Alley." *Buzzworm* 2, no. 4 (July/August 1990), 38–45.

_____. "Of Pollution and Poverty: Deadly Threat on Native Lands." *Buzzworm* 2, no. 5 (September/October 1990), 39–45.

Beegley, Sharon, Mary Hager, and Susan Agrest. "Maybe It Could Happen Here." *Newsweek* 105 (February 4, 1985), 24.

Beers, David, and Diana Hembree. "The New Atlanta: A Tale of Two Cities." *Nation* 244 (March 1987), 347, 357–360.

Bernard, Richard M., and Bradley R. Rice, eds. *Sunbelt Cities: Politics and Growth Since World War II.* Austin: University of Texas Press, 1984.

Berry, Brian J.L., ed. *The Social Burden of Environmental Pollution: A Comparative Metropolitan Data Source.* Cambridge, Mass.: Ballinger, 1977.

Bingham, Gail. "Resolving Environmental Disputes: A Decade of Experience." In Robert W. Lake (ed.), *Resolving Locational Conflict*, New Brunswick, N.J.: Rutgers University Center for Urban Policy Research, 1987, 314–323.

Blackwell, James E. *The Black Community: Diversity and Unity.* New York: Harper and Row, 1985.

Bloom, Jack. *Class, Race and the Civil Rights Movement.* Bloomington: Indiana University Press, 1987.

Bluestone, Barry, and Bennett Harrison. *The Deindustrialization of America.* New York: Basic Books, 1982.

Blum, Barbara. *Cities: An Environmental Wilderness.* Washington, D.C.: Environmental Protection Agency, 1978.

Breckenfield, Gurney. "Refilling the Metropolitan Doughnut." In David C. Perry and Alfred J. Watkins (eds.), *The Rise of the Sunbelt Cities.* Beverly Hills: Sage, 1977, 231–258.

Brown, K. W., J. W. Mullins, E. P. Richitt, G. T. Flatman, and S. C. Black. "Assessing Soil Lead Contamination in Dallas, Texas." *Environmental Monitoring and Assessment* 5 (1985), 137–154.

Brown, Michael H. *Laying Waste: The Poisoning of America by Toxic Chemicals.* New York: Pantheon Books, 1980.

_____. *The Toxic Cloud: The Poisoning of America's Air.* New York: Harper and Row, 1987.

Brownstein, Ronald. "The Toxic Tragedy." In Ralph Nader, Ronald Brownstein, and John Richard (eds.), *Who's Poisoning America: Corporate Polluters and Their Victims in the Chemical Age.* San Francisco: Sierra Club Books, 1982, 1–59.

Bryant, Bunyan, and Paul Mohai. *Race and the Incidence of Environmental Hazards.* Boulder, Colo.: Westview Press, 1992.

Bryant, Pat. "Toxics and Racial Justice." *Social Policy* 20 (Summer 1989), 48–52.

Bullard, Robert D. "Solid Waste Sites and the Black Houston Community." *Sociological Inquiry* 53 (Spring 1983), 273–288.

_____. "The Black Family: Housing Alternatives in the 80s." *Journal of Black Studies* 14 (Spring 1984), 341–351.

_____. "Endangered Environs: The Price of Unplanned Growth in Boomtown Houston." *California Sociologist* 7 (Summer 1984), 84–102.

_____. "Blacks and the American Dream of Housing." In Jamshid A. Momeni (ed.), *Race, Ethnicity, and Minority Housing in the United States.* Westport, Conn.: Greenwood Press, 1986, 53–68.

_____. "Blacks and the New South: Challenges of the Eighties." *Journal of Intergroup Relations* 15 (Summer 1987), 25–39.

_____. *Invisible Houston: The Black Experience in Boom and Bust.* College Station: Texas A & M University Press, 1987.

_____, ed. *In Search of the New South: The Black Urban Experience in the 1970s and 1980s.* Tuscaloosa: University of Alabama Press, 1989.

_____. "Ecological Inequities and the New South: Black Communities Under Siege." *Journal of Ethnic Studies* 17 (Winter 1990), 101–115.

_____. "The Environmental Justice Framework: A Strategy for Addressing Unequal Protection." Paper presented at the Resources for the Future Conference on Risk Management, Annapolis, Md. (November 1992).

_____. "In Our Backyards: Minority Communities Get Most of the Dumps." *EPA Journal* 18 (March/April 1992), 11–12.

_____. *People of Color Environmental Groups Directory 1992.* Flint, Mich.: Charles Stewart Mott Foundation, 1992.

_____. "Urban Infrastructure: Social, Environmental, and Health Risks to African Americans." In Billy J. Tidwell (ed.), *The State of Black America 1992.* New York: National Urban League, 1992, 183–196.

_____. *Confronting Environmental Racism: Voices from the Grassroots.* Boston: South End Press, 1993.

_____. "Environmental Racism and Land Use." *Land Use Forum: A Journal of Law, Policy & Practice* 2 (Spring 1993), 6–11.

_____. "Race and Environmental Justice in the United States." *Yale Journal of International Law* 18 (Winter 1993), 319–335.

_____. "The Threat of Environmental Racism." *Natural Resources & Environment* 7 (Winter 1993), 23–26, 55–56.

_____. "Waste and Racism: A Stacked Deck?" *Forum for Applied Research and Public Policy* 8 (Spring 1993), 29–35.

Bullard, Robert D., and Joe R. Feagin. "Racism and the City." In M. Gottdiener and C. V. Pickvance (eds.), *Urban Life in Transition.* Newbury Park, Calif.: Sage, 1991, 55–76.

Bullard, Robert D., and Beverly H. Wright. "Dumping Grounds in a Sunbelt City." *Urban Resources* 2 (Winter 1985), 37–39.

_____. "The Politics of Pollution: Implications for the Black Community." *Phylon* 47 (March 1986), 71–78.

_____. "Blacks and the Environment." *Humboldt Journal of Social Relations* 14 (Summer 1987), 165–184.

_____. "Environmentalism and the Politics of Equity: Emergent Trends in the Black Community." *Mid-American Review of Sociology* 12 (Winter 1987), 21–37.

Burden, Robert P. "The Forgotten Environment." In Lawrence E. Hinkle and William C. Loring (eds.), *The Effects of the Man Made Environment on Health and Behavior.* Washington, D.C.: U.S. Government Printing Office, 1977.

Buttel, Frederick R., and William L. Flinn. "Social Class and Mass Environmental Beliefs: A Reconsideration." *Environment and Behavior* 10 (September 1978), 433–450.

Carothers, Andre. "The Coming of Age of Sumter County." *Greenpeace* 12 (1987), 11–15.

Carroll Ginny. "When Pollution Hits Home." *National Wildlife* 29 (August/September 1991), 30–39.

Charles Stewart Mott Foundation. *Our Good Earth: Are We Living on Borrowed Time?* Flint, Mich.: Charles Stewart Mott Foundation, 1987.

Churchill, Ward, and Winona LaDuke. "Native America: The Political Economy of Radioactive Colonialism." *Insurgent Sociologist* 13 (Spring 1983), 51–63.

Collette, Will. "Somewhere Else USA: Fighting Back Against Chemical Dumpers." *Southern Neighborhoods* 9 (September 1985), 1–3.

Collin, Robert, and William Harris. "Race and Waste in Two Virginia Communities." In Robert D. Bullard (ed.), *Confronting Environmental Racism: Voices from the Grassroots.* Boston: South End Press, 1993, 93–106.

Collins, Daniel L., Andrew Baum, and Jerome E. Singer. "Coping with Chronic Stress at Three Mile Island: Psychological and Biological Evidence." *Health Psychology* 2 (1983), 149–166.

Colquette, Kelly C., and Elizabeth A. Henry Robertson. "Environmental Racism: The Causes, Consequences, and Commendations." *Tulane Environmental Law Journal* 5, no. 1 (1991), 153–207.

Commission for Racial Justice. *Toxic Wastes and Race in the United States: A National Report on the Racial and Socioeconomic Characteristics of Communities with Hazardous Waste Sites.* New York: United Church of Christ, 1987.

_____. *Proceedings: The First National People of Color Environmental Leadership Summit.* New York: United Church of Christ Commission for Racial Justice, 1992.

Costner, Pat, and Joe Thornton. *Playing with Fire.* Washington, D.C.: Greenpeace, 1990.

Cutter, Susan C. "Community Concern for Pollution: Social and Environmental Influences." *Environment and Behavior* 13 (1981), 105–124.

Davidson, Chandler, ed. *Minority Vote Dilution.* Washington, D.C.: Howard University Press, 1984.

Davis, King E. "The Status of Black Leadership: Implications for Followers in the 1980s." *Journal of Applied Behavioral Science* 18 (1982), 309–322.

Davis, Morris E. "The Impact of Workplace Health and Safety on Black Workers: Assessment and Prognosis." *Labor Studies Journal* 4 (Spring 1981), 29–40.

Domhoff, G. William. "The Growth Machine and the Power Elite: A Challenge to Pluralists and Marxists Alike." In Robert J. Waste (ed.), *Community Power: Directions for Future Research.* Newbury Park, Calif.: Sage, 1986, 53–75.

Dorman, Peter. "The Distributional Effect of the Uniform Air Pollution Policy in the United States." *Review of Radical Political Economy* 16 (Winter 1984), 151–164.

Douglas, Lee, and H. K. Lee. "Conclusions and Reservation." In Douglas Lee (ed.), *Environmental Factors in Respiratory Disease.* New York: Academic Press, 1972, 250–251.

Dunlap, Riley E. "Public Opinion on the Environment in the Reagan Era: Polls, Pollution, and Politics Revisited." *Environment* 29 (July/August 1987), 6–11, 32–37.

Edds, Margaret. *Free at Last: What Really Happened When Civil Rights Came to Southern Politics.* Bethesda: Adler and Adler, 1987.

Edelstein, Michael R. *Contaminated Communities: The Social and Psychological Impacts of Residential Toxic Exposure.* Boulder, Colo.: Westview Press, 1987.

Enterprise Foundation. *Dallas: A Survey of Poverty and Housing.* Dallas: Meadows Foundation, 1983.

Epstein, Samuel, Lester O. Brown, and Carl Pope. *Hazardous Waste in America.* San Francisco: Sierra Club Books, 1983.

Equal Employment Opportunity Commission. *Employment of Minorities, Women, and People with Disabilities in the Federal Government: EEOC Annual Report.* Washington, D.C.: Office of Federal Operations, EEOC, 1991.

Falk, William W., and Thomas A. Lyson. *High Tech, Low Tech, No Tech: Recent Industrial and Occupational Change in the South.* Albany: State University of New York Press, 1988.

Feagin, Joe R. "The Global Context of Metropolitan Growth: Houston and the Oil Industry." *American Journal of Sociology* 90 (May 1985), 1204–1230.

Feagin, Joe R., and Clairece Booher Feagin. *Discrimination American Style: Institutional Racism and Sexism.* Malabar, Fla.: Robert E. Krueger Publishing, 1986.

Fisher, Robert. *Let the People Decide: Neighborhood Organizing in America.* Boston: Twayne, 1984.

Ford, Larry, and Ernst Griffin. "The Ghettoization of Paradise." *Geographical Review* 69 (April 1979), 140–158.

Franklin, Ben A. "In the Shadow of the Valley." *Sierra* 71 (May/June 1986), 38–43.

Freeman, Myrick A. "The Distribution of Environmental Quality." In Allen V. Kneese and Blair T. Bower (eds.), *Environmental Quality Analysis.* Baltimore: Johns Hopkins University Press for Resources for the Future, 1972, 243–278.

Fuller, Chet. "I Hear Them Call It the New South." *Black Enterprise* 12 (November 1981), 41–44.

Furuseth, Owen J., and Mark S. Johnson. "Neighborhood Attitudes Toward a Sanitary Landfill: A North Carolina Study." *Applied Geography* 8 (1988), 135–145.

Gale, Richard P. "The Environmental Movement and the Left: Antagonists or Allies?" *Sociological Inquiry* 53 (Spring 1983), 179–199.

Gamson, William. *The Study of Social Protest.* Homewood, Ill.: Dorsey Press, 1975.

Geiser, Ken, and Gerry Waneck. "PCBs and Warren County." *Science for the People* 15 (July/August 1983), 13–17.

Gelobter, Michel. "The Distribution of Air Pollution by Income and Race." Paper presented at the Second Symposium on Social Science in Resource Management, Urbana, Illinois (June 1988).

_____. "Toward a Model of Environmental Discrimination." In B. Bryant and P. Mohai (eds.), *The Proceedings of the Michigan Conference on Race and the Incidence of Environmental Hazards.* Ann Arbor: University of Michigan School of Natural Resources, 1990.

Gianessi, Leonard, H. M. Peskin, and E. Wolff. "The Distributional Effects of Uniform Air Pollution Policy in the U.S." *Quarterly Journal of Economics* 56, no. 1 (1979), 281–301.

Gladwin, Thomas. "Patterns of Environmental Conflict over Industrial Facilities in the United States, 1970–78." In Robert W. Lake (ed.), *Resolving Locational Conflict.* New Brunswick, N.J.: Rutgers University Center for Urban Policy Research, 1987, 14–44.

Godsil, Rachel D. "Remedying Environmental Racism." *Michigan Law Review* 90, no. 394 (1991), 394–427.

Goldfield, David R. *Promised Land: The South Since 1945.* Arlington Heights, Ill.: Harlan Davidson, 1987.

Goldstein, I. F., and A. L. Weinstein. "Air Pollution and Asthma: Effects of Exposure to Short-Term Sulfur Dioxide Peaks." *Environmental Research* 40 (1986), 332–345.

Gottlieb, Robert, and Helen Ingram. "The New Environmentalists." *Progressive* (August 1988), 14–15.

Greenberg, Michael R., and Richard F. Anderson. *Hazardous Waste Sites: The Credibility Gap.* New Brunswick, N.J.: Rutgers University Center for Urban Policy Research, 1984.

Gunter, Booth, and Mike Williams. "The Cadillac of Dumps." *Sierra* 71 (January/February 1986), 19–22.

Haggerty, Michael. "Crisis at Indian Creek." *Atlanta Journal and Constitution Magazine* (January 20, 1980), 14–25.

Hamilton, Lawrence. "Concern About Toxic Waste: Three Demographic Predictors." *Sociological Perspective* 28 (1985), 463–486.

Harris, Art. "Too Busy to Hate." *Esquire* 103 (June 1985), 129–133.

Hays, Samuel P. *Beauty, Health, and Permanence: Environmental Politics in the United States, 1955–1985.* Cambridge, Mass.: Cambridge University Press, 1987.

Human Environment Center. *Minority Education for Environmental and Natural Resource Professions: Higher Education.* Washington, D.C.: Human Environment Center, 1981.

Humphrey, Craig R., and Frederick R. Buttel. *Environment, Energy and Society.* Belmont, Calif.: Wadsworth, 1982.

Institute for Southern Studies. *1991–1992 Green Index: A State-by-State Guide to the Nation's Environmental Health.* Durham, N.C.: Institute for Southern Studies, 1992.

Jacoby, Arthur P., and Nicholas Babchuk. "Instrumental and Expressive Voluntary Associations." *Sociology and Social Research* 47 (1973), 461–471.

Jaret, Charles. "Black Migration and Socioeconomic Inequality in Atlanta and the Urban South." *Humboldt Journal of Social Relations* 14 (Summer 1987), 65–105.

Jenkins, Craig J. "Resource Mobilization Theory and the Study of Social Movements." *Annual Review of Sociology* 9 (1983), 27–53.

Joint Center for Political Studies. *Black Elected Officials: A National Roster.* New York: UNIPUB, 1984.

Jones, J. M. "The Concept of Racism and Its Changing Reality." In Benjamin P. Bowser and Raymond G. Hunt (eds.), *Impact of Racism on White Americans.* Beverly Hills: Sage, 1981, 27–49.

Jordon, Vernon. "Sins of Omission." *Environmental Action* 11 (April 1980), 26–30.

Kasarda, John D. "Implications of Contemporary Distribution Trends for National Urban Policy." *Social Science Quarterly* 61 (December 1980), 373–400.

———. "Caught in the Web of Change." *Society* 21 (1983), 41–47.

Kasarda, John D., Michael D. Irwin, and Holly L. Hughes. "The South Is Still Rising." *American Demographics* 8 (June 1986), 32–40.

Kazis, Richard, and Richard Grossman. *Fear at Work: Job Blackmail, Labor, and the Environment.* New York: Pilgrim Press, 1983.

Kruvant, W. J. "People, Energy, and Pollution." In Dorothy K. Newman and Dawn Day (eds.), *American Energy Consumer.* Cambridge, Mass.: Ballinger, 1975, 125–167.

Kushner, J. A. *Apartheid in America: An Historical and Legal Analysis of Contemporary Racial Segregation in the United States.* Frederick, Md.: Associated Faculty Press, Inc., 1980.

Ladd, E. C. "Clearing the Air: Public Opinion and Public Policy on the Environment." *Public Opinion* (February/March 1982), 16–20.

Lash, Jonathan, Katherine Gillman, and David Sheridan. *A Season of Spoils: The Reagan Administration's Attack on the Environment.* New York: Pantheon Books, 1984.

Lavelle, Marianne, and Marcia Coyle. "Unequal Protection: The Racial Divide in Environmental Law." *National Law Journal* (September 21, 1992), 1–2.

Lazarus, Richard E., and Raymond Launier. "Stress-Related Transactions Between Persons and Environment." In Lawrence A. Pervin and Michael Lewis (eds.), *Perspectives in International Psychology*. New York: Plenum, 1978, 279–327.

Lee, Bill Lann. "Environmental Litigation on Behalf of Poor, Minority Children: Matthews v. Coye: A Case Study." Paper presented at the Annual Meeting of the American Association for the Advancement of Science, Chicago (February 9, 1992).

Lee, Douglas, and H. K. Lee. "Conclusions and Reservations." In Douglas Lee (ed.), *Environmental Factors in Respiratory Disease*. New York: Academic Press, 1972, 250–251.

Levine, Adeline. *Love Canal: Science, Politics, and People*. Lexington, Mass.: Lexington Books, 1982.

Lewis, Sanford, Brian Keating, and Dick Russell. *Inconclusive by Design: Waste, Fraud and Abuse in Federal Environmental Health Research*. Boston: National Toxics Campaign and Environmental Health Network, 1992.

Lineberry, Robert L. *Equity and Urban Policy: The Distribution of Municipal Public Services*. Beverly Hills: Sage, 1977.

Logan, John R. "Growth, Politics and Stratification of Places." *American Journal of Sociology* 84 (1978), 404–416.

Logan, John R., and Harvey Molotch. *Urban Fortunes: The Political Economy of Place*. Berkeley: University of California Press, 1987.

Love, Sam. "Ecology and Social Justice: Is There a Conflict?" *Environmental Action* 4 (1972), 3–6.

Mak, H. P., H. Abbey, and R. C. Talamo. "Prevalence of Asthma and Health Service Utilization of Asthmatic Children in an Inner City." *Journal of Allergy and Clinical Immunology* 70 (1982), 367–372.

Mandell, Daniel, Sanford J. Lewis, and National Toxics Campaign Fund. *The Formosa Plastics Story: A Report to the People of St. John the Baptist Parish*. Boston: National Toxics Campaign, 1990.

Mann, Eric. *L.A.'s Lethal Air: New Strategies for Policy, Organizing, and Action*. Los Angeles: Labor/Community Strategy Center, 1991.

Matney, William C., and Dwight L. Johnson. *America's Black Population: A Statistical View 1970–1982*. Washington, D.C.: U.S. Government Printing Office, 1983.

McCall, Nathan. "Atlanta: City of the Next Generation." *Black Enterprise* 17 (May 1987), 56–58.

McCarthy, John D., and Mayer Zald. *The Trend of Social Movements in America: Professionalism and Resource Mobilization*. Morristown, N.J.: General Learning Press, 1979.

McCaull, Julian. "Discriminatory Air Pollution: If the Poor Don't Breathe." *Environment* 19 (March 1976), 26–32.

Miller, Alan S. "Toward an Environment/Labor Coalition." *Environment* 22 (June 1980), 32–39.

Mitchell, Robert Cameron. "Silent Spring/Solid Majorities." *Public Opinion* 2 (August/September 1979), 16–20.

_____, ed. "Public Opinion on Environmental Issues." In Council on Environmental Quality, *The Eleventh Annual Report of the Council on Environmental Quality.* Washington, D.C.: U.S. Government Printing Office, 1980, 401–425.

_____. "Public Opinion and Environmental Politics in the 1970s and 1980s." In Norman J. Vig and Michael E. Kraft (eds.), *Environmental Policy in the 1980s: Reagan's New Agenda.* Washington, D.C.: Congressional Quarterly Press, 1984, 51–74.

Mitchell, Robert Cameron, and Richard T. Carson. "Protest, Property Rights, and Hazardous Waste." *Resources* 85 (Fall 1986), 6–9.

Mohai, Paul. "Public Concern and Elite Involvement in Environmental-Conservation Issues." *Social Science Quarterly* 66 (December 1985), 820–838.

Molotch, Harvey L. "The City as a Growth Machine: Toward a Political Economy of Place." *American Journal of Sociology* 82 (1976): 309–330.

Momeni, Jamshid A., ed. *Race, Ethnicity, and Minority Housing in the United States.* Westport, Conn.: Greenwood Press, 1986.

Morell, David. "Siting and the Politics of Equity." In Robert W. Lake (ed.), *Resolving Locational Conflict.* New Brunswick, N.J.: Rutgers University Center for Urban Policy Research, 1987, 117–136.

Morell, David, and Christopher Magorian. "Risk, Fear, and Local Opposition: 'Not in My Back Yard.'" In David Morell and Christopher Magorian (eds.), *Siting Hazardous Waste Facilities: Local Opposition and the Myth of Preemption.* Cambridge, Mass.: Ballinger, 1982, 21–46.

Morris, Aldon D. *The Origins of the Civil Rights Movement: Black Communities Organizing for Change.* New York: Free Press, 1984.

Morrison, Denton E. "The Soft Cutting Edge of Environmentalism: Why and How the Appropriate Technology Notion Is Changing the Movement." *Natural Resources Journal* 20 (April 1980), 275–298.

_____. "How and Why Environmental Consciousness Has Trickled Down." In Allan Schnaiberg, Nicholas Watts, and Klaus Zimmermann (eds.), *Distributional Conflict in Environmental-Resource Policy.* New York: St. Martin's Press, 1986, 187–220.

Morrison, Denton E., and Riley E. Dunlap. "Environmentalism and Elitism: A Conceptual and Empirical Analysis." *Environmental Management* 10 (1986), 581–589.

Nader, Ralph, Ronald Brownstein, and John Richard, eds. *Who's Poisoning America: Corporate Polluters and Their Victims in the Chemical Age.* San Francisco: Sierra Club Books, 1982.

Neiman, Max, and Ronald O. Loveridge. "Environmentalism and Local Growth Control: A Probe into the Class Bias Thesis." *Environment and Behavior* 13 (1981), 759–772.

Newman, Dorothy K., and Dawn Day. *The American Energy Consumer.* Cambridge, Mass.: Ballinger, 1975.

Nie, Norman H., C. Hadlai Hull, Jean G. Jenkins, Karin Steinbrenner, and Dale H. Bent. *Statistical Package for the Social Sciences.* New York: McGraw Hill, 1975.

Nieves, Leslie A. "Not in Whose Backyard? Minority Population Concentrations and Noxious Facility Sites." Paper presented at the Annual Meeting of the

American Association for the Advancement of Science, Chicago (February 9, 1992).

Oberschall, Anthony. *Social Conflict and Social Movement.* Englewood Cliffs, N.J.: Prentice-Hall, 1973.

Office of Technology Assessment. *Technologies and Management Strategies for Hazardous Waste Control.* Washington, D.C.: U.S. Government Printing Office, 1983.

O'Hare, Michael, Lawrence Bacow, and Debra Sanderson. *Facility Siting and Public Opposition.* New York: Van Nostrand Reinhold, 1983.

Omi, Michael, and Howard Winant. *Racial Formation in the United States: From the 1960's to the 1980's.* New York: Routledge and Kegan Paul, 1986.

Ong, Paul, and Evelyn Blumenberg. "Race and Environmentalism." Unpublished manuscript, Graduate School of Architecture and Urban Planning, UCLA, March 14, 1990.

Orum, Anthony M. "On Participation in Political Movements." *Journal of Applied Behavioral Science* 10 (April/June 1974), 181–207.

Page, Ann. "The Union Carbide Institute Plant: The Perception of Risk." Paper presented at the annual meeting of the Society for the Study of Social Problems, New York (August 27, 1986).

Pearlin, Leonard I., and Carmi Schooler. "The Structure of Coping." *Journal of Health and Social Behavior* 19 (March 1978), 2–21.

Perrin, Constance. *Everything in Its Place: Social Order and Land Use in America.* Princeton, N.J.: Princeton University Press, 1977.

Perry, David C., and Alfred J. Watkins, eds. *The Rise of the Sunbelt Cities.* Beverly Hills: Sage, 1977.

Pervin, Lawrence A., and Michael Lewis, eds. *Perspectives in International Psychology.* New York: Plenum, 1978.

Pollack, Sue, and JoAnn Grozuczak. *Reagan, Toxics and Minorities.* Washington, D.C.: Urban Environment Conference, Inc., 1984.

Popper, Frank J. "The Environmentalist and the LULU." *Environment* 27 (March 1985), 7–11, 37–40.

Porterfield, Andrew, and David Weir. "The Export of Hazardous Waste." *Nation* 245 (October 3, 1987), 340–344.

Portney, Kent E. "The Potential of the Theory of Compensation for Mitigating Public Opposition to Hazardous Waste Siting: Some Evidence from Five Massachusetts Communities." *Policy Studies Journal* 14 (1985), 81–89.

Preston, Michael, Lenneal J. Henderson, Jr., and Paul Puryear, eds. *The New Black Politics: The Search for Political Power.* New York: Longman, 1987.

Public Data Access, Inc. *Mortality and Toxics Along the Mississippi River.* New York: Greenpeace, 1988.

Rabin, Yale. "The Roots of Segregation in the Eighties: The Role of Local Government." In Gary A. Tobin (ed.), *Divided Neighborhoods: Changing Patterns of Racial Segregation.* Newbury Park, Calif.: Sage, 1987, 208–226.

Reynolds, Barbara. "Triana, Alabama: The Unhealthiest Town in America." *National Wildlife* 18 (August 1980), 75.

Rice, Bradley R. "Atlanta: If Dixie Were Atlanta." In Richard M. Bernard and Bradley R. Rice (eds.), *Sunbelt Cities: Politics and Growth Since World War II.* Austin: University of Texas Press, 1984, 31–57.

Roberts, Ron E., and Robert Marsh Kloss. *Social Movements: Between the Balcony and the Barricade,* 2nd ed. St. Louis: C. V. Mosby, 1979.

Robinson, Isaac. "Blacks Move Back to the South." *American Demographics* 9 (June 1986), 40–43.

Russell, Dick, "Environmental Racism." *Amicus Journal* 11, no. 2 (Spring 1989), 22–32.

Schnaiberg, Allen. *The Environment: From Surplus to Scarcity.* New York: Oxford University Press, 1980.

_____. "Redistributive Goals Versus Distributive Politics: Social Equity Limits in Environmentalism and Appropriate Technology Movements." *Sociological Inquiry* 53 (Spring 1983), 200–219.

Schnaiberg, Allan, Nicholas Watts, and Klaus Zimmermann, eds. *Distributional Conflict in Environmental-Resource Policy.* New York: St. Martin's Press, 1986.

Schueler, Donald. "Southern Exposure." *Sierra* 77 (November/December 1992), 42–49.

Schwartz, J., D. Gold, D. W. Dockey, S. T. Weiss, and F. E. Speizer. "Predictors of Asthma and Persistent Wheeze in a National Sample of Children in the United States." *American Review of Respiratory Disease* 142 (1990), 555–562.

Seley, John, and Julian Wolpert. "Equity Issues and Location." In Roger E. Kasperson (ed.), *Equity Issues in Radioactive Waste Management.* Cambridge, Mass.: Oelgeschlager Gunn, and Hain, 1983, 69–93.

Shlay, Ann B., and Peter Rossi. "Keeping up the Neighborhood: Estimating the Effect of Zoning." *American Sociology Review* 46 (December 1981), 703–719.

Shrader-Frechette, K. S. *Risk and Rationality: Philosophical Foundations for Populist Reforms.* Berkeley: University of California Press, 1992.

Sills, David L. "The Environmental Movement and Its Critics." *Human Ecology* 13 (1975), 1–41.

Slaughter, Jane. "Valley of the Shadow of Death." *Progressive* 49 (March 1985), 50.

Smith, J. N. *Environmental Quality and Social Justice in Urban America.* Washington, D.C.: The Conservation Foundation, 1974.

Starr, Mark, Mary Hager, William J. Cook, and Carolyn Friday. "America's Toxic Tremors." *Newsweek* (August 26, 1985), 18–19.

Stewart, R. B. "Paradoxes of Liberty, Integrity, and Fraternity: The Collective Nature of Environmental Quality and Judicial Review of Administration Action." *Environmental Action* 7, no. 3 (1977), 474–476.

Taeuber, Karl. "Racial Segregation: The Persisting Dilemma." *Annals of the American Academy of Political and Social Science* 442 (November 1978), 87–96.

_____. "Racial Residential Segregation, 28 Cities, 1970–1980." Mimeograph. CDE Working Paper, University of Wisconsin, Madison, 1983.

Taeuber, Karl, and Alma K. Taeuber. *Negroes in Cities: Residential Segregation and Neighborhood Change.* Chicago: Aldine, 1965.

Taylor, Dorceta E. "Blacks and the Environment: Toward an Explanation of the Concern and Action Gap Between Blacks and Whites." *Environment and Behavior* 21 (March 1989), 175–205.

Taylor, Ronald A. "Do Environmentalists Care About Poor People?" *U.S. News and World Report* 96 (April 2, 1982), 51–52.

Templet, Paul H., and Stephen Farber. *The Complementarity Between Environmental and Economic Risk: An Empirical Analysis.* Baton Rouge: Louisiana State University Institute for Environmental Studies, 1992.

Tilly, Charles. *From Mobilization to Revolution.* Reading, Mass.: Addison-Wesley, 1978.

Tobin, Gary A. *Divided Neighborhoods: Changing Patterns of Racial Segregation.* Newbury Park, Calif.: Sage, 1987.

U.S. Bureau of the Census. *State and Metropolitan Area Data Book 1982.* Washington, D.C.: U.S. Government Printing Office, 1982.

U.S. Bureau of the Census. *Number of Inhabitants: West Virginia.* Washington, D.C.: U.S. Government Printing Office, 1982.

U.S. Department of Housing and Urban Development. *Report of the President's Commission for a National Agenda for the Eighties.* Washington, D.C.: U.S. Government Printing Office, 1980.

U.S. Environmental Protection Agency. *Environmental Equity: Reducing Risk for All Communities.* Washington, D.C.: Environmental Protection Agency, 1992.

U.S. Environmental Protection Agency. *EPA Headquarters Cultural Diversity Survey: Draft Final Report.* Washington, D.C.: Environmental Protection Agency Cultural Diversity Task Force, 1992.

U.S. Environmental Protection Agency. "Geographic Initiatives: Protecting What We Love." *Securing Our Legacy: An EPA Progress Report 1989–1991.* Washington, D.C.: Environmental Protection Agency, 1992.

U.S. Environmental Protection Agency. "Koppers Site Update: EPA Announces Amended Record of Decision for Site." *EPA Update* (March 5, 1992).

U.S. Environmental Protection Agency. *Women, Minorities and People with Disabilities.* Washington, D.C.: Environmental Protection Agency, 1992.

U.S. Environmental Protection Agency. *Toxic Release Inventory & Emission Reductions 1987–1990 in the Lower Mississippi River Industrial Corridor.* Washington, D.C.: Environmental Protection Agency, Office of Pollution Prevention and Toxics, May 13, 1993.

U.S. General Accounting Office. *Siting of Hazardous Waste Landfills and Their Correlation with Racial and Economic Status of Surrounding Communities.* Washington, D.C.: General Accounting Office, 1983.

United Church of Christ Commission for Racial Justice. *Proceedings: The First National People of Color Environmental Leadership Summit.* New York: Commission for Racial Justice, 1992.

Urban Environment Conference, Inc. *Taking Back Our Health: An Institute on Surviving the Toxic Threat to Minority Communities.* Washington, D.C.: Urban Environment, Inc., 1985.

Vallette, Jim. *The International Trade in Wastes: A Greenpeace Inventory.* Washington, D.C.: Greenpeace, 1989.

Van Liere, Kent, and Riley E. Dunlap. "The Social Bases of Environmental Concern: A Review of Hypotheses, Explanations, and Empirical Evidence." *Public Opinion Quarterly* 44 (Summer 1980), 181–197.

Vig, Norman J., and Michael E. Kraft, eds. *Environmental Policy in the 1980s: Reagan's New Agenda.* Washington, D.C.: Congressional Quarterly Press, 1984.

Walsh, Edward J., and Rex Warland. "Social Movement Involvement in the Wake of a Nuclear Accident: Activists and Free-Riders in the TMI Area." *American Sociological Review* 48 (December 1983), 764–780.

Wernette, D. R., and L. A. Nieves. "Breathing Polluted Air: Minorities Are Disproportionately Exposed." *EPA Journal* 18, no. 1 (March/April 1992), 16–17.

West, Pat, J. M. Fly, F. Larkin, and P. Marans. "Minority Anglers and Toxic Fish Consumption: Evidence of the State-Wide Survey of Michigan." In B. Bryant and P. Mohai (eds.), *Race and the Incidence of Environmental Hazards*. Boulder, Colo.: Westview Press, 1992, 100–113.

Willie, Charles V. *The Caste and Class Controversy*. Bayside, N.Y.: General Hall, 1979.

Wilson, William J. "The Black Underclass." *Wilson Quarterly* (Spring 1984), 88–99.

_____. *The Truly Disadvantaged: The Inner City, the Underclass, and Public Policy*. Chicago: University of Chicago Press, 1987.

Wood, James L., and Maurice Jackson, eds. *Social Movements: Development, Participation and Dynamics*. Belmont, Calif.: Wadsworth, 1982.

Wright, Beverly H., and Florence Robinson. "Voluntary Buy-Outs as an Alternative Damage Claims Arrangement: A Comparative Analysis of Three Impacted Communities." Baton Rouge, Southern University Institute for Environmental Issues and Policy Assessment (December 15, 1992), pp. 10–11.

Zwerdling, Daniel. "Poverty and Pollution." *Progressive* 37 (January 1973), 25–29.

APPENDIX:
RESOURCES AND
CONTACTS

◆

In the 1990s, the quest for environmental justice has taken root in every region of the United States. Hundreds of grassroots environmental groups are working on an array of problems and issues. Many of these groups do not have the word *environment* in their name or do not focus exclusively on environmental issues. Some work alone, whereas others have formed loose alliances, coalitions, and networks with other grassroots and mainstream environmental groups.

Some of the national environmental groups have taken steps to diversify their boards and staffs and to incorporate environmental justice into their action agendas. However, grassroots groups continue to provide the critical leadership and organizing needed to defend people-of-color communities that are threatened by toxins and other hazards. Communities of color look to their own organizations to shoulder the responsibility of leading their struggle: This was also the case in the push for open housing, equal employment opportunities, voting rights, and school desegregation.

A list of regional and national groups that are working on environmental justice issues follows. In addition, a list of grassroots groups of color is included to demonstrate the diversity of the environmental justice movement. This list is by no means exhaustive.

National and Regional Groups

Asian American Legal Defense Fund
99 Hudson Street, 12th Floor
New York, NY 10013
Margaret Fung (212) 966–5932

Black Environmental Science Trust
c/o UCAR, P.O. Box 3000
Boulder, CO 80307
Michelle Simpson (303) 497–8680

Center for Constitutional Rights
666 Broadway
New York, NY 10012
Matthew Chachere (212) 614–6464

Center for Ecology and Social Justice—IPS
1601 Connecticut Avenue NW
Washington, DC 20009
Richard Hofrichter (202) 234–9383

Center for Environment, Commerce, and Energy
733 6th Street SE, #1
Washington, DC 20003
Norris McDonald (202) 543–3939

Center for Policy Alternatives
1875 Connecticut Avenue NW, #710
Washington, DC 20009
Richard Regan (202) 387–6030

Center for Third World Organizing
1218 East 21st Street
Oakland, CA 94606
Rinku Sen (510) 533–7583

Citizens' Clearinghouse for Hazardous Waste
119 Rowell Court, Box 6806
Falls Church, VA 22040
Lois Gibbs (703) 237–2249

Commission for Racial Justice
475 Riverside Drive, Suite 1948
New York, NY 10015
Charles Lee (212) 870–2077

Congressional Black Caucus Foundation, Inc.
1004 Pennsylvania Avenue SE
Washington, DC 20003
Arthur Johnson (202) 675–6730

Conservation Law Foundation
62 Summer Street
Boston, MA 02110
Stephanie Pollack (617) 350–0990

Earth Island Institute
300 Broadway, Suite 28
San Francisco, CA 94133
Carl Anthony (415) 788–3666

Environmental Action
1525 New Hampshire NW
Washington, DC 20036
Ruth Caplan (202) 745–4870

Environmental and Energy Study Institute
122 C Street NW, Suite 700

Washington, DC 20001
Diane Schwartz (202) 628–1400

Environmental Defense Fund
1875 Connecticut Avenue NW, 10th Floor
Washington, DC 20009
Guy Williams (202) 287–3500

Environmental Health Network
P.O. Box 16267
Chesapeake, VA 23328
Linda King (804) 424–1162

Environmental Law Institute
1616 P Street NW
Washington, DC 20036
Tobie Bernstein (202) 939–3869

Environmental Support Center
1731 Connecticut Avenue NW, #200
Washington, DC 20009
James Abernathy (202) 328–7813

Friends of the Earth
1025 Vermont Avenue NW, Suite 300
Washington, DC 20003
Fred Millar (202) 783–7440

Greenpeace
1436 U Street NW
Washington, DC 20009
Damu Smith (202) 462–1177

Health Watch
2030 Glenwood Road
Brooklyn, NY 11210
Norma Goodwin (718) 434–5311

Highlander Research and Education Center
1959 Highlander Way
New Market, TN 37820
Larry Wilson (615) 933–3443

Indigenous Environmental Network
P.O. Box 279
Bemidji, MN 56671
Tom Goldtooth (218) 679–3959

INFORM
381 Park Avenue South
New York, NY 10016
Joanna Underwood (212) 689–4040

Joint Center for Political and Economic Studies
1301 Pennsylvania Avenue NW, Suite 400
Washington, DC 20004
Eddie Williams (202) 626–3500

Lawyers' Committee for Civil Rights Under Law
1450 G Street NW, Suite 400
Washington, DC 20005
Deeohn Ferris (202) 662–8333

Legal Environmental Assistance Foundation (LEAF)
1115 North Gadsden
Tallahassee, FL 32303
Suzie Ruhl (904) 681–2591

Mexican American Legal Defense and Educational Fund
National Office
634 South Spring Street
Los Angeles, CA 90014
Valerie Small Navarro (213) 629–2512

Minority Health Professionals Foundation
720 Westview Drive SW
Atlanta, GA 30310
John C. Smith (404) 752–1973

NAACP
National Office
4805 Mount Hope Drive
Baltimore, MD 21215
Benjamin F. Chavis, Jr. (410) 358–8900

NAACP Legal Defense and Educational Fund
315 West Ninth Street, #208
Los Angeles, CA 90015
Bill Lann Lee (213) 624–2405

National Audubon Society
666 Pennsylvania Avenue SE, Suite 200
Washington, DC 20003
Adaora Lathan (202) 547–9009

National Black Leadership Roundtable
1025 Connecticut Avenue NW, Suite 610
Washington, DC 20036
Walter Fauntroy (202) 296–0250

National Coalition Against the Misuse of Pesticides
701 E Street SE, Suite 200
Washington, DC 20003
Jay Feldman (202) 543–5450

National Conference of Black Lawyers
1875 Connecticut Avenue NW, Suite 410
Washington, DC 20009
Adjoa Aiyetoro (202) 234–4830

National Conference of Black Mayors
1430 West Peachtree Street, Suite 700
Atlanta, GA 30309
Keith Hinch (404) 892–0127

National Council of La Raza
810 1st Street NE, Suite 300
Washington, DC 20009
Magdalena Prada (202) 289–1380

National Health Law Program
1815 H Street NW, Suite 705
Washington, DC 20006
Jane Perkins (202) 887–5310

National Medical Association
1012 10th Street NW
Washington, DC 20001
Tracy M. Walton, Jr. (202) 347–1895

National Rainbow Coalition
1110 Vermont Avenue NW, #410
Washington, DC 20005
Dr. John T. Wolfe, Jr. (202) 728–1180

National Wildlife Federation
Cool It Project
1400 16th Street NW
Washington, DC 20036
Monica Spann (202) 797–6631

Natural Resources Defense Council
40 West 20th Street
New York, NY 10011
Vernice Miller (212) 727–4461

Physicians for Social Responsibility
1101 Fourteenth Street NW, Suite 700
Washington, DC 20005
Julia A. Moore (202) 898–0150

**Puerto Rican Legal Defense
and Educational Fund**
99 Hudson Street, 14th Floor
New York, NY 10013
Ruben Franco (212) 219–3360

Sierra Club
730 Polk Street
San Francisco, CA 94109
Vivien Li (415) 776–2211

Sierra Club Legal Defense Fund
400 Magazine Street, #401
New Orleans, LA 70130
Nathalie M. Walker (504) 522-1394

Southern Christian Leadership Conference
334 Auburn Avenue NE
Atlanta, GA 30303
Joseph Lowery (404) 522-1420

Southern Environmental Law Center
201 W. Main Street, #14
Charlottesville, VA 22901
Richard A. Parish (804) 977–4090

Southwest Network for Environmental and Economic Justice
211 10th Street SW
Albuquerque, NM 87102
Richard Moore (505) 242–0416

The Panos Institute
1717 Massachusetts Avenue NW, #300
Washington, DC 20036
Don Edwards (202) 483–0044

Trial Lawyers for Public Interest
1625 Massachusetts Avenue NW, #100
Washington, DC 20036
Jim Hecker (202) 797–8600

People-of-Color Groups
in the Southern United States

Alabama

Alabama New South Coalition
P.O. Box 851
Tuskegee, AL 36088
Latrease Rutland (205) 727–5967

Beat-10 Action Group
Route 1, P.O. Box 36425
Beatrice, AL 36425
Ezra Cunningham (205) 789–2256

Federation of Southern Coops/Land Assistance Fund
P.O. Box 95
Epes, AL 35460
Cleo Askew (205) 652–9676

Institute for Human Development
P.O. Box 809
Eutaw, AL 35462
Carol P. Zippert (205) 372–3344

Lowdnes County Concerned Citizens
P.O. Box 102
Haynesville, AL 36040
Elbert Means (205) 548–2271

Pine Grove Concerned Citizens
Bennett Road 13–865
York, AL 36925
Elijah Ivory (205) 652–2754

Southern Rainbow Education Project
46 East Patton Avenue
Montgomery, AL 36105
Gwen Patton (205) 288–5754

West Alabama Farmers Association
214 Boligee Street, P.O. Box 598
Eutaw, AL 35462
Aaron Hodges (205) 372–3373

Arkansas

Arkansas Land and Farm Development Corp.
Route 2, P.O. Box 291
Brinkley, AR 72021
Roy H. King, Jr. (501) 734–1140

District of Columbia

Anacostia RAP (Recycling Action Project)
2425 17th Street SE
Washington, DC 20020
Brenda Lee Richardson (202) 889–2102

Concerned Citizens of Brentwood
2202 13th Street SE
Washington, DC 20018
Alice Walker (202) 260–1919

D.C. ACORN (Association of Community Organizations for Reform Now)
739 8th Street SE

Washington, DC 20003
Melanie Marcus (202) 547–9292

People of Color Caucus on Ecology
2028 Fulton Place NE
Washington, DC 20018
Yewande D. Dada (202) 832–2419

River Terrace Community Organization
3393 Blaine Street NE, #3D
Washington, DC 20019
George Gurley (202) 399-1722

Florida

Black Rhino Vegetarian Society
Route 3, P.O. Box 292
American Beach, FL 32034
MaVynee Betsch (904) 261–3468

Farmworker Association of Central Florida
815 S. Park Avenue
Apopka, FL 32703
Tirso Moreno (407) 886–5151

Wolf Mountain Press
P.O. Box 7573
Naples, FL 33941
Oannes Pritzker (813) 353–2164

Georgia

Carver Hills Neighborhood Association, Inc.
P.O. Box 93947
Atlanta, GA 30377
Arnold D. Weathersby, Sr. (404) 799–5382

Citizens for Environmental Justice
P.O. Box 1841
Savannah, GA 31401
Mildred McClain (912) 233–0907

Citizens League Opposed to Unwanted Toxins (CLOUT)
1107 Lower Brookfield Road
Tifton, GA 31794
Brenda Iglehart (912) 382–9767

Clark-Atlanta University
Public Policy Center
Atlanta, GA 30314
Bob Holmes (404) 880–8089

Minority Health Professionals Foundation
720 Westview Drive SW
Atlanta, GA 30310
John Smith (404) 752–1973

Newtown Florist Club
1067 Desota Street
Gainesville, GA 30501
Faye Bush (706) 536–1359

Southern Organizing Committee (SOC)
P.O. Box 10518
Atlanta, GA 30313
Connie Tucker (404) 243–5229

Toxic Communication and Assistance Project (T-CAP)
Albany State College
504 College Drive
Albany, GA 31705
Barbara Sullivan (912) 430–4813

**Work Action Key Efforts in Uniting People
(WAKEUP, Inc.)**
P.O. Box 572, 107 Broad Street
Sparta, GA 31087
Lillie Webb (706) 444–5896

Louisiana

Ascension Parish Residents Against Pollution
P.O. Box 478
Geismer, LA 70734
Amos J. Favorite, Sr. (504) 673–6939

Citizens Against Nuclear Trash
Route 4, P.O. Box 229
Homer, LA 71040
Elmira Wafer (318) 927–3367

Coalition for Community Action
332 Old Rafer Mayer Road
Baton Rouge, LA 70807
Mary McCastle (504) 775–9607

Deep South Center for Environmental Justice
Xavier University
New Orleans, LA 70125
Beverly H. Wright (504) 483–7508

Gulf Coast Tenants Organization
1866 N. Gayoso Street

New Orleans, LA 70119
Pat Bryant (505) 949–4919

North Baton Rouge Environmental Association
421 Springfield Road
Baton Rouge, LA 70807
Florence T. Robinson (504) 775–0341

Maryland

Blacks Against Nukes
8603 Geren Road
Silver Spring, MD 20901
Gregory Johnson

I. C. Green
609 Montpelier Street
Baltimore, MD 21212
Morning Sunday (410) 235–5270

Jobs with Peace
100 S. Washington Street
Baltimore, MD 21231
Sr. Katherine Corr (410) 342–7404

Mississippi

African Americans for Environmental Justice
P.O. Box 8
Macon, MS 39341
John Gibson (601) 726–5411

Brickfire
101 N. Jefferson Street
Starkville, MS 39759
Helen Taylor (601) 323–5321

Concerned Citizens of Choctaw
401 Oswald Road
Philadelphia, MS 39350
Linda Farve (601) 656–7664

Jesus People Against Pollution
P.O. Box 464
Columbia, MS 39429
Charlotte Keys (601) 736–3327

Rural Organizing and Culture Center
103 Swinney Lane
Lexington, MS 39095
Ann Brown (601) 834–3080

Southern ECHO, Inc.
P.O. Box 10433
Jackson, MS 39289
Leroy Johnson (601) 352–1500

North Carolina

Center for Community Action
P.O. Box 723
Lumberton, NC 28359
Mac Legerton (919) 739–7851

Center for Women's Economic Alternatives
P.O. Box 1033
Ahoskie, NC 27910
Sarah Fields-Davis (919) 332–4179

Halifax Environmental Loss Prevention (HELP)
P.O. Box 61
Tillery, NC 27887
Gary R. Grant (919) 826–3244

Land Loss Prevention Project
P.O. Box 179
Durham, NC 27702
David Harris (919) 682–5969

Leadership Initiative Project
Rt. 1, Box 119
Kittrell, NC 27544
Angela Brown (919) 496–7940

Native American Cultural Center
P.O. Box 2410
Pembroke, NC 28372
Donna Chavis (919) 521–2433

North Carolina Fair Share
P.O. Box 12543
Raleigh, NC 27605
John Worchek (919) 832–7130

Shiloh Coalition for Community Control and Improvement
Route 2, P.O. Box 77
Shiloh in Morrisville, NC 27560
Angaza Laughinghouse (919) 941–5716

Southerners for Economic Justice
P.O. Box 240
Durham, NC 27702
Leah Wise (919) 683–1361

United Church of Christ
Commission for Racial Justice
Office of Rural Racial Justice
P.O. Box 187
Enfield, NC 27823
Vivian Lucas Wynn (919) 437–1723

United Farmers Organization
P.O. Box 176
Oak City, NC 27857
Debbie Strickland (919) 798–4721

Warren County Concerned Citizens
P.O. Box 506—Warren County
Warrenton, NC 27589
Dollie Burwell (919) 257–3265

Oklahoma

Citizens Against Toxics (CAT)
220 S.E. Queenstown
Bartlesville, OK 74006
Melissa Mohundro (918) 333–7989

East Side Environment Coalition
524 N. Nebraska
Oklahoma City, OK 73117
Minnie Jones (405) 235-7113

Eco-Law Institute
110 W. Delaware
Tahlequah, OK 74464
Jackie Warledo (918) 456–3235

Environmental Pollution and Health Concerns Coalition, Inc.
1301 Martin Luther King Avenue
Oklahoma City, OK 73117
John H. Bowman III (405) 427–1330

Garden Community Environmental Citizen Group
4216 N.E. 16th Terrace
Oklahoma City, OK 73121
Nanna M. Mason (405) 427–2121

Native Americans for a Clean Environment (NACE)
P.O. Box 1671
Tahlequah, OK 74465
Lance Hughes (918) 458–4322

Otoe-Missoullia Tribe of Oklahoma
Route 1, P.O. Box 62

Red Rock, OK 74651
Willis Robedeaux (405) 723–4466

South Carolina

Citizens Local Environmental Action Network
P.O. Box 50529
Columbia, SC 29250
Ron Nixon (803) 252–9837

Tennessee

Jonah, Inc.
1472 Shaw Road
Brownsville, TN 38012
Rosemary Derrick (909) 772–2208

Students, Mothers, and Concerned Citizens, Inc.
1249 Cannon Street
Memphis, TN 38106
Mary D. Taylor (901) 942–9877

Texas

Advocacy, Inc.
225 Cage Street
Phar, TX 78577
Rose E. Torres (512) 783–8400

Border Agricultural Workers Union
514 S. Kansas Street
El Paso, TX 79901
Carlos Marentes (915) 532–0921

Centro de Salud Familiar La Fe, Inc.
700 S. Ochoa Street
El Paso, TX 79901
Antonio Carraco (915) 545–4550

Coalition for Justice in the Maquiladoras
P.O. Box 4717
Brownsville, TX 78523
Domingo Gonzales (512) 541–8354

Concerned Citizens
102 Vera Cruz Street
Rosenberg, TX 77471
Alice Flores (713) 342–5598

Farm Worker Health and Safety Project
259 S. Texas Street

Weslaco, TX 78596
Evonne Charboneau (512) 968–9574

Gulf Coast Coalition for Public Health
864 Central Boulevard
Brownsville, TX 78520
Margaret Diaz (512) 541–5231

Indigenous Women's Network
13621 FM 2769
Austin, TX 78726
Marsha Gomez (512) 258–3880

Lower Rio Grande Valley Nature Center
P.O. Box 8125, 301 S. Border Street
Weslaco, TX 78596
Betty Ashworth (512) 969–2475

LULAC (League of United Latin American Citizens)
  Task Force on Toxics and Latinos
1214 Montana Street
El Paso, TX 79902
Carlos Calderon (915) 544–0441

Mexican American Legal Defense and Educational Fund
Regional Office
140 E. Houston, Suite 300
San Antonio, TX 78205
Guadalupe T. Luna (512) 224–5476

Northeast Community Action Group
7027 Hopper Road
Houston, TX 77016
Pat Reaux (713) 449–5830

PODER (People Organized in Defense of Earth and Its Resources)
1207 E. 2nd Street
Austin, TX 78702
Susana Almanza (512) 482–0503

Shape Community Center
3903 Almeda Road
Houston, TX 77004
Delloyd Parker (713) 521–0629

Southwest Public Workers' Union
P.O. Box 830706
San Antonio, TX 78283
Chavel Lopez (512) 299–2666

Texas Center for Policy Studies
P.O. Box 2618

Austin, TX 78768
Antonio Diaz (512) 474–0811

Texas Network for Environmental and Economic Justice
P.O. Box 771
Austin, TX 78767
Antonio Diaz (512) 474–0811

Texas Network for Environmental and Economic Justice
P.O. Box 52341
Houston, TX 75501
Arthur Shaw (713) 691–6809

Texas Rural Legal Aid
P.O. Box 1658
Plainview, TX 79072
Trini Gamez (806) 293–2625

United East Austin
1000 Glen Oaks Court
Austin, TX 78702
Gilberto Rivera (512) 477–2352

West Dallas Coalition for Environmental Justice
5101 Goodman Street
Dallas, TX 75211
Luis D. Sepulveda (214) 330–7947

Virginia

Citizens for a Better America
P.O. Box 356
Halifax, VA 24558
Cora Tucker (804) 476–7757

First Nation Financial Project
69 Kelly Road
Falmouth, VA 22405
Debra Levy (703) 371–5615

Task Force for Historic Preservation of the Minority Community
P.O. Box 25604
Richmond, VA 23260
Earline Smith (804) 788–1709

ABOUT THE BOOK
AND AUTHOR

◆

To be poor, working class, or a person of color in the United States often means bearing a disproportionate share of the country's environmental problems. Starting with the premise that all Americans have a basic right to live in a healthy environment, *Dumping in Dixie* chronicles the efforts of five African American communities, empowered by the civil rights movement, to link environmentalism with issues of social justice. In the second edition, Bullard speaks to us from the front lines of the environmental justice movement about new developments in environmental racism, different organizing strategies, and success stories in the struggle for environmental equity.

Robert D. Bullard is a professor of sociology at the University of California, Riverside and visiting professor in the Center for Afro-American Studies at UCLA.

INDEX